Below the Fairy City

A Life of Jerome K. Jerome

by

Carolyn W. de la L. Oulton

Victorian Secrets 2012

Published by

Victorian Secrets Limited
32 Hanover Terrace
Brighton BN2 9SN

www.victoriansecrets.co.uk

Below the Fairy City: A Life of Jerome K. Jerome by Carolyn W. de la L. Oulton

Cover design © Ramona Szczerba (www.winonacookie.etsy.com)
Composition by Catherine Pope

A catalogue record for this book is available from the British Library.

ISBN 978-1-906469-37-5

CONTENTS

ACKNOWLEDGEMENTS

Anyone who knows Frank Rodgers's articles on Jerome K. Jerome will rightly suspect that I have benefited from his expertise. And no one who has met him will be in the least surprised to hear of his unparalleled generosity in placing his fifty years of research at my disposal – not to mention personally photographing Marguerite Jerome's diary and beaming it over from Guatemala. He has also saved me from at least some of the errors into which I would otherwise have blithely tumbled. Of his many detailed emails my personal favourite begins, 'Dear Carolyn. No no no!' when I had been guilty of a particularly egregious mistake.

Thanks are also due to the Jerome K. Jerome Society for welcoming me into their midst and to the Society of Authors for allowing me to quote from Jerome's unpublished MSS. Mark Richards gave me access to his superb Jerome collection, Victoria Arrowsmith-Brown supplied background on the firm and the photograph of J.W. Arrowsmith, and Gina Wilson allowed me to quote from the unpublished biography of W. W. Jacobs written by her late husband Aubrey Wilson. Thanks are likewise due to Sarah Crowley for allowing me to quote the unpublished writings of her grandmother Nell Jacobs.

I have, as always, made good use of other people's time, and I am grateful to the following in particular: Ruth Vyse for supplying me with copies of vital material from the Walsall Local History Centre; staff at the Cannock Chase Mining Museum; Alison Kenney of the Westminster Archives Centre (no they don't make them like this any more), who found me the uncatalogued records of the Philological School within twenty minutes, saying that she remembered seeing them once in the 1980s; Gill Culver and Kirsty Bunting for information on the Playgoers' Club; Andrew Crowther for information on the Savage Club; Helen Davis, who lent me her transcript of the 2010 Passion Play; Vicky Davis (everyone should have a friend whose mother speaks Russian); Hazel Malpass of the Marlow Society; the indefatigable Jean Wooler at the British Library; staff at the National Portrait Gallery, the Theatre Museum, the Bodleian and the Harry Ransom Center at the University of Austin, Texas; Anne Humpherys for sharing her work on *TO-DAY*; Beth Palmer for allowing me to quote from her unpublished conference paper on *The Era*; Mark Connelly for talking me through the political and media context of World War I and Jacqui for hearing 'perfectly chilled chardonnay' when I said I'd love a cup of tea.

Catherine Pope's suggestions for the MS were enlightening and if the Pluck Fund were still in operation Jerome would surely owe her a medal.

My family are by now quite used to spending their holidays in museums and churchyards, for which they likewise deserve thanks.

FOREWORD

by Jeremy Nicholas

It's extraordinary, given that he is the author of one of the best-known and most widely-read books in the English language, that there is no statue to Jerome K. Jerome. Equally strange, there have only ever been four commercially published books devoted to him. The earliest was Alfred Moss's hagiographic *Jerome K. Jerome – His Life and Work* (Selwyn & Blount, 1928). There was nothing further till 1974 and *Jerome K. Jerome* (Twayne Publishers, Inc. of New York) a useful survey of Jerome's varied output by the American academic Ruth Marie Faurot. The most detailed and engaging so far followed in 1982: *Jerome K. Jerome – A Critical Biography* by Joseph Connolly (Orbis Publishing) though, like Faurot's work, it contains many minor factual errors. Some of these were corrected in *Idle Thoughts on Jerome K. Jerome* published by the Jerome K. Jerome Society in 2009 to coincide with the sesquicentenary of his birth, not a study of his life and career, more a Jeromian cornucopia.

Two other books have focused on particular aspects of Jerome's work. *Slang and Cant in Jerome K. Jerome's Works* by Olaf E. Bosson (W. Heffer & Sons, Cambridge), an almost unreadably stodgy thesis, appeared as early as 1911. Far more alluring and illuminating was R.R. Bolland's *In the Wake of Three Men in a Boat* (Oast Books, 1995) which examined the episodes in the novel that referred to real life events.

These half dozen works hardly amount to a ringing endorsement from the literary establishment. The reasons for this are many and varied. There is the 'lightweight' tag of which Jerome tried so hard to rid himself. The early books (*On the Stage – and Off, The Idle Thoughts of an Idle Fellow, Three Men in a Boat*) established him as an entertainer writing in a humorous style of which *Punch* and other journals thoroughly disapproved. As a serious novelist Jerome never rivalled his hero Dickens (though he came close in the semi-autobiographical *Paul Kelver*), nor as a playwright did he approach the dramatic gifts of Wilde or Shaw (though *The Passing of the Third Floor Back* enjoyed long popular success). His prolific journalism for *TO-DAY* and *The Idler*, both of which publications he edited, was not the kind of writing to attract the dissemination of the literati. Yet who of Jerome's contemporaries embraced the different writing disciplines of humourist, novelist, journalist, essayist and dramatist? Who, indeed, has *ever* done so – and with the same degree of success?

All of which makes Carolyn Oulton's present volume doubly welcome, both a valuable addition to the tiny Jerome canon, and an illuminating, scholarly study of parts of JKJ's life and career that have never been fully scrutinized before. She has had a great deal to explore and correct.

Jerome was a public figure for forty years, much interviewed, much written about, yet many aspects of his life remain confused and even mysterious. This was a man who died famous – and relatively recently (1927), recent enough, in fact, that only a few months ago the present writer received a letter from an elderly gentleman who, as a small boy, had been introduced to Jerome as he lay dying in Northampton hospital and had shaken the great man's hand. In the early 1980s, during the run of my one-man version of *Three Men in a Boat* at London's May Fair Theatre, a lady of a certain age came up to me after the performance and told me in a strong foreign accent how much she had enjoyed the evening. We talked further. She seemed to know a great deal about Jerome, and I said as much to her. 'Oh well, I should know something,' she replied. 'You see Harris was my uncle.' To reinforce the point, Mrs May Walker, who at the age of two became a surrogate daughter of the Jeromes when her parents worked for the family as housekeeper and gardener, died in October 2003, just before her 100th birthday.

Part of the biographical confusion was of Jerome's own making. The account of his early life as told in his autobiography *My Life and Times* (1926), is a mixture of fact and fantasy, some of it doubtless invented and passed on by his father, a man of whom the more one knows the less one finds appealing. JKJ chooses not to tell us that his three older siblings were christened with the surname Clapp and that his father only changed the family name to Jerome when they moved to Walsall, shortly before JKJ's birth. Nor does he reveal that he was christened Jerome Clapp Jerome, nor that he changed his name only when he decided to make writing his profession. However, JKJ is not responsible for the absurd story of his being named after General George Klapka (1820-92), exiled hero of the Hungarian revolution who, it was stated, had been invited by Jerome Clapp Jerome (JKJ's father) to the Jerome home in Appledore, Devon, to write his memoirs. Subsequently, 'Klapka,' writes Alfred Moss, 'visited the Jeromes in Walsall, and in all probability was with them at the time of their youngest son's birth, and in honour of their famous guest they named him Jerome Klapka.' (Jerome makes no reference to Klapka in *My Life and Times* and the tale seems to have gained currency only after Jerome's death: Moss's biography, dedicated to 'Mrs and Miss Jerome', appeared in 1928.) No one bothered to challenge these fictions until a few years ago when they were easily disproved by the simple expediency of examining various relevant documents and birth certificates. Amongst its many other merits, Dr Oulton's study is the first to debunk the myths and present the facts in context.

The narrative of Jerome's early years is, though, just one area of his life that has never previously been properly researched and assessed. Another is Jerome's work as an editor, an aspect of his career on which Dr Oulton lays particular emphasis. And it is the editorial content of *The Idler* and, especially, *TO-DAY* that reveals a virtually unknown and very different side to Jerome. It was the side surely inherited from his father, the preacher and religious zealot, and from his God-fearing, Bible-soaked mother. Judging some of Jerome's opinions by present day standards makes queasy acquaintance. He was by no means alone among his contemporaries in holding what are, in the twenty-first century, unspeakably stupid views on the 'negro', on women and their role in society, and other contentious issues, views which, to be fair to Jerome, he subsequently moderated or renounced. Even allowing for the passage of time, however, Carolyn Oulton's research reveals a pompous moraliser masquerading as an intellectual whose editorials of often muddled thinking frequently read like the reactionary musings of a club bore.

The corollary of this side of him, another similarly unknown characteristic he shared with his father, is Jerome the campaigner. As early as 1885 we find him writing to *The Times* about cruelty to horses, pleading 'that their suffering may be relieved'. In 1909 he chaired the first meeting of the National Equine Defence League. During a lecture tour of America in 1913, he courageously denounced the then horrific vogue for lynching and the country's vile treatment of black men and women. He came close to being lynched himself. Was it idealism, obstinacy or naivety that led him to take on the enormously wealthy businessman Samson Fox in a libel case in 1897? Jerome's crusading magazine *TO-DAY* had charged him with fraud.

Jerome lost – ruinously so – yet one cannot help but admire the courage of a man standing so resolutely by his convictions.

So, as Carolyn Oulton shows in these pages, there is rather more to Jerome than larking about with chums on the Thames. In fact it would be hard to imagine a more different Jerome to the one whom the world remembers solely as the author of one of the funniest books ever written. That, of course, is part of the fascination. 'No man will ever write the true story of himself,' wrote Jerome in the introduction to *My Life and Times*. This was clearly so in his case, but that true story needs and, indeed, deserves to be told. The only thing stranger than there being no statue to Jerome is that it has taken so long for anyone to write that story. But here, at last, it is.

Jeremy Nicholas
President, Jerome K. Jerome Society
January 2012

PREFACE

As a young child I remember yelling with laughter as I first listened to the story of George's shirt. The reader, as I recall, actually had tears rolling down his face. Recently I was told the story of a woman who never forgave her sister for reading her Jerome's masterpiece when she had mumps – every time she laughed it made her face hurt.

Three Men in a Boat is a very, very funny book. Everyone knows that. But it took an encounter with a twelve-foot trampoline to make me realise the sheer genius of expression that lies behind the comedy. I began by watching the erection of this new purchase from the safety of a swing seat. I said, inevitably, 'I like work. It fascinates me. I could sit and look at it for hours.' Having sat and looked at it for considerably more than the ninety minutes advised on the box, I felt the work would benefit from my involvement. Time passed. Children commented helpfully that this was taking longer than they had expected. The crisis came when we realised that having hammered various poles and parts of our thumbs successfully into place, the safety net was now firmly moored inside out. I said we just needed to move the netting over the frame. He (jetlagged but determined) said we needed to re-thread it anti-clockwise. The children again said this was taking longer than they'd expected. I explained the principle whereby you put on a duvet cover by putting your hands in the top corners inside out. He said then it would be upside down and we should do it 'like this', rotating his damaged thumbs. Twice I demonstrated the duvet technique and got tangled up in the netting. Twice more he rotated his thumbs and I pretended to know what he meant. For the next half-hour we took it in turns to berate the children and twist the netting, finally lodging the offside in a convenient tree. How and why the frame magically jumped into place as we all stood glaring at each other, no one has since been able to explain. But in the inimitable scene where J, Harris and George are putting up canvas in the gathering dusk, Jerome *does* explain it. Every moment of the agony is spread out for the reader's consumption, with the finesse only possible to a writer of acute observation and the rare power to put in words exactly what he means. In the words of a twentieth-century critic, Ruth Faurot, 'the art of making everyday incidents a source of shared amusement, seemingly without effort, is Jerome's forte.'[1]

In his own time, critics were keen to attribute Jerome's humorous bent to his reading of Mark Twain, and in turn speculation continues as to Jerome's influence on a younger comic writer, P. G. Wodehouse. Both friends of J. M. Barrie and both at different times members of his cricket team the Allahakbarries, it would be extraordinary if they had not met, but there is no evidence that they ever did. If Jerome was Wodehouse's literary hero (again, he should have been but there is no evidence that he was), there is no doubt as to who filled that role for Jerome himself. As a child he was convinced that he had met Dickens, but was later unable to prove it because in the course of a long and fascinating conversation about writing, he had thoughtlessly forgotten to ask the name of the man sitting next to him.

If they could have met again twenty years later they would have had even more to discuss. Like Dickens, Jerome was fascinated by the manners and mores of the lower-middle class and like him, he would struggle to shake off the persistent association of his name with an early humorous novel.

'Everything has its beginning, and it seems to me that the most natural and satisfactory beginning for anyone who is finally to attain to the culture of his mind and the widening of his sympathies lies in fiction. Each grade of society has its faithful record there, and it is difficult for one who reads widely the best fiction to feel very deeply any class prejudice.'[2] In his own lifetime it was his very ability to capture middle-class experience in comic form that so enraged reviewers, who promptly dubbed Jerome a 'new humourist'. 'New' in the 1890s carried a range of possible meanings. The Victorian period prided itself on advances in technology, but in the conservative rumblings that seem to come with the end of centuries, newness may also be associated with a perceived abandonment of tradition or standards, or even of morality. The *fin-de-siècle* press devoted much ink to the various demerits of 'the new journalism', 'the new humour' and most controversially of all, the 'New Woman'. But if many critics dismissed the new humour – their persistence in doing so suggests that they took it more seriously than they claimed – at least one influential voice was raised on its behalf. In a speech to the bohemian Vagabonds Club, Hall Caine made what now seems the unlikely connection between Jerome and Thomas Hardy, explicitly addressing the class bias that impelled late Victorian attitudes:

> And in the time to come, when people want to arrive at a picture of
> our own generation, to know how we lived and amused ourselves,
> and what sort of folks we were, as well as what Acts of Parliament
> we passed and what wars we waged, which are the documents they
> will have to go to? Will they be the Blue-Books, the newspapers,
> the Whitakers, the Hazells, and the "Who's Who" of the period? I
> daresay they will go to these sources, but it is not too much to say
> that they will also go to whatever is left of the poor despised light
> literature of the present moment—the Wessex novels of Mr. Hardy,
> the Scotch stories of Sir J. M. Barrie and Ian Maclaren, the Cockney
> sketches of Mr. Jerome and Mr. Pett Ridge, and perhaps a great
> many other good things besides.[3]

As a picture of his generation Jerome's comedy is both revealing and
deceptive; the idyllic bachelor world inhabited by J, George and Harris, as
its early readers would have understood, is under perpetual threat, a point
made forcefully by the body of a woman that floats past the boat just as the
comedy reaches its height.

Elsewhere in his fiction and notably in his journalism, Jerome is overtly
serious, and he was always conscious of the deprivation and tragedy that might
at any moment engulf the respectable but not affluent classes he represents.
As Faurot noted in 1974, 'He particularly understood the discouraged
individual.'[4] Much of his fiction in the 1890s in particular reflects the 'failed'
and often lonely lives of workers in the metropolis.

This is the story he tells in *Paul Kelver*, the partly autobiographical novel he
published in 1902. Faurot sensibly warns against reading Jerome's fiction as
straight autobiography, commenting that 'any writer putting his own life into
his novel has the advantage of a schizophrenia that permits truthfulness when
useful – and artistic license when needed.'[5] Nonetheless, Jerome encourages
the reader to trace the events of his life in the novel, even bequeathing to the
hero the names of his own mother and aunt – Marguerite Jerome becomes
Maggie Kelver, while Frances Jones is even more thinly disguised as Aunt
Fan (a then popular corruption of Frances). In a transparent allusion to his
father's misfortunes in the coal fields of Staffordshire, Aunt Fan caustically
warns Luke Kelver at one point not to drop his son down a mine (the small
hero of the story convincingly wonders why his parents take this good advice

amiss). In later chapters Paul will lose his father just as Jerome himself did in 1871; again like Jerome, Paul will subsequently find his place in the often hostile world of the city, watched over by an adult narrator whose presence in the chapter headings gives the novel, as Faurot argues, an allegorical status something like *The Pilgrim's Progress*.

Jerome was, as his friends vainly pointed out in his lifetime, a profoundly serious as well as a gifted comic writer. This was 'The Other Jerome' as he has been called in a subsequent effort to recover this side of his work.[6] As the editor Martin Green rightly says, 'the popular conception of him as simply a writer of a couple of very funny books does him an injustice.'[7] His campaigning journalism in the 1890s testifies to the strength of his convictions – he once told a reader of his journal *TO-DAY* that protesting against cruelty to animals in its pages was more important than maintaining circulation. He also protested repeatedly against the respectable dictates that would judge people by their failures and not by their efforts to overcome them, commenting wryly in 1898, 'An oyster has no evil passions, therefore we say he is a virtuous fish.'[8]

While he was outspoken on subjects that mattered to him, Jerome was by nature a shy man and a notably private one. He could never resist a good story and could be cavalier with the facts of his own life, a trait that makes him a fascinating if not an easy biographical subject. Some humorous advice on giving interviews from his friend and colleague Barry Pain could have been written with him in mind:

> Nothing conceals one's real self better than an interview, except more interviews. Vary the information which you give to the interviewers; never tell two of them the same thing, and never tell any one of them anything approaching the truth. Always see a proof; it is possible that the interviewer may have observed some little thing correctly, and it is necessary to strike it out. In this way, by the careful disposal of dummies supposed to be you, you will detract public attention from your real self and attain the privacy and reserve which your good taste demands.[9]

Jerome's good taste certainly demanded a certain distance between himself and his public, and his famous humour provided just such a barrier. It was his misfortune, as he knew himself, that this very success precluded many of his readers from noticing when he *was* being serious. He was in fact a far more complex figure than his opponents ever wanted to recognise.

He himself was never sure about the nature or value of his public achievements, writing in 1898, 'What grand acting parts they are, these characters we write for ourselves alone in our dressing-rooms. ... And the house is always crowded when we play. Our fine speeches always fall on sympathetic ears, our brave deeds are noted and applauded. It is so different in the real performance.'[10] Since his death, critics have continued to treat Jerome badly, leading a Russian scholar to assume in 1995 that, 'In England, Jerome is almost forgotten, and English people are always amazed at evidence of his unfading popularity amongst Russian readers.'[11] He has been the subject of two previous biographies, one by Alfred Moss written shortly after his death and a second by Joseph Connolly in 1982. But his place in the complex world of *fin-de-siècle* literary London remains to be fully explored. In 2009 we saw the 150th anniversary of his birth and the issue of a commemorative volume by the Jerome K. Society, in what was otherwise something of a critical vacuum. He might have derived solace from the thought that while a number of significant writers were born in the same year, including Sir Arthur Conan Doyle and Mary Cholmondeley, it was only Tennyson (born half a century earlier in 1809) whose landmark year was widely acknowledged.

While this book attempts to offer a new interpretation of Jerome and his oeuvre, it is by no means definitive, and inevitably there are moments when my own interests are out of step with Jerome's, or when one of us has an unfair advantage. Protestations aside, he knew more about boats than I ever will, but I knew more about the course of World War I when I started writing than he could possibly have done in December 1914 when he wrote of 'our chivalrous, kindly, cheery lads in khaki ... pouring out their blood for England's honour'.[12]

When I made my first attempt as a biographer I was given two excellent pieces of advice: one was, don't do it. The second was to ask myself, do you like this person – you'll be spending a lot of time with them. In all honesty there are things about Jerome that I find downright irritating and it is always tempting to edit out the awkward moments, the less appealing traits of personality that emerge in the course of research. But as Jerome himself said:

> Of what value is a man's life to the world if the truth is never to be spoken? What lesson can we learn from an artificial word-built thing, constructed of lies and gush? If a man's life is worth the telling, it is worth the telling truthfully. ... We want to know what a man was, not

what some journalistic Mrs Grundy thinks he ought to have been. Let us know of his follies and his failings, that we may understand his virtues and heroisms. Let us understand how a man cursed with this temperament, hampered by that folly, yet managed, on the whole, to do his work worthily. We want to get at a man's real self, at his real inside. ... The man for whom other men's lives are written is the man who can see through the follies into the great heart of his hero, who loves him all the better for knowing that he was human, like the rest of us...[13]

In many ways Jerome speaks to our own time, and not just in his insight that laughter dispels tension in all sorts of ways. His views on making education relevant are highly topical, as is his insistence on social responsibility. His opposition to female employment – what, he said, could be more important than bringing up the next generation? – too often reads like period sophistry. After all, why should motherhood be incompatible with a career, and what about the fathers? But if we are apt to dismiss his rhetoric as belonging to a bygone generation, the continued use of loaded terms such as 'working mother' (significantly the equivalent term for a man who works to support his children is 'family man') shows that we are not out of the woods quite yet. Again, he was mystified by women's readiness to torture themselves in pursuit of the wasp waist, but the 'size zero debate' would not have surprised him in the least. As a figure he has eluded and frustrated me, inspired and annoyed me, and then just in time he has made me laugh all over again. I have shouted at him in public places and warned him not to do things over a century too late. In trying to spend time 'with him', I never know how close I have got. In this I suspect I share the uncertainty of most of his vast range of acquaintances. And yes, I like him.

PROLOGUE

On 9 June 1870 the London evening papers announced that the great novelist Charles Dickens had died. In a barely respectable house in East Poplar an eleven-year-old boy 'slipped quietly from the room. I do not think that anyone noticed my going. Reaching my attic, I closed the door and softly turned the key. I hoped they would forget me. Then pushing aside the low chest of drawers, I opened the window, and putting my elbows on the sill, stared out across the maze of chimney-pots to where the light still lingered beyond the dark mass of the city; and after a while tears came to my relief.'[14] The child's improbable name was Jerome Jerome (his father Jerome Clapp, had reinvented himself as Jerome Clapp Jerome some years before the birth of his son) and he wanted to be a writer. More to the point, he was convinced that he himself had met Dickens less than a year before.[15]

With hindsight Jerome was bewildered by his own reaction, 'Even if all this had been so, a chance encounter of a few minutes' duration does not so bind you to a stranger that, neglectful of home lessons and indifferent to your supper, you see the whole world blurred through tears because of his going.'[16] Nonetheless it was with the death of Dickens that a lifelong preoccupation with the man and his work, specifically *David Copperfield*, would begin. According to Jerome's memoir, the meeting is fairly truthfully recorded in his 1902 novel *Paul Kelver*. In the novel Paul visits Victoria Park one summer evening and finds himself drawn to a man sitting on a bench. 'He was a handsome, distinguished-looking man, with wonderfully bright, clear eyes, and iron-grey hair and beard. I might have thought him a sea-captain, of whom many were always to be met with in that neighbourhood, but for his hands, which were crossed upon his stick, and which were white and delicate as a woman's.'[17] The normally shy Paul is surprised to find himself drawn out by this strange man, specifically 'the magic of his bright eyes',[18] and confides to him that he wants to be a writer. They discuss their shared enjoyment of Dumas, Walter Scott and Victor Hugo, before the man asks casually what the young Paul thinks of Dickens. It is at this point that Paul unfortunately comments on his appreciation of Dickens's humour, especially in *The Pickwick Papers*. Rather wonderfully he enthuses, 'I like so much where Mr. Pickwick –', only to be interrupted with, 'Oh, damn Mr. Pickwick!'[19] Just as it seems he can do no worse, he goes on to admit that his mother finds parts of Dickens a trifle 'vulgar', but this he supposes is because she has no sense of humour. As Paul realises that he must go home, the strange man reminds him that he has never asked him who he is. More fascinated even than his alter ego Paul, the real Jerome evidently took to haunting the park in hopes of seeing the strange man again, but only realised who it was a few months later when he came across a portrait of Dickens in a gallery and felt convinced that the eyes were sparkling at him in token of recognition.[20]

If they could have met again twenty years later they would have had even more to discuss. Like Dickens, Jerome was fascinated by the manners and mores of the lower-middle class and, like him, he would struggle to shake off the persistent association of his name with an early humorous novel. Notably, both were drawn to the darker side of London life; while the glamorous West End did little for Jerome's imagination, he wrote with feeling of the overworked clerks and lonely women in the poorer districts in the East, for whom life was a constant struggle. After all, he had come so close himself to being 'chained here, deep down below the fairy city that was already but a dream'.

CHAPTER ONE

'If only they would fling the right books' 1805 – 1870

According to different sources Jerome Clapp was variously born in 1805, 1808 and 1810,[21] probably in Queen Square, Bath. What is known is that he was the youngest of three or possibly four children born to a watchmaker, Benjamin Clapp, and his wife Ann (née Ewens). His sister Sarah married a solicitor, John Shorland in 1823; a year later his brother William, a doctor, married another Shorland sibling, Mary Ann. Both marriages took place in London, suggesting that the younger generation had moved to the metropolis in search of better career prospects than Somerset had to offer. William Clapp's three sons all became doctors, sensibly using instead the family name of Woodforde. John and Sarah's son Robert would later marry his cousin, Jerome's daughter Paulina.[22] William and Mary Ann's daughter Marianna married a William Marris, with whom she had four children; this family too would play a crucial part in the affairs of Clapp's famous son, the writer Jerome K. Jerome.

The older Clapp children were clearly upwardly mobile by the time the young Jerome was of an age to choose a profession. This may quite possibly explain some of the more outrageous fabrications surrounding not only his own early life, but also the antecedents of Marguerite Jones, the woman he would marry in 1842. The confusion begins with the account given by his famous son Jerome K. Jerome in *My Life and Times* (1926), in which he claims that his father attended the Merchant Taylors' school. The records of the London school show beyond doubt that Jerome Clapp was never there.[23] Perhaps deriving inspiration from his uncle's profession, Jerome goes on to assert blithely that his mother's father had been a Swansea solicitor (in fact his profession is given on Jerome's and Marguerite's marriage certificate' as 'draper'). Jerome's final invention – that near his first home in Devon 'relics were discovered proving beyond all doubt that the Founder of our House was one 'Clapa', a Dane, who had obtained property in the neighbourhood about the year Anno Domini one thousand'[24] – is surely not meant to be taken seriously.

What is known is that the young Jerome Clapp attended the non-conformist Rothwell Academy in Northamptonshire in the early 1820s, although he never became a member of the chapel there.[25] By December 1823 it seems almost certain that he was already a member of the Independent Chapel in Marlborough, where he then appears to have occupied a preaching post. According to his son he was presented with a silver salver by the congregation in June 1828.[26] This salver may well have been a tribute on his departure, although the records show simply that he left at some unspecified date to go to Cirencester with another member of the chapel, a Mrs Morgan, in whose house in Bideford he was still boarding in 1841.[27]

Clapp appears in the records in Cirencester from 1830, moving to become minister of the Boulton Lane Chapel in Dursley in 1835. Here, according to Alan Argent, he demonstrated 'initiative and vision' as well as a characteristic readiness to campaign 'for his congregation and his principles', unsuccessfully opposing a move to levy rates for the repair of the churchyard at a time when nonconformists were legally obliged to contribute to Church of England funds.[28] During his time here Clapp was also instrumental in reuniting the breakaway Boulton Lane Chapel with the nearby Dursley Tabernacle, from which it had originally seceded.[29]

In 1840 Clapp was invited to become the new minister of the Independent congregation in Appledore, Devon, a promising appointment given that the chapel had been recently extended to accommodate up to 570 people.[30] It seems that he also fell in love in this year.[31] He is listed in the 1841 census as a dissenting minister, living with two other boarders and a servant in the house of Anne Morgan in a house on Marine Parade, Appledore. In August 1841, he again took up a determined political stance, campaigning against the Corn Laws on behalf of his parishoners. According to the *Sheffield and Rotherham Independent* he seconded a resolution that, 'The Corn Laws must be abolished … upon religious principles'.[32] He appears in the papers again in 1849, in support of the Peace Congress Movement for Arbitration Instead of War, and forming a deputation with the philanthropist J. Passmore Edwards to all the borough towns in Cornwall. The *Daily News* noted that Clapp and

Edwards were well received in Devonport, despite the town's naval interests.[33]

On 7 June 1842 Clapp had married Marguerite Maire Jones in the Great Meeting House, Bideford. Like her husband, Marguerite was a non-conformist and presumably at this time a total abstainer,[34] and she is supposed to have told her son Jerome in later life 'how she and her sister, when they were girls, would often have to make their way to chapel of a Sunday morning through showers of stones and mud'.[35] Marguerite's father had already died by this point,[36] but her mother Mary witnessed the register (she wrote her own name, in itself an indication that she had received some level of education, even if she had not married a solicitor). Contrary to Jerome K. Jerome's later claim, her presence also suggests (assuming she was the beneficiary of her husband's will) that Marguerite did not initially bring a 'modest fortune' to her new husband.

In the following year the Clapps suffered the distress of two family deaths. In August the fourteen-year-old Arthur Shorland was staying with his uncle when he drowned in the Torridge and, as the resident minister, Clapp himself officiated at the funeral.[37] Only a few weeks later the death of Mary Jones at fifty-seven from polyps of the womb[38] may explain how her son-in-law apparently acquired a local farm shortly after his marriage; it is likely that Marguerite and her older sister Frances, grotesquely immortalised by Jerome K. Jerome as the irascible Aunt Fan in *Paul Kelver* (1902), inherited the house from Mary Jones. Frances would continue to live with the family until just before her death in 1874. By 1857 Clapp's growing gentility is suggested by the 'esquire' appended to his name.[39]

On 11 May 1845 the couple's first child, Paulina Deodata, was born. By the time she was joined by Blandina Dominica on 4 December 1847, the family is recorded as living at the eight-bedroomed Odum House in Appledore.[40] This initial success is worth bearing in mind – given the spectacular failure of Clapp's later investments, it is easy to write him off as a Micawberish optimist possessed of more energy than business acumen, and his surviving son actively promoted this view in his mature writing. If so, this same son was also enthusiastic about new business ventures and he repeatedly defended the working class against middle-class condescension. Clapp was also of course still active in the ministry, preaching at the new Wesleyan Chapel in Milk Street and Bedminster Chapel as late as 1853.[41]

Although Clapp appeared to prosper as both preacher and gentleman farmer, a series of reverses seems to have begun in 1852 with his decision to mine his land for silver, following a fraudulent advertisement in the local press. Clapp's fortune appears to have withstood this first misadventure, but more trouble was to follow in 1854 when he became involved in an undignified scuffle with one of his congregation over a proposed meeting to appoint new trustees of a chapel fund.[42] On 11 June 1855 a third child, Milton Melanchton, was born to the Clapps, before they abruptly departed for Walsall in September.[43]

Here Clapp joined the Bridge Street Congregational Chapel, dramatically changed his name to Jerome Clapp Jerome and was elected deacon, chairing the church's finance committee in August 1856.[44] But rumours of scandalous behaviour followed the erstwhile Clapp to his new town, prompting a flurry of correspondence between the North Devon Association of Congregational Ministers and the Congregational Church, Walsall. In January 1857 twenty members, including Jerome, seceded from the Church. When a new building, Ephratah Chapel, opened for worship in January 1859, however, Jerome did not become its minister, although he remained active in the ministry, speaking on total abstinence principles.[45]

Nor were his business ventures going well. A failed interest in a Staffordshire ironworks was compounded by a further failure in the coal industry. Jerome K. Jerome later claimed that it was on his own first birthday that his father broke the news of his bankruptcy to Marguerite, although the early entries of Marguerite's diary have since disappeared. What had happened, according to their son, was this:

> It was the beginning of the coal boom in Staffordshire, and fortunes were being made all round him, even by quite good men. In my father's case it was the old story of the man who had the money calling in to his aid the man who had the experience. By the time my father had sunk his last penny, he knew all that was worth knowing about coal-mining; but then it was too late.[46]

Coal seemed at first to be a fail-safe option. The first shafts on Cannock Chase officially opened on 9 September 1853,[47] and the *Daily News* assured its readers that 'in all probability in very few years that district will be the most productive coal field of Staffordshire.'[48] In 1855 the *Derby Mercury* confirmed that 'The coal trade is exceedingly active.'[49] So what went wrong in Jerome's case?

He had begun in June 1858 by leasing fifty-one acres of mineral land with three shafts. Many years later his youngest child recalled, 'the contrast between the squalid slums of the collieries and the green hills and fields in their vicinity.'[50] Jerome then extended his lease with a further twenty-eight adjoining acres for an additional £16,293 over sixteen years. As recent historians have noted, 'The terms of this agreement were very stringent and left Jerome virtually "ham strung" with little room for mistake.'[51] Clearly mistakes were made, Jerome's pit fell prey to flooding and by 1860 it was all over.[52]

During this crisis the family's fourth and last child was born on 2 May 1859. Regardless of the inevitable confusion, his parents named him Jerome Clapp Jerome, the result being that he was known in the family as Luther for some years. The 1861 census, taken on 7 April, suggests that Jerome C. Jerome, colliery proprietor, was still living in Walsall with his wife, her sister and four children. Tellingly, they were employing only one servant and were now living in a terraced house, 23 Lichfield Street. It is likely that they moved to Stourbridge later in this year.[53] Their sudden poverty would not only reduce the family's standard of living, but also divide them. Marguerite Jerome's diary shows that her husband had moved to London, probably in December 1861, when in a rather jumbled entry she noted, 'Received dear Jerome's first account of his housekeeping. Gracious father soon reunite and we will consecrate ourselves for thy service – Prince Albert died.'[54] It was the first Christmas they had spent apart in twenty years. Jerome had taken premises in Narrow Street, Limehouse, in a last-ditch attempt to make money in the ironmongery business. He himself had acquired a small house in Sussex Street, Poplar, from where he seems to have sent home cheerful reports and as much money as he could afford, while all but starving himself on five shillings a week. It is not entirely clear how long the ironmongery business attracted Jerome's attention, and the last of his capital, but he was associated around this period with the business of a Mr Wood, a Walsall friend with substantial means who had business interests in London. Mr Wood appears intermittently in Marguerite's diary as carrying parcels between herself and Jerome as well as contributing funds to a programme of lectures.

But events in Stourbridge were set to take another turn for the worse. On 23 January 1862 Marguerite noted in her diary that Milton had been ill for several days with a severe attack of croup (an illness associated with children, croup constricts the airways, making it increasingly difficult to breathe) and was now much worse. He was under medical care but at this time there was no known cure. On the evening of 25th Jerome arrived and was able to walk about with his son in his arms, but after progressively weakening for three days, and at the young age of six and seven months, Milton himself knew quite well that he was dying. A horror-struck Marguerite detailed his last words over this period, creating a vivid picture of a child of simple faith and equally enquiring mind, who tried in vain to interest his younger brother in biblical passages (Jerome was two-and-a-half and presumably had little idea what was going on). Marguerite herself seems to have responded with extraordinary courage to the impending death of her small son, the tragedy of which he himself was perhaps too young to realise. 'I said, My dear would you like to see Jesus he said yes', and she told him that she thought it would not be long. Later he asked her, 'Mamma shall I be able to tell when my spirit is leaving my body[?]'. But the voice of a curious and articulate child, too young to have fully learned the accepted register of 'ars moriendi' (the art of dying), is nowhere more apparent than in his speculating about where his blood would go after his death.[55] Milton died on 26 January, the day after his father had rushed up from London to be with him. As was traditional, he was photographed in his coffin[56] before being buried in the High Street Congregational Church in Stourbridge[57] on 30 January, by a cruel coincidence also his father's birthday. It is not clear whether his mother and sisters attended the funeral (it was not common at this time for women to follow loved ones to the grave) but in any case the young Jerome would almost certainly have remained at home.

Despite the tragedy of Milton's sudden death the family finances were sufficiently pressing for Marguerite to take in 'a little boy to educate' in February,[58] a particularly poignant way of making ends meet given the death of her own young son a few weeks earlier. Around the same time Paulina left the family home, presumably for the first of her posts as governess, although she was not quite seventeen.[59] Her frequent returns home over the following months suggest that this work was either fairly local or disappointingly intermittent. Jerome Senior seems to have returned to London shortly after the funeral, appearing in the diary for a brief visit in April. His grief is registered by Marguerite as appearing in 'a beautiful piece of poetry' on 17 June, a suggestive detail that may have informed the presentation of his fictional counterpart in *Paul Kelver* many years later.

In June Paulina's latest engagement came to an end;[60] by September Jerome had bought a house in Poplar and was preparing for the rest of his family to move in.[61] His small son's impressions of childhood trauma begin, not with the loss of his older brother, which he may not have fully registered at a conscious level, but with this departure from the town of his birth. A few months before his own death he told the townspeople of Walsall:

> I went to London, accompanied by my family. I arrived there without
> even the traditional half-crown – with literally nothing in my pocket
> but a clockwork mouse, and he wouldn't go, for the reason that a
> large lady, who had got into our carriage at a wayside station – it
> may have been Birmingham – had unfortunately trodden on him.
> It sounds a triviality, but it was my first real grief, so far as I can
> remember.[62]

Jerome would later give a vivid fictional account of his arrival in
London and how 'I slept downstairs that night, on the floor, behind a screen
improvised out of a clothes-horse and a blanket.'[63] Jerome's first impressions
of London were probably impossible for him to recapture himself in later life.
But he would allow Paul Kelver, coming to the city as a boy, an extraordinary
perspective. It is the adult narrator who informs the boy's dazzled relation,
but the passage is important in suggesting how the adult Jerome had come
to figure the city in which he grew up and the impact it had had on his
childhood:

> We passed through glittering, joyous streets, piled high each side
> with all the good things of the earth – toys and baubles, jewels and
> gold, things good to eat and good to drink, things good to wear and
> good to see – through pleasant ways where fountains splashed and
> flowers bloomed. The people wore bright clothes, had happy faces.
> … The children ran and laughed. London, thought I to myself, is the
> city of the fairies.
>
> It passed, and we sank into a grim city of hoarse, roaring streets,
> wherein the endless throngs swirled and surged as I had seen the
> yellow waters curve and fret, contending, where the river pauses,
> rock-bound. Here were no bright costumes, no bright faces, none
> stayed to greet another; all was stern, and swift, and voiceless.
> London, then, said I to myself, is the city of the giants. … and these
> hurrying thousands are their driven slaves.
>
> But this passed also, and we sank lower yet until we reached a third
> city, where a pale mist filled each sombre street. … And wearily

to and fro its sunless passages trudged with heavy steps a weary people, coarse-clad, and with dull, listless faces. And London, I knew, was the city of the gnomes who labour sadly all their lives, imprisoned underground; and a terror seized me lest I, too should remain chained here, deep down below the fairy city that was already but a dream.[64]

This was a London defined largely by physical deprivation. The Thames was notoriously filthy, not least because of the sewage routinely dumped in it by the populace, and 'by the 1850s there were some sixty sewer outlets into the river. ... All vomited filth into the tideway.'[65] There were complaints about the stench caused by the removal of 'soil' (sewage) in open waggons,[66] and a commissioner in 1863 began a statement with an ominous warning against the moral dangers of overcrowding: 'Before starting on my rounds with the district visitors of Limehouse, Walworth, Poplar, Shoreditch, Stepney, and Whitechapel, where the poor and the criminal are massed, I am most anxious to impress on the reader's mind the vices of the system under which London is growing.'[67]

One reason for Jerome's fascination with Dickens is their shared experience of the East End of London. In a foreword to an edition of *Our Mutual Friend* Jerome admitted that as a boy he had gone with his father to hunt out or imagine the 'originals' of different scenes and characters from the book, and even as an adult 'I have never been able to regard *Our Mutual Friend* as a mere story.'[68]

Given Jerome's abiding fascination with the city, it is significant that he predicates Paul's response on the dual themes of enchantment and the need to escape. In *My Life and Times* Jerome would confirm the effect of these hopeless streets on his own character:

I have come to know my London well. Grim poverty lurks close to its fine thoroughfares, and there are sad, sordid streets within its wealthiest quarters. But about the East End of London there is a menace, a haunting terror that is to be found nowhere else. The awful silence of its weary streets. The ashen faces, with their lifeless eyes that rise out of the shadow and are lost. It was these surroundings in which my childhood was passed that gave to me, I suppose, my melancholy, brooding disposition. I can see the humorous side of things and enjoy the fun when it comes; but look where I will, there seems to me always more sadness than joy in life.[69]

Jerome's ability to 'see the humorous side of things' is of course what made him famous. That he was also a pessimist is one of the very few personal revelations in his published non-fiction.

Overall these first months in Poplar seem to have been a reasonably settled time. Marguerite recorded the anniversary of Milton's death, as she would continue to do every year. But she also received 'a handsome present' from her husband on her birthday, 10 March, and on the same day Paulina and Blandina were taken to see the illuminations in honour of the marriage of the Prince of Wales. A few days later Jerome had his wallet stolen with £15 in it, but pursued the thief and recovered his property, a courageous act in the crime-ridden East End.[70]

But by the end of April the family was once again in financial trouble. Changed circumstances meant that Paulina could not have a watch for her birthday on 3 May. By the end of July they were forced to tell Eliza, the maid, that they could no longer afford to keep her,[71] a loss that would have entailed an enormous amount of extra work for Marguerite. Early in November Jerome accepted a new situation in some kind of banking concern and was paid £50.[72] Nonetheless, by 15 January 1864 Marguerite had received 'most fearful intelligence', that there was no money that quarter to meet the family's liabilities.[73]

Despite the end of their working relationship, Wood continued to involve himself with the family in general, and seems to have taken a particular interest in one or both sisters during this period. Her brother later remembered visits to Stoke Newington with Blandina, to take tea with 'a very old gentleman – or so he appeared to me – with a bald, shiny head and fat fingers',[74] whom he assumes to have been the man in question. It was at the instigation of Wood that Jerome somehow found more money to put into a plan for a new railway. As his son sadly put it, 'from where to where, I cannot say… For us it led from Poverty to the land of Heart's Desire'.[75] The scheme was probably connected with the 'railway mania' in London during the 1850s and 60s, including a proposed line connecting Stepney, Poplar and Limehouse.[76] As Jerry White explains, 'Through the 1850s new railway developments had stalled while capital was scarce and companies merged and restructured. Yet demand for rail travel continued to grow.' This seemed an ideal time to invest in such a venture. But if all the projected lines were sanctioned a quarter of the city would need to be demolished to make way for them, and a parliamentary committee on Metropolitan Railway Communication decided on a substantial overground exclusion zone.[77] Again, the new venture came to nothing and Marguerite was forced to admit that, 'Every effort my dear Jerome has made has proved unsuccessful.'[78]

The year 1865 seems to have been relatively uneventful. There were visits to the Marris cousins and to the Woodfordes at Plaistow; Paulina was troubled by persistent ill health. This was also the year that the six-year-old Jerome stopped taking sugar in his tea and implored his parents to let him join in family prayers. Poignantly he was the same age as his precociously religious older brother Milton had been when he died. Jerome rarely discussed his brother in later life, at least in writing, but he may even have felt that as the only remaining son, he had to compensate for his mother's loss. On 30 November his uncle Marris sent him a box of bricks. On a gloomier note, in 1866 the millenarian Dr Cummings prophesised the end of the world.[79] Jerome later regretted that as a result of his teachings 'my young blood used to be everlastingly chilled by weekly prognostications of doom'.[80]

That January, Wood finally proposed to Paulina but, to her mother's evident relief, 'God graciously preserved her from being influenced by his wealth'.[81] By the summer the family's financial prospect was presumably brighter than it had been for some time, as a replacement for Eliza was found.[82]

But domestic upheavals were not the only problem in the summer of 1866. It was at this moment that London suffered one of its periodic outbreaks of cholera, with an estimated 70 per cent of the casualties occurring in the East End.[83] As Michelle Allan points out, cholera was associated with pollution or lack of hygiene, and so by extension with the urban poor themselves. This was the class among which the Jeromes were now living but with whom they were so determined not to be associated. Allan posits 'a provisional generalization about the meanings of filth for the educated members of the middle class in mid-Victorian cities: the problem of filth was at once a physical danger (defined as such by an emergent scientific authority), a demoralizing influence, and a social threat; moreover, it was inextricably tied to perceptions and anxieties about the urban poor, who were themselves insufficiently contained'.[84] This anxiety would be sufficient explanation for the fictional Mrs Kelver's pretence that the family employs a servant long after this has become a practical impossibility. But in the summer of 1866 the threat was not simply moral, it was quite literal, with Poplar and Limehouse 'giving sad witness to the deadly character of this fatal disorder.'[85]

It must have been with some relief that Jerome Senior put behind him the scandal surrounding his departure and returned to Appledore this summer, leaving his wife to contemplate, 'Oh what changes have we passed thro' since last I saw that spot. Well our Father's love has never waned or changed to us.'[86] On 13 October Paulina was married to her cousin Robert Shorland in a quiet service in Margate. None of her own family were present. A few weeks later Marguerite and Blandina went to visit her new home in Seville Villa, Colney Hatch, but the house in Poplar was inevitably lonely without her. One stroke of luck came unexpectedly that December, in the form of a £50 legacy, which was immediately paid into the building society.

How long this money remained in the building society is unclear, but ominously there was no gas in the house by 5 January, and when the snow did begin to thaw it transpired that the roof was leaking and Jerome and Marguerite were forced to lie in bed with the rain dripping down on them. As a successful editor Jerome would suggest with feeling that young men on the verge of matrimony might spend their leisure time in 'acquiring some knowledge of the duties of a householder, and of the various traps which are laid for him'. Specifically he pointed out that, 'The small boy who is destined to become a householder learns a great many things, but ... does not know anything about water-pipes, and takes a house where the water-supply must definitely be cut off every winter when there is a slight frost.'[87]

It was not just the Jeromes who were suffering. In the winter of 1866-67 an estimated 16,000-18,000 artisans were 'in a state of absolute starvation' in the areas of Poplar, Millwall, Limehouse and Bromley'.[88] A local relief fund reported that by the middle of March they had given assistance to something like 2,000 families.[89] At around this time smallpox was on the increase in the most notorious parts of the East End, including Poplar.[90]

But these events did not directly affect the Jeromes. For his eighth birthday 'Luther' received a bird cage from his parents, a bible from one of his sisters and a hymn book from the other. At this young age he also became an uncle when Paulina gave birth to her first child in August. In the autumn he joined the Band of Hope, a child's evangelical organisation of the type much mocked by Dickens, whose mission was to promote the principles of sobriety and teetotalism. In this summer Jerome Senior meanwhile seems to have purchased a property in Notting Hill.

But the family's troubles were far from over. Paulina's health was still a source of concern and Blandina was obliged to stay with her for a period of some weeks over the winter of 1867-8, leaving the house 'desolate' and her younger brother 'amusing himself by getting up a show alone poor little fellow' while his mother wrote to the girls.[91] Sickness in Poplar continued on such a scale that the local surgeon claimed that he had so many cases on his hands it was impossible to see them all himself.[92] On 26 April Mr Wood died and a few days later a letter arrived from the owners of the farm in Appledore, objecting to an intended visit of Marguerite and the children. Evidently not everyone in Appledore was prepared to be formally reconciled with the Clapp Jeromes. Notwithstanding this frosty response, the holiday went ahead in July, and Marguerite was gratified that 'They seemed to remember all my acts of kindness which I had long ago forgotten and quite overwhelmed me with their love and affection. We enjoyed ourselves excessively[.] My visit has been to me like the refreshing rain after a long and heavy drought.'[93] Jerome confirmed in later life that this visit had partaken of the stuff of fairy tale. He had, he admitted, no memory of the countryside in the time before Poplar, and (ironically in the tones of Paul Kelver entering London) he described how, 'There were no lamps that I could see, but a strange light was all about us, as if were were in fairyland. It was the first time that I had ever climbed a hill.'[94] After the insufficient diet of his London life, 'There were picnics on the topmost platform of the old, grey, ruined tower that still looks down upon the sea. And high teas in great farmhouses, and with old friends in Bideford, where one spread first apple jelly and then Devonshire cream upon one's bread, and lived upon squab pies and junkets, and quaffed sweet cider out of goblets, just like gods.'[95]

Unfortunately the child was accidentally left behind on the way back. As his mother laconically reminded herself, 'tho' we left Jerome behind at Salisbury they forwarded him by express and we met on the platform.'[96] Jerome's more spirited account has his younger self cast adrift at Taunton, where a stout man in uniform placed him under the care of a sympathetic lady to whom he confided on the way up that he was keeping a diary. 'For, unknown to all but my aunt Fan, I was getting together material for a story of which I myself would be the hero. ... By some magic, as it seemed to me, the kind lady and myself reached Paddington before my mother got there, so that, much to her relief, I was the first thing that she saw as she stepped out of the train.'[97] A more significant literary encounter, Jerome's meeting with the man who cried 'Damn Mr Pickwick', probably took place at around this time.

Also at this time the nine-year-old Jerome was finally able to go to school.

He later placed this opportunity in the context of Forster's Education Act, although in fact this did not become law until 1870. But education was clearly in the air in the late 1860s, as Jerome said, 'There was fear that we should all be over educated – that England would become too intellectual and the common people waste their time in thinking.'[98]

Education, as Jerome observes here, was both a product and determiner of class status. In later years he would himself be mocked in the press for supposedly lacking the tone associated with middle-class schooling. In the event, he received a bare four years' formal education. A contemporary later remembered that he 'was very reserved, he made no close acquaintances and rarely volunteered a statement. He was generally dreamy, but at the same time was a pugnacious boy; he was proud and sensitive.'[99] These are just the sort of memories entertained by Dickens about his own behaviour – such reserve and sensitivity are embodied in David Copperfield, who would become one of Jerome's favourite fictional characters and who had, like him, 'come down in the world' from a seemingly stable middle-class background dangerously close to the indigent working class.

With his usual flair, Jerome K. Jerome would later cite his mother's diary for December as proudly noting that he passed the entrance exam with flying colours. In fact, she notes more prosaically in November that he was presented by a Mr Halford and there is no mention of any exam.[100] He did tell an interviewer in 1926 that he had been prevented from getting an exhibition by dreadful toothache on the last day of the exam.[101] He was one of three pupils to be presented in 1869, and interestingly his father is entered in the records as 'Jerome Clapp Jerome, formerly iron & coal master, now accountant.'[102] On 21 August the elder Jerome mysteriously returned to Devon. By November he was ill with spasms, a sign of worse things to come.

For the younger Jerome all seemed to be going well. On 16 December 'Jerome came home much pleased he is top in Mr Floyd's room which includes geography, history & scripture history by 7 subjects. The boys clapped him and he received 3 cheers as being one of the top boys in all the classes. He is moved on to the third form.'[103] In fact, whatever he may have told his mother, Jerome emerged more respectably than gloriously from his four years of formal education. In the semi-autobiographical *Paul Kelver* the narrator condemns the sheer inappropriateness of the education offered to children who would soon have to earn their own living, 'We were the sons of City men, of not well-to-do professional men, of minor officials, clerks, shopkeepers, our roads leading through the workaday world. Yet quite half our time was taken up in studies utterly useless to us. How I hated them, these youth-tormenting Shades! ... Horace! why could not that shipwreck have succeeded? – it would have in the case of anyone but a classic.'[104] Jerome strongly objected to the Education Bill of 1896 on the grounds of such apparent irrelevance, 'The education that the farm peasant and the farm labourer now receive is of little use to them. ... The Government School Board is only of service to those who would have been educated without the interference of the state.'[105]

He later commented ruefully on Carlyle's definition of school as a place where youth is confined and has books flung at it: 'If only they would fling the right books, it would be something.' Indirectly casting light on his personal drive and ambition, Jerome attributed his own command of French and German in later life to the efforts of 'shabby, careworn ladies and gentlemen, their names forgotten, who, for a sadly inadequate fee of sixpence to ninepence an hour, put their fine learning at my disposal.'[106] He was always modest about these acquirements, joking in 1905 that his German was understood best in Holland, although the Dutch G was impossible. 'The Dutchman appears to keep his G in his stomach, and to haul it up when wanted. Myself, I find the ordinary G, preceded by a hiccough and followed by a sob, the nearest I can get to it. But they tell me it is not quite right, yet.'[107]

Jerome's school exam papers from the period survive for a variety of subjects: Scripture History, Latin, Greek, English Language, French, German, History and Geography. If its idea of instilling knowledge is anything to go by, certainly the teaching method was not inspiring. 'Quote the passage beginning "Would he were fatter," and ending "and therefore are they dangerous,"' runs one question on *Julius Caesar* in 1867. Jerome himself was asked in 1869, 'Did Shakespeare invent the plot of the Merchant of Venice?'[108] By Easter he had been marked for 'application, regular attendance, and general good conduct', coming twenty-seventh out of forty-four overall. On 10 April Marguerite records receiving a letter, telling her that her son's school fees would be paid by 'an unknown friend' provided he conducted himself creditably. In the 1870 annual exam he obtained a certificate of merit, but in 1872 (his final year) he came 15th in the list, a creditable enough performance but hardly a pass 'with flying colours'.

Jerome never acquired much faith in the school system, although his grounds for distrust varied over the years. In his mid-thirties he was outraged by the case of a clergyman who had been fined ten shillings for thrashing a schoolboy at the school's request, arguing that, 'Everyone who has had anything to do with education knows that for boys of a certain nature, given to certain offences, a thrashing is the most remedial punishment.'[109]

Long afterwards he came to see corporal punishment as an altogether more shady affair:

> Justice may occasionally condone the whip; but the long martyrdom inflicted upon youth in the name of Education shows human nature in an ugly light. All cruelty has its roots in lust. The boy has been beaten, one fears, not for his own good, but for the pleasure of the Domini. When magisterial gentlemen pass eulogisms on the rod, and old club fogies write to the papers fond recollections of the birch, I have my doubts. They like to think about it.[110]

The best he could find to say of his own particular school was that 'In one respect it might be cited as a model. Corporal punishment was never employed.'[111]

The journey to school meant an early start and, including waiting for trains, it took something like two hours each way.[112] The journey became easier after the summer of 1870, when the family moved to Colney Hatch in north London to be nearer Paulina and her children. They moved to 77 Springfield Villas (later 42 Springfield Street) in August. Otherwise 1870 was not a good year, although the assumption of knowledge in Marguerite's brief diary entries makes it difficult to piece together the details. A speculative account might read something like this: the Notting Hill property seems to have been owned jointly with a board or organisation of some kind, and while Marguerite made a number of trips in to the city to see directors, she made little headway. In March she was told that they would take £670 for the property.[113] Interestingly, she saw the responsibility for raising this huge sum as hers alone, a response that is perhaps suggestive of her husband's failing health or simply despondency at this time. Successive entries refer to her hopes of obtaining a mortgage, but the struggle was soon acknowledged to be a useless one and the problem now became how to sell her interest in the property for a reasonable sum.

In the middle of all this Paulina had a daughter, on 2 April. It was a few weeks after this that the Jeromes's servant eloped with an unnamed man, adding to the general stress until Mary Ann appeared on 27 May. As if all this was not enough for the family to contend with, there was evidently trouble with back rent and bills.

Given the stress the whole family was under, his parents may not have realised that their youngest child was facing his own misery in the early weeks of June, following the death of Dickens on the 9th of the month. Marguerite's diary refers wearily to negotiations with men in the city and on 23 July she records, 'Agreement with Walters to sell this house for 210£, 10 paid down the whole to be complete within 1 calendar month.' It must therefore have been with some relief that she was able to record on 1 August, 'Took a house in the Springfield Road. May God bless us there.' Given the poor state of her husband's health by this time, Marguerite must have been only too glad of such help as Mary Ann was able to offer. They moved in on 11 August. Paulina seems to have helped her parents financially around this time, allowing them to get through another year 'and God will provide for the next.'[114]

In January 1871 the young Jerome of course returned to school. While the 1871 census shows that Jerome Clapp Jerome was now of no occupation, the presence of two servants, rather than simply a maid-of-all-work might suggest an improvement in the family's situation. However, it is possible that one of these two women was a nurse brought in for Jerome's final illness (on 21 January Marguerite notes the receipt of £7 collected among old friends). She now spent a sovereign buying her husband 'a nice warm dressing gown' on 2 June but he only wore it once. As she wrote the next day, 'the Lord called him home this morning, at ½ past 9 o'clock. A momentary summons and he is gone to receive the reward of his labouring & sufferings for so many years.'

With a certain degree of artistic licence, the fictional autobiography *Paul Kelver* places the death of Paul's father on his birthday. Otherwise the description of what happened may reflect the reality as remembered by Jerome. He describes the cries of the first costermonger of the morning and his mother opening the bedroom door inch by inch. Paul reflects:

> I had never seen death before, and could not realise it. All that I could see was that he looked even younger than I had ever seen him look before. By slow degrees it came home to me, the knowledge that he was gone away from us. For days – for weeks – I could hear his step behind me in the street, his voice calling to me; see his face among the crowds, and hastening to meet him, stand bewildered because it had mysteriously disappeared. But at first I felt no pain whatever.[115]

On 15 August 1871 Marguerite and the thirteen-year-old Jerome moved to a house in St John's Villas, a row of smaller houses just east of Springfield Villas. Blandina would have stayed with her mother and brother between governessing posts. On 12 November 1871 Marguerite's diary recorded Jerome's anger when a boy threw a stone at him. This small incident, occurring at a time when he must have felt emotionally vulnerable, is noteworthy both for the close relationship Jerome clearly had with his mother, and for his changing perspective – in this brief account the child is infuriated rather than demoralised by his treatment at the hands of street boys.

Some time in 1872 or '73 Marguerite seems to have relaxed her religious principles sufficiently to sanction Blandina's visiting the theatre to see *Babel and Bijou* at Covent Garden. In fairness to Marguerite, this suspicion of theatres was shared by many purity campaigners; despite the best efforts of manager reformers such as the famous Shakespearean actor William Macready, some of the London theatres were still used as a base for prostitutes soliciting clients. But, as an amused Jerome K. Jerome later remembered:

> In my parents' time, among religious people, the theatre was regarded as the gate to Hell. … My mother was much troubled, but … eventually gave her consent. After my sister was gone my mother sat pretending to read, but every now and then she would clasp her hands, and I knew that her eyes, bent down over the book, were closed in prayer. My sister came back about midnight with her face radiant as if she had seen a vision. … It was two o'clock in the morning before she had finished telling us all about it and my mother had listened with wide-open eyes; and when my sister suggested that one day she must adventure it, she had laughed and said that perhaps she would.[116]

This incident is important not least for the significance Jerome himself accords to it over fifty years later. He treats his mother's mistrust of the stage humorously, but having written over thirty plays in the course of his career, he was clearly very conscious of the gap between his parents' attitudes and his own. *Paul Kelver* suggests one obvious reason: it is at about this stage that Paul (and possibly, therefore, Jerome) is increasingly plagued by religious doubt.

In *My Life and Times* Jerome offers a devastating critique of his parents' evangelical belief in 'a God who loved you if you were good; but, if you were wicked, sent you, after you were dead, to a place called Hell, where you were burnt alive for ever and ever. My mother had the idea that it was not really for ever and ever … But that was only her fancy; and perhaps it was wrong of her to think so.'[117] The child's fear of such a God surely explains Jerome's later anxieties about the innate 'brutality' of man as well, quite possibly, as his related suspicion of 'lust' in any form. It also resonates with later accounts of a reserved and private man who differed so markedly from his public persona. While he himself placed the blame for his 'brooding, melancholy disposition' on his persecution by other children, he also remembered his fear of heaven as presented to him by his parents:

> Gold entered a good deal into the composition of it. You wore a golden crown, and you played upon a golden harp, and God sat in the centre of it – I pictured it a bare, endless plain – high up on a golden throne; and everybody praised Him: there was nothing else to do. My mother explained that it was symbolism. All it meant was that we should be for ever with the Lord, and that He would take away all pain. But it was the ever-and-everness of it that kept me awake of nights. A thousand years – ten thousand – a million! I would try to count them. And still one would be no nearer to the end. And God would always be there with His eyes upon one. There would never be any getting away by oneself, to think.[118]

As a successful editor and author in the late 1890s he told a correspondent that, 'It always used to puzzle me as a child where came the line of demarcation between the good who went to Heaven and the wicked who went to Hell. … I cannot think of my God as the proprietor of Hell.'[119]

Chapter Two

'a strange new creature that would not know me' 1871-1888

At around the time of the theatre incident, when Jerome was fourteen, he left school and got a job with the London and North-Western Railway at Euston station. In later life he would get much humorous mileage out of the railway system, with its undependable departure times and the inevitable confusion over platforms: 'Of course, I don't want to tie a train down to any particular platform, or, for the matter of that, to any particular part of a platform. I am an individualist in all things, and I like to see a certain amount of wholesome freedom everywhere; but, if there were somebody at Waterloo who knew something about the South-Western trains, it would be a boon to travellers.'[120]

He had received a bare four years of formal education, an awareness that must have come home to him repeatedly in later years. It may have been now that he began to feel the crushing sense of life narrowing that he later described as the moment of change between boyhood and manhood, 'I had the feeling I was being changed, as if by some malignant fairy's wand, into a strange new creature that would not know me, and that I should hate. My thoughts and dreams and visions he would not understand. He would drive them away.'[121]

Given his later comments, it is not likely that Jerome otherwise regretted this rather abrupt end to what would have been by modern standards a brief school career (tellingly by his own account he would prove inept in his later sally into teaching). Although his older sister was doing well academically, it was not unusual for a lower-middle-class boy without substantial family income to receive a bare education before starting work. Jerome would be earning £26 a year with an annual rise of £10 and overtime for the asking.[122]

As David Fink has argued, his first paid employment was probably arranged through the good offices of the LNWR Superintendent, George Potter Neele, who presumably met the Jeromes in the 1840s and '50s, when he was based in Walsall as Superintendent of the South Staffordshire Railway.[123] By the spring of 1874, Aunt Fan was presumably in need of more nursing care than they were able to provide and went to a nursing home in South Kensington.[124] She died just over a month later, the telegram summoning Marguerite having come just too late. Ironically, she and Blandina had visited Frances a few days earlier on 31 May and reported her as being 'very happy and comfortable'. Now she arrived in South Kensington by the first train, only to find that her sister was 'safe in glory'.[125] Meanwhile, on 21 May 1874 the remaining family had moved to Holloway in north London,[126] the last house that Jerome would live in with his mother. The final entries in the diary are brief and dispiriting:

> 6 June. Paulina Bland and I followed the dear remains to its last resting place.

> 7 June. My wedding-day.

> 10 June. Dear Papa's burial day.

> 11 June. Dear Milton's birth-day.

Marguerite Jerome died on 21 July 1875 of strangulation of the bowels and exhaustion. She had already chosen her memorial, 'The Long waiting days are over / They've received their wages now / For they've gazed upon their Master, And <u>his</u> name is on their brow.'[127] Blandina was away when it happened, presumably with an employer, but the sixteen-year-old Jerome was with his mother when she died. It was now that his religious doubts became particularly troubling. Without her influence 'my prayers were few and far between – occasional cries for help such as a shipwrecked swimmer might fling out into the darkness without any real hope of response.'[128] In *Paul Kelver* the impending death of the hero's father has a comparable effect:

> There was no firm foothold anywhere. What were all the religions of the world but narcotics, with which Humanity seeks to dull its pain, drugs in which it drowns its terrors, faith but a bubble that

death pricks?

I do not mean that my thoughts took this form. I was little more than a lad, and to the young all thought is dumb, speaking only with a cry. But they were there – vague, inarticulate. Thoughts do not come to us as we grow older; they are with us all our lives. We learn their language – that is all.[129]

Jerome would admit towards the end of his life that his knowledge of the two or three years immediately after his mother's death was 'confused and disjointed'.[130] Just old enough to be considered independent, he was forced to find affordable lodgings and support himself. Tellingly, what he remembered most about this period of his life was not the fight for survival at such a young age; it was the loneliness. In *My Life and Times* he recalled:

The chief thing about [these years] was my loneliness. In the daytime I could forget it, but when twilight came it would creep up behind me, putting icy hands about me. I had friends and relations in London who, I am sure, would have been kind; but my poverty increased my shyness: I had a dread of asking, as it were, for pity. I seem to have been always on the move, hoping, I suppose, to escape from solitude.[131]

He would use this experience to stunning effect in his fiction, especially in *Paul Kelver*. In the year after his mother dies, Paul inhabits a number of cheap lodging houses while working as a clerk for a meagre salary. He makes no friends of his own and haunts the parks watching the passers-by. As he explains:

Sometimes a solitary figure would pass by and glance back at me – some lonely creature like myself longing for human sympathy. In the teeming city must have been thousands such – young men and women to whom a friendly ear, a kindly voice, would have been as the water of life. Each imprisoned in his solitary cell of shyness, we looked at one another through the grating with condoling eyes; further than that was forbidden to us.[132]

On one occasion a young woman sits beside him on a bench and the lonely Paul impulsively stretches out his hand to her for a moment before she walks away, and he never sees her again.

Whether Jerome drew on his earlier novel as an aide-memoire for his autobiography is of course uncertain, but tellingly one passage reads, 'For those first twelve months after my mother's death I lived alone, thought alone, felt alone. In the morning, during the busy day, it was possible to bear; but in the evenings the sense of desolation gripped me like a physical pain.'[133] Similarly, the experience of living alone in lodgings creates a painful undercurrent in both texts. In one of Jerome's temporary lodgings he apparently heard a noise suggestive of a man hammering with his hands on the wall. Later his hanged body was discovered by the landlady coming round for the rent.[134]

It is impossible to ascertain exactly where Jerome lived in the years 1875 to 1878 – by his own account he would have had few correspondents, and if any of his landlords and landladies did recognise a shy young clerk in the almost grotesquely successful author of *Three Men in a Boat* over a decade later, there is no record of their having come forward. His first known address is 36 Newman Street, in the Fitzrovia district, significant not least because it was here that he met his first lifelong friend George Wingrave, thinly disguised as 'George' in *Three Men in a Boat*. It is also the address from which his first extant letter is addressed in November 1880, enquiring about admission to the British Museum and dramatically changing his middle name of Clapp for the more impressive K. (Klapka) on which legends of his father's encounter with the Hungarian general were later based.[135] The very formal tone of this letter, with its careful grammar and convoluted syntax ('Any information you could give me that would facilitate my deriving the advantages of this institution I should deem a great favour'), is revealing both for its suggestion of social insecurity and as proof that the writer later lambasted as ''Arry K. Arry' adopted slang terms in his fiction quite self-consciously. While Jerome refers to reading books in the British Museum, as one would expect, the only extant record relates to his ordering a volume on 19 November 1880.[136]

It is not known whether this initial foray into the museum was auto-didactic or connected with Jerome's early journalism. However, something is known of where he had been between April 1878 and this abortive relationship with the British Museum in late-1880. The youngest child of Jerome C. Clapp, dissenting minister, and his wife, who had felt such distress at the thought of her daughter visiting the theatre, had spent the last two years on the provincial stage.

It is likely that Jerome had, as his memoir suggests, been attracted to the theatre for some time before he was able to take up acting as a career. As he put it in *On the Stage – and Off: the brief career of a would-be actor.*

> There comes a time in every one's life when he feels he was born to
> be an actor. Something within him tells him that he is the coming
> man, and that one day he will electrify the world. Then he burns with
> a desire to show them how the thing's done, and to draw a salary of
> three hundred a week.
>
> This sort of thing generally takes a man when he is about
> nineteen, and lasts till he is nearly twenty.[137]

He later remarked that 'I might have become a matinee idol. But Fate
preserved me. After a year or two, I returned to London: this time chiefly
with pawn tickets in my pocket.'[138]

For his first venture onto the boards Jerome at least did not have to
move far from his familiar surroundings. In the first few months, between
April and December 1878,[139] he played a number of roles at Astley's, a
theatre renowned for its exotic melodramas. They opened with *Dolly Varden*,
based on *Barnaby Rudge* (not the first and by no means the last coincidence
persistently linking Jerome to Dickens), before moving on to *Mazeppa* and
Lost in London (a further irony, as the author Watt Phillips may well have been
an unacknowledged influence on *A Tale of Two Cities*). It is not clear what
roles Jerome played in these productions, but by his own account he played
the policeman in Manville Fenn's *Land Ahead*.[140] If this entry onto the boards
was exciting at one level, it was also a precarious existence. Jerome may well
have known Joseph Mathews, a renowned master carpenter who had worked
in a number of theatres including Astley's. Little is known of him, except
that in 1850 he was the victim of an assault by a drinking partner while
working at the Strand, and was hospitalised after being thrown forcibly into
the orchestra.[141] But at the time when Jerome was acting at Astley's, Mathews
suffered a fatal accident and an appeal was placed in the theatrical paper *The
Era* for funds for his widow and children, living in Lambeth.[142] Such stories at
the very start of his career would surely have reminded Jerome himself that
there were no guarantees in this profession.

But if there were setbacks, equally there were evident opportunities,
not least through the advertisement columns of *The Era*. Beth Palmer sees
The Era and its later rival *The Stage* as 'attempting to *construct an image* of the
professional and respectable actor, even if that image did not match up
seamlessly with the realities of theatrical life in late-Victorian Britain.' Palmer

notes that with a circulation of 5,000 in the 1870s, *The Era* was strategically placed to become indispensable as a directory for theatre professionals,[143] and it is likely that Jerome was consulting it in these years.

Nonetheless, when the season finished at the end of November he began looking around for alternative work and after the exhilaration of his first season felt free to hand in his resignation to the North-Western Railway. Predictably his older sisters were horrified. As he put it:

> I chucked the North-Western Railway, and joined a touring company. My sisters were much troubled. At Euston, I was earning seventy pounds a year, and I might become general manager. I pointed out to them that, instead, I might become London's leading actor with a theatre of my own. But they only cried.[144]

In fact, he later complained that, having once shown an aptitude for comic parts, he was never thereafter allowed to play a romantic role.[145] It is almost certain that his next engagement was with Our Girls' Company, who opened with a pantomime in Torquay just after Christmas. The available evidence suggests that Jerome was appearing as Dick Whittington's cat.[146] Poignantly his 1902 autobiographical novel contains a scene in which the hero's father falls in love with a dangerously fascinating woman, and the child bitterly regrets the resentment he feels for his mother when she will not allow her rival to take him to the pantomime. The production is *Dick Whittington*.

It was during his engagement in Torquay that Jerome later claimed to have assumed the stage name Harold Crichton, only to find that he would be acting with a genuine Haldane Crichton, who subsequently taught him dancing and tumbling.[147] As a touch of humour it is pure Jerome. Except that, unbelievably, it is probably true. Jerome had left the company by early February after a brief tour of the south. He next turns up in Auguste Creamer's company, in a production at the Theatre Royal in King's Lynn, a port town near the east coast. At precisely this time Haldane Crichton and his wife were announcing their availability from their home in 34 Newman Street,[148] just two doors down from the lodgings Jerome would famously occupy with George Wingrave in 1880. As well as teaching him the rudiments of clowning, Crichton may well have been indirectly responsible for one of Jerome's most enduring and creatively productive friendships.

Meanwhile, Creamer's company left King's Lynn for Great Yarmouth in April 1879 and then went on to Stockport, near Manchester, for six nights in June. It is likely that Jerome parted company with them here, although the ostensible clues he leaves in *My Life and Times* may be no more than an elaborate joke. He remembers that he left while touring through a large town, presumably Stockport, and paints affectionate thumbnail sketches of an ironmonger called Hopsam and a landlady by the name of Miss Pinkeen. That this last has a certain Dickensian flavour ceases to be a surprise after consultation of the local records. Neither a Hopsam nor a Pinkeen appears in Yarmouth or Stockport around this time.[149] Nor does either name appear anywhere in the country on the census of 1881, the nearest available year to Jerome's tour of 1879.

By his own account, he next joined one of the few remaining stock companies, which he left after five months for a 'fit-up', essentially a mobile stage company and therefore at the very bottom of the profession. It is important to remember that, according to research done by Josephine Harrop, very few touring shows would have travelled by rail, depending instead on horse-drawn carts.[150] Jerome gives the date of his return to London as October[151] (from the context this has to refer to 1879) and his final departure for a provincial tour as late-December.[152] By May the following year the manager had absconded and Jerome had returned to London penniless.[153]

Paulina would presumably have come to his aid had she been aware of his circumstances. Blandina was probably not in London (the 1881 census taken in April shows that she was in Norfolk as governess to four children in a family called Brown). There were also the Marris cousins in Berners Street who might have helped. But the same combination of pride and embarrassment presumably stopped Jerome asking for help now, as it had done in the first period of his bereavement five years earlier. Now twenty-one, the would-be actor, who had suffered years of respectable poverty with his hapless parents and rejected the North Western Railway for a career on the stage, found himself living on the streets.

There is no extant record of how long this existence lasted, but it may have been for up to six months. By the time he came to write his memoir Jerome was deceptively matter-of-fact, even grimly humorous in his manner of handling what must have been a traumatic period of his life:

> On wet nights I would have to fork out ninepence for a doss-house.
> The best I ever struck was one half-way up Pentonville Hill, where
> they gave you two blankets; but one had to be early for that. ...
> It was a jungle sort of existence. Always we slept with everything

belonging to us, even to our leaky boots, underneath our pillow; and would start up with our hands clenched if a mouse crept across the floor. Round the common frying-pan, where we cooked our breakfast, when it ran to it, we stood on guard, ready to defend our skimpy rasher or our half-starved-looking bloater, if need be, with our lives.[154]

From having been, just a few years earlier, the shabby-genteel child of parents who had known better times, tormented by the street boys because, as his mother told him, he was 'a gentleman', Jerome now appeared doomed to a life at the very bottom of the social pile. The memory of these few months would inform his social outlook for the rest of his life. Unlike Dickens, whose life Jerome's own experience would uncannily echo in many respects, he had no hesitation in acknowledging this phase of his existence following his own rise to fame and comparative fortune. Looking back in the 1920s, Jerome would present a strange picture of himself as a young man, with the accomplishments of speaking both French and German, and the ability to outswear a cab driver: 'I discovered that there was but one way of teaching him Christian behaviour; and that was by knowing more bad language than he had ever learnt, and getting it in first. How could he know that I had slept in doss-houses, shared hay-ricks with tramps? I had the further advantage over him of being able to add vituperation both in French and German.'[155] But just as Dickens's tortures in the blacking warehouse were greatly increased by the fear that there would be no escape, so Jerome must have dreaded growing old on the streets of London.

He seems to have been rescued quite by chance, he later claimed through a meeting with an old friend who had himself fallen on hard times and generously introduced Jerome to his own network of newspaper editors. Luckily for Jerome, he turned out to have a flair for writing, and from as early as November 1880 he was making a living as penny-a-line journalist. Who this friend was Jerome does not say, but at around this time he may well have renewed his friendship with (one might almost say the real) Haldane Crichton. From the proximity of their lodgings, already noted above, it seems most likely that Crichton took his namesake under his wing, found him somewhere to live, and quite possibly even some precarious employment. By his own account Jerome conducted the work with such panache as the limitations of the form allowed. Certainly his retelling of this part of his career leaves no poetically-licenced stone unturned. He claims for instance to have reported on Irving's first appearance in *The Bells*. This is unlikely, given Jerome would have been twelve at the time, although it is tempting to identify him as the author of an admittedly rather late fanfare in the *Penny Illustrated Paper and Illustrated Times* on Irving's revival of the play in 1883.[156] Again, he recalls, with considerable enjoyment, writing a report of the evangelical Spurgeon's sermon based on a joke about the weather, 'It's damned hot (a long pause) in Hell'.[157] It is a good story, but had in fact been doing the rounds since at least 1864, when it was attributed to the Rev. A. Mursell of Manchester.[158] For the rest of his life Jerome retained a passionate conviction in the power of journalism to influence social direction. He was clearly joking when he said in the more fortunate days of 1886 that, 'I thought once that the life of a journalist was as near heaven as I could ever hope to get; I have since come to earnestly trust that this will not prove to be the case.'[159] Enjoyable or not, penny-a-lining was hardly a viable long-term career, and he next turned his attention – somewhat bizarrely, given his avowed dislike of the English educational system – to teaching. His friend, the writer Coulson Kernahan later asked him how he had got on as a teacher - 'Not at all – *nor did the boys*'[160] came the reply.

In the 1881 census Jerome (by now K) Jerome is listed as a shorthand writer to a solicitor, although his continued residence at 36 Newman Street, with an equestrian perfomer for Astley's as his landlord, testifies to his continued fascination with a less pedestrian way of life. His enquiry to the British Museum a few months earlier similarly suggests that he had no intention of spending his life writing legal documents. What does impress, incidentally, is his obvious aptitude for learning, as well as his determination and persistence. As the cursory record shows, at some point between his return to London in the spring of 1880 and the census of April 1881, the man who would later dub himself 'an idle fellow' had somehow managed to learn shorthand. Almost certainly this was the Pitman system, which he later recommended as the only one for practical purposes,[161] rather than the fiendish Gurney system described by Dickens. Jerome makes the link quite explicitly in *My Life and Times*, 'Dickens had started his career as a Parliamentary reporter. It seemed to me I could not do better than follow in his footsteps.'[162]

It would be gratifying to picture Jerome frantically scribbling, pad perched on knee, while his new friend Wingrave declaimed in the manner of Traddles speechifying for David Copperfield. The reality of their meeting was, in fact, more prosaic. The story goes that their landlord suggested they should take rooms together in order to save on the rent. Where Jerome can claim to echo the early career of David Copperfield (or for that matter one of Dickens's shabby genteel clerks) is in his desperate attempt to cultivate the vices.

The 1880s was a decade of change, perhaps most visibly in the metropolis. Not least, women became more visible in the city and their place more hotly contested, as they started to infiltrate the offices and form their own clubs. As Emma Liggins has recently shown, 'The labelling of bachelor girls … indicated the new associations of singleness with Bohemianism, professional work, access to higher education, ladies' clubs and new living spaces for women in the city.'[163]

This was also a decade of controversy surrounding the now notorious Contagious Diseases Acts, under which the police in a number of naval towns were given power to arrest suspected prostitutes and have them compulsorily examined and treated for venereal disease. While the purity lobby, famously including Josephine Butler, had protested against the Acts since their introduction in the 1860s, there were powerful voices in favour of their extension to all the major towns. As Trevor Fisher explains, 'For many public health reformers, regulation of prostitution to protect the public from venereal disease was a logical step forward after regulating sewage and water supplies to protect the nation from cholera.'[164] 1886 finally saw the repeal of the Acts, a year after the raising of the age of consent under the Criminal Law Amendment Act (a wide-ranging piece of legislation later used to bring about the downfall of Oscar Wilde).

In this fraught context there was limited opportunity for meeting men socially, but women alone in the streets might be deemed sexually available and therefore not respectable (this is precisely the dilemma faced by Monica Madden in Gissing's *The Odd Women*). As Deborah Epstein Nord puts it, 'The metropolis offered anonymity, community, and distance from provincial and familial expectations, but it also proved a difficult and threatening place to be a woman alone. … Just as there was no wholly adequate social or economic structure for the independent existence of the genteel single woman, so there was no wholly respectable context for her appearance in the city landscape.'[165]

In Jerome's male-focused account, the usual strategy for picking up women was to pretend to have met them before, but he dodges the issue of sexual adventure with a tactful reference to holding hands on a bench, implying that something or nothing might come of it. He himself seems never to have been particularly successful in getting to the hand-holding stage – it is hard to read his account of taking 'the lady's preliminary rebuff … as final dismissal' and shrinking 'scarlet into the shadows' without a sympathetic shudder.

He did practise other vices – in the year before he died he commented grimly that 'with pluck and perseverance one attains to all things – even to the silly and injurious habit of pumping smoke into one's heart and liver'.[166] But if smoking was an acquired taste, alcohol was even more of a problem. The advantage of porter over claret, he decided, was that 'one gulped it down, and so got it over quicker'.[167] How Wingrave coped with these trials of young manhood, Jerome is too loyal to divulge. In later life he would become, with unimpeachable respectability, a manager for Barclay's Bank.

Despite his own rather mixed experience Jerome would always be fascinated by the world of theatre (some of the most successful comic episodes in *Paul Kelver* are based on his brief career as an actor). There is some evidence to suggest that he may have continued to act intermittently for years afterwards – he told an American actress that he had played in the copyright performance of Israel Zangwill's *Merely Mary Ann* in 1904.[168] But in particular he was sympathetic to struggling dramatists, as correspondence with *The Era* in 1885 testifies. At this stage of his life he seems to have taken an almost Micawber-like pleasure in writing letters, and now he held forth on the subject of managers' readers. He supported a previous correspondent who had opined that a fellow playwright was hardly likely to be impartial in recommending rival work. Moreover, he argued, managers were shirking one of their most crucial tasks in not personally reading new MSS submitted to them:

> Some years ago, when my name was even less known than it is now, I submitted a piece to a certain manager. Six months afterwards it was sent back to me, accompanied by a hurried note, in which I was addressed as "Miss Jacobs" and in which the manager stated he had read my little farce (it was a one-act drama of a pathetic character) with much pleasure and begged to return it herewith: which he did in the same envelope in which I had sent it, *and with the seal unbroken*.[169]

When a vituperative 'reader of plays' got involved in the debate Jerome seized on his letter with obvious enjoyment, pointing out that the reader's attitude to other dramatists was hardly impartial, 'He contemptuously dubs them Smith and Brown. ... He thinks the inhabitants of the infernal regions must sympathise with those who have to peruse their work. ... Such is the spirit in which he views the duties he is employed to discharge.'[170]

In this instance Jerome is not simply adopting a satirical pose, he is letting off steam after years of trying to place his own work, and with the assurance of a young writer who has finally achieved volume publication. At a distance of over twenty-five years *My Life and Times* tells the familiar story with the author's customary panache. After successfully placing one story 'about a maiden who had given her life for love and been turned into a waterfall'[171] in a short-lived periodical, there was nothing:

> The others, with appalling monotony, had been returned to me again and again: sometimes with the editor's compliments and thanks, and sometimes without; sometimes returned with indecent haste, seemingly by the next post; sometimes kept for months – in a dustbin, judging from appearances.[172]

Despite the self-mockery Jerome pointedly asks 'if the smart journalists who make fun in the comic papers of the rejected contributor have ever been themselves through that torture-chamber.'[173]

Jerome's defensive, and soon to be highly successful strategy, was to mock his own failures, a stance he adopts in *On the Stage – and Off: the brief career of a would-be actor*. Humour aside, this first book is, as Jeremy Nicholas suggests, 'a remarkably vivid and useful source on life in the theatre of the 1880s.'[174]

The idea apparently came to him while reading Longfellow's poem 'Gaspar Becerra'. In the first lines of the poem, 'By his evening fire the artist / Pondered o'er his secret shame; / Baffled, weary, and disheartened,/ Still he mused, and dreamed of fame.' Finally the artist realises that he must abandon far flung visions and 'take this lesson to thy heart: That is best which lieth nearest; / Shape from that thy work of art.' After the initial success of his one story in *The Lamp*, the young writer was still struggling with perpetual rejection and 'it came to me that Longfellow was telling me not to bother about other people's troubles – those of imaginary maidens turned into waterfalls, and such like – but to write about my own'. In his enthusiasm Jerome wrote to thank Longfellow, who to his credit wrote back:

My Dear Young Friend,

Your letter has given me much pleasure. I am happy to know that any words of mine have cheered and strengthened you. With my best wishes for your happiness and success in life,

I am, yours very truly,

Henry W. Longfellow.[175]

Jerome persevered. In June 1882 he wrote to Clement Scott, an influential drama critic for the *Daily Telegraph* and *The Theatre*, 'I beg to submit to you enclosed first pages of Reminiscences, which if you approve of, I propose continuing from month to month. – You will see at a glance the nature of the thing, so I abstain from any comment here, merely mentioning that the circumstances related here are my actual experiences.' The postscript, 'I enclose envelope to save you trouble', is in line with professional practice.[176] Clearly Scott used the envelope, as Jerome wrote again by return of post: '... you can have no idea of the desperate uphill struggle a young fellow without influence has before he can get the smallest piece of his work accepted, or you would not be surprised at his taking a perhaps inexcusable course in his efforts to gain a footing in journalism'. By the time of World War I he had become increasingly wary of the power wielded by newspaper syndicates, but continued to represent the journalist's vocation as a kind of moral crusade:

> We did not then anticipate that there would come a time when the entire Press of the country, practically speaking, would be in the hands of one or two rich men, working together for their own purposes. In those days, one man owned one paper and believed what he published. Journalism was a noble and interesting profession and, but for an incurable tendency towards romancing, that had been my trouble ever since I was a boy, I might have stuck to it.[177]

As far as his account of his stage career went, he realised himself that his rejected MS was not suitable for the general press, and he would therefore never get it published if 'I go about the matter in the usual dreary way.' Would Scott therefore advise him whom to approach, or better still, recommend him to another paper? 'It is the first foothold that is so hard to obtain. ...

I am aware how extraordinary such a request from an utter stranger must appear to you, but a little assistance of this kind would be such a help to me just at present that I venture to cast modesty to the winds in my pursuit of it.'[178] Scott seems to have been responsive to this request, and Jerome wrote him a series of letters over the next few years, thanking him for advice and friendly notices of his first plays. When Scott himself suffered disaster in 1899 and was forced to resign from the *Daily Telegraph*, Jerome (also in exile by this point) in turn wrote to offer his advice and support. Many years after his death in 1904 Jerome insisted that Scott in some respects at least, 'however old-fashioned his views may have been, easily beat the modern dramatic critics in his wonderful power of describing a production in detail and singling out fine points of acting'.[179]

On the Stage – and Off, ironically about his failure to establish himself on the stage, was finally published as a serial in *Play* in 1883. It was probably at this time that Jerome first met another failed actor and, later, famous novelist, Eden Phillpotts. Phillpotts, who made his name with *Children of the Mist* in 1890, published his first stories in *Play*, which he later claimed was kept afloat by Jerome's anecdotes of his time on the stage.[180]

At around this time Jerome and Wingrave moved to new lodgings in Tavistock Place.[181] During these years Jerome at least was a regular attender at theatrical first nights, where he would energetically shove his way through the crowd to obtain pit or gallery tickets, depending on the state of his finances. As he laconically put it, 'The queue system had not yet been imported. It came from Paris. We despised the Frenchies for submitting to it.'[182] It was on one of these occasions that he met Carl Hentschel, later immortalised as Harris in *Three Men in a Boat*. Unlike Jerome, Hentschel himself was not an aspiring writer, but became highly successful in his own right. Jerome later claimed that he was Polish. In fact, although he had been born in Poland in 1864, he was actually the son of an American Russian, who had come to England and set up a wood-engraving company, subsequently inventing the Hentschel colour type process and revolutionising the means of newspaper illustration.[183] In testament to his own standing, his obituary mentions his identity as "Harris" only in the very last line. In later days Jerome doubtless approved of Hentschel's attempt to limit public speeches. On the occasion of a dinner for the Bartholomew Club in 1904 Hentschel made the decision as President to distribute the speeches in advance and take them 'as read'.[184]

As well as his friendship with Hentschel, Jerome's 'first night' habit brought him into contact with a number of other young men who would become important in various ways. Among them G. B. Burgin, who later became his subeditor on *TO-DAY*, listed J. M. Barrie, Coulson Kernahan, Bernard Partridge and George A. Lewes.[185] It is not clear exactly when Jerome's friendship with Barrie began, but Kevin Telfer suggests that '... Jerome and his friends were among a group of men that Barrie was beginning, for the first time in his adult life, to engage with socially, after the lonely years of university and the start of his time in London'. Jerome remembered with amusement that he had inadvertently procured Barrie a wife in finding for him the only actress he knew who 'was young, beautiful, quite charming, a genius for preference, and able to flirt'.[186] Jerome generously suggested Mary Ansell, who had been cast for a part in Jerome's *Woodbarrow Farm*, produced by his own travelling company. The next time he met her she was married to his friend.[187]

On 18 March 1884 Jerome became a founding member of the Playgoers' Club, inaugurated in the Dane Inn Coffee House in Holywell Street by Heneage Mandell and Hentschel, with Addison Bright, later theatrical agent, as President (Hentschel would be President in 1902-3, 1914-16 and at the time of his death in January 1930). According to Burgin, J. M. Barrie was a member in 1885, but attended only once. Unfortunately, no one else was there but the 'charwoman' and, as he afterwards wrote to Hentschel, she thought he had designs on the library and eyed him with such suspicion that he never came again.[188]

The format of the Club was a weekly meeting held at the Hotel Cecil in the Strand, at which a topic was proposed, seconded and debated by the members. From the start Jerome's name appears as debating contested points such as whether too much staging detracts from the acting of a play (21 May 1884) and whether farce could be taken too seriously (1 July 1884).[189] He was proposed but not elected to the committee in the second general meeting of 10 June 1884, and served as President from 1889 to October 1891,[190] taking the Chair at the annual dinner in 1890 and 1891.[191] It was during this time that the Club had its celebrated debate on the merits or demerits of Ibsen. Jerome spoke against and noted some aggressive reactions, notably from George Bernard Shaw, with whom he would have further disagreements over the years. One point of contention was their different attitude to the drama and, as Faurot notes, Shaw, 'who wrote many reviews of the plays of the 1890's, criticized sometimes gently and sometimes harshly the plays of Jerome'.[192] In 1904 Shaw told Wells that, 'If you imagine that you have so artfully concealed your brains that [managers] will accept you unsuspiciously as a disciple of

Jerome K. Jerome, you err most prodigiously.'[193] At this stage Jerome noted that:

> The general feeling of the club is clearly anti Ibsenite but the mere talking power (embracing as it does the Socialist contingent) was on his side. … For myself I feel that Ibsen is a great genius but I am growing to hate him as a teacher… He sees nothing but the evil side of all things. God knows there is plenty of evil in the world. It doesn't need a genius to see it. But there is good in everything…. If art is only to make life more hideous for us – if it is only to show us the evil & teach us hopelessness then art is a curse to humanity.[194]

Coincidentally, his friend Rose Norreys would become an important apologist for Ibsen in 1891 when she played Nora in *A Doll's House*, explaining in an interview that, 'I thoroughly love the character. It could not suit me better if Ibsen had written it for me. It suits me better than parts which *have* been written for me.'[195] Jerome would drastically modify his own stance over the next few years, as he revised his notions of the role of literary and dramatic art.

At around the time of the Playgoers' debates Jerome established the weekly *Playgoer* with Heneage Mandell. Israel Zangwill (who became, according to his biographer, 'probably the most famous Jew in the English-speaking world')[196] was a contributor, Phil May and Bernard Partridge were its leading artists, and it was the first platform for the sketches that would become *Stage-Land: Curious Customs and Manners of its Inhabitants*.

In 1888 Jerome had agreed to subscribe to *Punch* on behalf of the club (just in time to get the full benefit of that journal's satire of his own work over the next few years). In November of that year he wrote a long and impassioned defence of the club to Clement Scott, who had been shocked by its supposed rowdiness. Jerome insisted that, on the contrary, 'the whole influence of the club is against all kinds of rows'.[197]

While the available records cover only the period 1884-1891, it is clear that he was still a member in 1895, when he protested against the conduct of rowdy members and so brought on a contretemps with Reginald Geard of the *Morning Leader*.[198] The club weathered this controversy, only to split a few years later in 1900, in an acrimonious row over new premises.

Writing the club's history in 1905 W. H. Findon clearly blamed Hentschel for high-handed behaviour, although he thanks him in a note for supplying details of the club's early history and acknowledges his 'ebullient energy'[199] in the early years (Burgin similarly described him as 'the indefatigable Carl Hentschel ... possessed of more persuasive and pervasive dynamic force than any man I have ever met').[200] In the end it was the club's very success that brought about the split. An Extraordinary General Meeting on 7 March 1900 had agreed to move to larger premises after negotiations broke down for the taking of an additional floor in the Hotel Cecil. At a special meeting on 20 July it was agreed to take premises on Charing Cross Road, but Hentschel insisted on overriding the appointed committee and putting the resolution to an AGM. In the subsequent altercation he threatened to resign unless the 'three musketeers' Frederick Hess, Louis Harfeld and W. R. Bennett went instead.

The Era sided wholeheartedly with Hentschel, explaining to its readers that Hentschel had objected to the election of Louis Harfeld as vice president, on the grounds that the vote had been strategically geared and did not represent the wishes of the body of members. The 'musketeers', it claimed, wanted not only to 'move the club into new premises' but 'generally alter its tone and character.'[201] The writer of the article, describing himself as 'an old member', finished up with the assurance that:

> I can only congratulate Mr Hentschel and his friends on their escape from its ranks. One thing "goes without saying" – every Playgoer of the old school, every Playgoer who was in sympathy with the early aims and objects of the club, must leave it at once. Of course, no theatrical manager or leading actor or actress will now care to be present at the banquets of the club. The title of "the Playgoers" may be retained, but the character of the club is entirely, essentially altered.[202]

Findon was himself in the Chair on the occasion of the dispute and would claim in his history that, 'Hentschel made the fatal mistake of deeming himself indispensable. Without him, he thought, the Playgoers' Club must go to the wall.'[203] In the event two hundred original members did go with him.[204] It was Findon who later wrote the manifesto to members stating that, 'Mr Carl Hentschel, ignoring club etiquette, took the public into his confidence through the medium of the Press, and made common property of affairs which had no right of discussion outside the Club walls.'[205] By this he seems simply to have meant that Hentschel, in founding the Old Playgoers' Club in opposition to the original club from which he had seceded, had advertised in the press. But certainly the press enjoyed itself enormously with the row. In its 'The Man About Town' column for instance, *Judy* offered its readers a picture of 'a stormy session' in the Victoria Hall of the Hotel Cecil.[206]

Predictably, Jerome himself appears in the press as lecturing to the breakaway Old Playgoers' Club in 1903[207] and it is likely that he had resigned with Hentschel in 1900, at the time of the dispute. The American writer Douglas Sladen remembered that 'The old Playgoers'' was a most breezy place, where no one was allowed to speak for more than a few minutes, unless he could bring down the house with his wit. The ordinary person making a good sound speech was howled down.'[208]

Israel Zangwill, on the other hand, would remain in the rival club, becoming President in 1904. But these internecine scuffles belong to a later stage of the club. When Jerome joined in 1884 the arrangements seem to have been soon formalised, but the atmosphere remained suitably bohemian and convivial, at least for a time.

Bram Stoker was a member, and it was presumably through Addison Bright that Jerome met his fellow lodger, the artist Bernard Partridge, 'one of the handsomest men in London' and Jerome's close friend and collaborator for many years, until a rash decision about the casting of a play came between them.

Something of the atmosphere in these bohemian clubs was captured in 1894 by an American visiting London, who wrote enthusiastically that, 'No sooner is an American known to be a stranger here than a hearty welcome is extended him. If he writes, paints or does anything in the artistic vein the Authors' Club, the Savage and other clubs make him an honorary member for as long a period as he is in England, with all the privileges of ordinary membership.'[209]

It was while he was moving in these new circles that Jerome approached the novelist F. W. Robinson, who had recently begun a new magazine called *Home Chimes*. Robinson asked to meet him and commissioned a series of essays, which became *The Idle Thoughts of an Idle Fellow*, collected by Field & Tuer in 1886. His fellow contributors, several of whom either were or became close friends, included Swinburne and his friend Watts-Dunton, Westland Marston (who had known Dickens) and his son, the poet Philip Marston, Coulson Kernahan, William Sharp, Coventry Patmore (author of the notorious mid-century poem *The Angel in the House*), Bret Harte, Israel Zangwill and J. M. Barrie. It was Swinburne who arranged for Jerome to review E. Nesbit, then an up-and-coming poet and an admirer of his poetry likewise, who later contributed to *The Idler*.[210] It was also in the pages of *Home Chimes* that Jerome first predicted the success of the actress Rose Norreys, [211] who would become his friend and staunch supporter.

But in the 1880s mixing in these circles at all must have been intoxicating – little wonder that Jerome's first biographer Alfred Moss should comment, 'It was no small matter that a clerk living in lodgings on twenty-five shillings a week should find himself associated with some of the most eminent writers of the day.'[212] In fact, many of these writers, like Jerome himself, were still struggling to make their way. Robinson told G. B. Burgin, whom he had met at a Vagabonds' dinner, 'You must be one of my boys. I've already collected Barrie, Jerome, Kernahan, Eden Phillpotts, and a dozen others. Though the magazine doesn't pay, it helps you youngsters to train on for a generation of readers I shall never see.' As Burgin confirmed, 'It did not pay. How could it possibly pay when the circulation was so small?'[213]

These contacts, and the experience of working with Robinson, would prove invaluable when Jerome came to set up his own journal a decade later. He later remembered fondly that, 'In those days, there was often a fine friendship between an editor and his contributors. There was a feeling that all were members one of another, sharing a common loyalty. I tried when I became an editor myself to revive this tradition; and I think to a great extent that I succeeded.'[214] Not least, he later claimed that he was one of the friends who persuaded Phillpotts to expand a short story about a Faustian pact into what became *A Deal With the Devil*, serialised in *TO-DAY* in 1894.[215]

Over the next few years Jerome began to consolidate his new position as a respectable citizen through the time-honoured practice of writing indignant letters to *The Times*. It is quite possible that the young man with journalistic experience of his own, a ticket for the British Museum and a latent desire to make his name as a writer, was also using the paper as a means of self-promotion. As he observed himself in *My Life and Times*, it was not least 'a handy way of keeping one's name before the public.'[216] Although the humorous account he gives of a conversation with J. M. Barrie may be an invention of the moment, it is none the less entertaining for that. Apparently Barrie had told him that this particular paper would only publish correspondence from married men or mothers. Accordingly, Jerome published a letter of protest against nude art following on from a letter by a 'British Matron'.[217] Both letters did indeed appear in the 'Letters to the Editor' section of the paper in 1885. The British Matron having complained that as men and women were socially prohibited from appearing naked in public, nude portraits were by extension an outrage to decency, Jerome chimed in with his agreement 'that the human form is a disgrace to decency, and that it ought never to be seen in its natural state. But "A British Matron" does not go far enough, in my humble judgement. She censures the painters, who merely copy Nature. It is God Almighty who is to blame in this matter for having created such an indelicate object.'[218]

Years later he remembered that of the epithets hurled indignantly at him for this piece of satire, 'blaspheming' was the one that most upset his female relatives.[219] However, religion was presumably not a subject he could easily discuss with his sisters and, despite his evident delight in the tirades of the British matron, it was probably at about this time he ' passed through a period of much mental suffering'. As he acknowledged, 'The beliefs of childhood cling close. One tears them loose at cost of pain.'[220]

Even among his friends Jerome seems to have struggled to find a sympathetic listener, with the exception of the Jewish Israel Zangwill, who nonetheless failed to convince him of God's ultimate purpose.[221] One source of his doubt may actually have been the Christian belief in the equality of all mankind. Inclining to a eugenicist view of humanity based on racial, gender and intellectual hierarchies, Jerome initially mistrusted socialism on just these grounds. In 1895 he expressed doubts of universal salvation, arguing that a large number of people were simply not useful enough to warrant immortality: 'One contemplates with a certain feeling of despair the idea that the ever-increasing numbers of the human race will continue to march on through eternity. May it not be that the possibility of acquiring an immortal soul is given to each man, and may not eternal sleep be the fittest and the kindest ending for many of the shadowy figures that flit, unheeding and unthinking, across the momentary light-lit space we call life?'[222]

By this stage it was becoming increasingly acceptable to express religious doubt and, in 1896 Jerome was addressing an established audience when he claimed that the most dogmatic Christians privately expressed heterodox opinions. Still yearning for religious consolation in the face of his own rational disbelief he confessed, 'It seems to me we are living in an artificial atmosphere. ... It haunts me – this idea of a dead religion – a machine beneath which the fire has died out, still beating the air by reason only of the momentum instilled into it in the past. ... Will there, in the near future, arise a religion that the coming generation will passionately embrace with the fervent hope with which man once embraced Christianity, Mohammedanism and Buddhism?'[223]

Still perplexed by doubts in 1926 he explained:

> There were three subjects about which, when I was a young man, respectable folk were not supposed to talk: politics, sex, and religion. I remember how fervently my early editors would seek to impress upon me this convention. Round about me must have been many sharing my doubts and difficulties. We might have been of help to one another. But religion, especially – even in Bohemian circles – was strictly taboo. ... Books dealing with the subject from the free-thinker's point of view I knew existed: but for such I had no use. The usual standard works in support of orthodox opinion I did read. I do not think it altogether my fault that, instead of removing, they had the effect of increasing my perplexities.[224]

Many years after his own religious crisis he said that Carlyle's *Sartor Resartus* 'should be a second Bible to a young man.'[225] Following his publication of his views on art, Jerome seems by his own account to have become addicted to writing to *The Times*. 'I wrote upon the dangers of the streets – dogs connected to old ladies by a string; the use of the perambulator in dispersing crowds; the rich man's carpet stretched across the dark pavement and the contemplative pedestrian. I advised "Paterfamilias" what to do with his daughters. I discussed the possibility of living on seven hundred a year.' The letter on nude art, and Jerome's account of writing it as a way of getting published, are of course hilarious. But in fact he had previously written at least three letters to *The Times*, all of which had met with sufficient approval to ensure their appearance within a day or two of being written. Shortly before his encounter with the British Matron, he had involved himself in a discussion about health and safety (the carpet article cited above). A man had successfully claimed damages after tripping over a piece of matting laid in the pavement and Jerome, who whatever his view on the conditions of the Strand, was never particularly impressed by upper-class affectation, reproved the unsympathetic journalist, who 'has evidently never fallen a victim to this system of Belgravian atrocity. I have; and am, as a consequence, strongly in favour of any step tending to put a stop to it.'[226] In December he penned a further protest against the road conditions, impelled by his concern for the horses forced to work in them, 'I suppose a vestry (which, like a corporation, has no soul to be damned and no body to be kicked) cannot be punished for its brutal supineness... In this damp, foggy weather the oily slime known as

London mud lies an inch deep on every thoroughfare, and over its slippery, treacherous surface the tortured horses have to fight and struggle with their heavy loads.'[227] Much earlier, on 20 September 1883, he had complained of the Strand that, 'The pavements are slippery with slimy dirt, every vehicle that passes covers one with a shower of the mud through which it has to plough its way, and getting from one side to the other is like crossing an Irish bog.'[228] On 7 August he wrote indignantly that a young man had been what we would now term 'mugged' walking down Oxford Street, and 'If we Englishmen were not rapidly becoming a pack of mean-spirited curs, such occurrences would be impossible in a great city. No thief would dare attempt such an insult to civilization if he did not know that out of the whole street full of gaping idiots no one had the pluck' to intervene, instead electing to run 'round the corner and feebly cry "police."'[229]

In these letters he can be seen testing his literary powers, with the humour for which he was soon to become famous, but also with the cascading lists and acute observation of objects most associated with Dickens, 'What between peg-tops and tip-cats, coals being taken in and dust being taken out, beer barrels being let down publichouse cellars, shop-boys' brooms, scavengers' carts, perambulators, poodles, and idiots who carry their umbrellas under their arms, &c, the London streets are quite lively enough.'[230] This letter on 'Mat Traps' is incidentally revealing for its insight into Jerome's own habits. Dickens famously said that the London streets provided the only environment in which he felt he could work. Jerome appears to have shared this habit, writing in 1888 '...that is always my favourite working-ground, the streets. They are my study, my den, my library; and the more thronged and noisy they are, the better I am able to work.'[231] In later life he said that he could only work in the country, but he always remembered how as a young man in London:

> For a work-room I often preferred the dark streets to my dismal bed-sitting-room. Portland Place was my favourite study. I liked its spacious dignity. With my notebook and a pencil in my hand, I would pause beneath each lamp-post and jot down the sentence I had just thought out. At first the police were suspicious. I had to explain to them. Later they got friendly; and often I would read to them some passage I thought interesting or amusing. There was an inspector – a dry old Scotchman who always reached Langham church as the clock struck eleven: he was the most difficult. Whenever I made him laugh, I went home feeling I had done good work.[232]

His 1885 correspondence with *The Times* confirms his nocturnal habit, although typically he deflates the romantic trope of the solitary writer observing teeming streets: 'At night we who love to walk and ponder look for a little happiness. We choose a quiet street or square, and, lighting a cigar, anticipate the luxury of a comparative dawdle. Before we have gone 20 yards we find ourselves on our noses, with a grinning flunkey standing over us, wanting to know why the —— we cannot look where we are going.'[233]

The reference to walking and pondering, humorously as it is treated here, is significant. It was in 1885 that Jerome published his first book, *On the Stage – and Off*, with Field & Tuer, three years after its rejection by Clement Scott. It sold well from the outset, and one journalist captured the mood when he said that as the usual reviewer was busy, he had taken on the task of reviewing the book, and 'to such of the population of these islands as are not included in the eight thousand previous purchasers, we can strongly recommend the expenditure of one shilling necessary to put them in possession of a copy.'[234]

Even in the account Jerome gave many years later, and through the usual self-deprecating humour, the excitement is palpable:

> My first book! He stands before me, bound in a paper wrapper of a faint pink colour, as though blushing all over for his sins. '*On the Stage – and Off*. By Jerome K. Jerome' (the K very large, followed by a small j; so that by many the name of the author was taken to be Jerome Kjerome).[235]

One might note in passing that complications with naming (already likely enough for a Jerome Jerome, son of a Jerome Jerome) seem to have haunted the writer all his life. In an age where the use of either first or surname was a vital index to the level of intimacy between men, this particular appellation must have proved excruciating. Moreover, it seemed that no one could pronounce it correctly – despite his insistence that it should be pronounced 'Jĕrōme K. Jĕrōme'.[236] *Punch* did get it right, seemingly only for the pleasure of mocking him – in 'Our Booking-Office', a review of *Told After Supper*, the Baron de Bookworms explains to readers that 'Jerome K. Jerome' is more easily pronounced as 'Jerumky Jerum',[237] a jibe Jerome alludes to indirectly in his conversation with an American journalist in discussing his hope that Americans, unlike his English readers, would adopt his own pronunciation of his name and stop calling him 'Jeroam'. But it was not to be and, over 150 years after his death, he is still known to his numerous readers as Jĕrōme K. Jĕrōme.

In his first book Jerome had eschewed melodrama in favour of realism, deciding as he later put it, 'I would tell the world the story of a hero called Jerome who had run away and gone upon the stage'.[238] Now his thoughts returned to the drama and in June 1886 he licensed his first play, the one-act *Barbara*. It is a sentimental piece, focusing on an orphan who feels mysteriously like a sister to the man her friend loves, and who is too poor to propose. In the final denouement Barbara learns that she is the missing heiress to a fortune, but as she is believed dead, the money is set to go to her brother. Inevitably, this brother is the man who cannot marry her friend unless he inherits the money, and so Barbara is unable to reveal her true identity. Jerome read it to Rose Norreys, who took it to the manager Charles Hawtrey and stood over him until he had read it. Hawtrey in turn referred Jerome to his brother George to sort out the terms, advising him (rightly as it turned out) not to sell the copyright.[239] Jerome remained grateful to Norreys, remembering nostalgically how he used to visit her in Chelsea Gardens before his marriage, when 'Half young Bohemia used to squeeze itself into her tiny drawing-room, and overflow into the kitchen. ... Bernard Partridge and myself were generally the last to leave.'[240]

It must have been a shock when her unexpected collapse in 1895 led to her confinement in Colney Hatch Lunatic Asylum, close to Jerome's childhood home.[241] A fund was raised for her through *The Era* and a female admirer tried to take charge of her. However, her condition made this impractical and instead she was taken to Bethlehem Hospital, until a second fund was launched by *The Era* in 1899 to have her sent to a hospital in Kent as a private patient. Jerome admitted in his autobiography that he could never face visiting her there, and prayed her forgiveness. His name does not appear on the list of subscribers in 1899,[242] presumably because he was out of the country. Strangely, he implies that she died in Colney Hatch, where 'She had kind women friends ... who watched over her.'[243] That a sense of guilt would prevent his finding out what had actually happened to her is in keeping with Jerome's behaviour on other occasions, notably his later response to Bernard Partridge. In fact Norreys survived Jerome by some years, dying in 1940.

Barbara certainly justified her confidence. The *Era* reported that Jerome had received a double call to the curtains and that:

> Truth to tell *Barbara* is a very interesting little piece, giving promise
> of even greater things. It is well written, and the plot, what there
> is of it, is constructed without too many signs of that clumsiness
> which so often reveals the hand of the amateur in stage-craft.[244]

Jerome was rightly pleased by the success of the play, and was subsequently able to sell the American rights to J. K. Emmett.[245]

As a published playwright Jerome could now speak with something like authority on the subject of amateur companies and burst forth in another letter to *The Era* in September. He pointed out that these companies were good friends to the dramatist, regularly paying fees to perform plays in which the regular players had lost interest, thereby extending their life.[246]

Despite his passion for the stage, he knew better than to trust himself to the writing of drama for a living. As he had already shown in *On the Stage — and Off*, he had a flair for humorous episodic prose, which would stand him in good stead a few years later as the editor of two concurrent journals. In 1886 he published *The Idle Thoughts of an Idle Fellow: A Book for an Idle Holiday*. Facetiously dedicated to his pipe, the book offers a joyous riposte to the mid-Victorian earnestness demanded of writers in his youth, and so evident in his quondam hero Dickens. In the preface he explains that, 'What readers ask now-a-days in a book is that it should improve, instruct and elevate. This book wouldn't elevate a cow. I cannot conscientiously recommend it for any useful purposes whatever.'[247]

Notwithstanding the comic preface, Jerome used the first essay to introduce his preoccupation with urban poverty, a condition his own experience had taught him to be very different from the threadbare but picturesque scenes of popular fiction. Unlike the aspiring writers created by Thackeray or Gissing, who know their success must depend on disguising their precarious status, Jerome, almost belligerently, insists that:

> I can speak with authority on the subject of being hard up. I have been a provincial actor. If further evidence be required, which I do not think likely, I have been a "gentleman connected with the press". I have lived on fifteen shillings a week. I have lived a week on ten, owing the other five; and I have lived for a fortnight on a great-coat.[248]

This is not an admission one can imagine Dickens making. Indeed, Jerome is quite clear that despite the placing of the essay, this is one of the few subjects on which he is not prepared to joke. As he points out:

> There have been a good many funny things said and written about hardupishness, but the reality is not funny, for all that. It is not funny to have to haggle over pennies. It isn't funny to be thought mean

and stingy. It isn't funny to be shabby, and to be ashamed of your address. No, there is nothing at all funny in poverty – to the poor. It is hell upon earth to a sensitive man; and many a brave gentleman, who would have faced the labours of Hercules, has had his heart broken by its petty miseries.[249]

Although the details of those first years after his mother's death were still vivid in his mind, this was no longer Jerome's position. With the serialisation of *Idle Thoughts*, and an established position as a 'regular' at *Home Chimes*, he could justifiably feel himself secure. But he was not yet able to pursue a writing career full-time. As if to remind himself of this fact, he gave his work address rather than Tavistock Place on the MS of *Barbara* when submitting it for licence. Whether this was the same office where he had taken shorthand in the census year of 1881 is not clear, but *My Life and Times* confirms that he was now working for Charles Hodgson, a solicitor in Adelphi Street, the Strand. Suddenly Jerome's preoccupation with the state of the Strand in winter makes a lot more sense.

It was at this point that he sustained another family tragedy, in the shape of Paulina's death from acute bronchial pneumonia on 28 September.[250] During this time he had also apparently remained in touch with his Marris cousins in Berners Street, although there is no way of knowing how close his relationship with them had been since his mother's death. In 1881, when Jerome had recently returned to London and found his feet again, William Marris had just married a Georgina Elizabeth Nesza,[251] with whom he went on to have a daughter, Elsie. It is unclear when Jerome first met Georgina, or what his relationship with William was like during these years. But the marriage was clearly not a happy one. As Frank Rodgers points out, there is a telling inscription in the leather-bound first edition copy of *On the Stage – and Off* (now held in the Bodleian) 'To the "leading lady" on his own Stage of Life' and dated April 1885. By July 1887 Georgina was publicly accusing her husband of adultery, indeed of bringing his mistress to the marital home and even expecting his wife to drink tea with her. Furthermore, she claimed that he was 'a man of intemperate and dissipated habits and of violent temper' who had thrown glasses, plates and boots at her, thrown her across the room and almost into the path of passing vehicles, and threatened their daughter with violence.[252]

While disaster was overtaking the Marris family in Berners Street, Jerome was to all appearances enjoying himself enormously, according to his second light-hearted account of stage traditions. In a useful discussion of Victorian stage conventions Judith Flanders notes that, 'Melodrama simplified an increasingly complex world' with predictable plots and instantly recognisable fixed types, each identified by mannerism and costume. This dressing of particular parts was useful to both audience and cast, and indeed:

> permitted stock companies to function: the rustic, the 'heavy', the heroine, the comic servant, were all a standard type, with standard make-up and a standard costume. Each week, therefore, a new drama could draw in the same audiences to watch similar characters in different situations, which were also standard: the last-minute reprieve from the gallows, the overheard conversation, the long-lost foundling child, the secret marriage.[253]

This was the drama in which Jerome had acted and which he lovingly mocked in *Stage-Land: Curious Manners & Customs of its Inhabitants,* published in 1889, with illustrations by *Punch* artist Bernard Partridge. In light of Jerome's long vilification by this journal it is surprising that so many of his colleagues and friends were connected with it, Phil May also being one of its cartoonists. Notably, Jerome's humour sedulously avoided the personal, taking liberties with the stage in general in its critique of theatrical stock types: 'The hero has his own way of making love. He always does it from behind. The girl turns away from him, when he begins (she being, as we have said, shy and timid), and he takes hold of her hands, and breathes his attachment down her back.'[254] Of the Comic Man he notes:

> He follows the hero all over the world. This is rough on the hero.
> What makes him so gone on the hero is that, when they were boys together, the hero used to knock him down and kick him. The comic man remembers this with a glow of pride, when he is grown up; and it makes him love the hero and determine to devote his life to him.[255]

Fresh from his work as a legal clerk Jerome also had great fun with the vagaries of stage law, which he claimed he had spent six months vainly trying to understand. The only points on which he claimed he was clear were:

> That if a man dies, without leaving a will, then all his property goes to the nearest villain.

> But that if a man dies, and leaves a will, then all his property goes to

whoever can get possession of that will.

That the accidental loss of the three and sixpenny copy of a marriage certificate annuls the marriage.

That the evidence of one prejudiced witness, of shady antecedents, is quite sufficient to convict the most stainless and irreproachable gentleman of crimes for the committal of which he could have had no possible motive.

But that this evidence may be rebutted, years afterwards, and the conviction quashed without further trial by the unsupported statement of the comic man.[256]

Years later he would describe it as 'a sort of curse to every play I have written since. In it, of course, I made fun of all stage characters and business, including, naturally, my own. But I have had so much of my own chaff thrown back at me, whenever I have produced a play, that I have become quite used to the process.'[257] This tone of mock resignation is designed to suggest that Jerome is still paying over twenty years later for a youthful indiscretion. He had perhaps forgotten that as recently as 1905 he had been having fun with precisely the same set of conventions:

Stage people are not allowed to put things right when mistakes are made with their identity. If the light comedian is expecting a plumber, the first man that comes into the drawing-room has got to be a plumber. He is not allowed to point out that he never was a plumber; that he doesn't look like a plumber; that no one not an idiot would mistake him for a plumber. He has got to be shut up in the bath-room and have water poured over him, just as if he were a plumber... Not till right away at the end of the last act is he permitted to remark that he happens to be the new curate.[258]

In a much earlier letter to Clement Scott, however, Jerome observed that he had mocked the drama of his day only affectionately, much as Dickens had mocked Pickwick while he loved him, for 'is it not one's friends that one likes best to chaff[?] ... I find people take form so desperately seriously now-a-days'. He was 'glad to see your advice is to shut our ears to this new criticism that would reform the drama – altogether. As you say nothing is easier than to sneer – nothing easier than to pull down.' Commenting that some contemporary writers would have hounded Shakespeare back to deerstalking, he complained bitterly that they termed virtue 'bourgeois' and 'would squeeze every drop of humanity out of all art.'[259] In various forms this would be Jerome's complaint throughout his writing career.

At this stage of his life Jerome was nothing if not conservative, and in January 1888 he became a Special Constable, with a view to putting down rioters in the metropolis. Encountering 'a mob of two or three hundred wild and repulsive-looking ruffians ... I rushed into their midst, determined to quell them or perish in the attempt; but was informed that they were only gentlemen, like myself, waiting to be sworn in as constables.'[260] He goes on to describe a scene in which the constables themselves are threatened with the Riot Act, to which he characteristically appends, 'N.B. This account is slightly exaggerated, but not much.'[261] What he had wanted, Jerome tells his readers, 'was to do deeds of startling heroism, and to come home with a broken head (not too much broken, but just broken enough), and excite the pity and admiration of my female relatives; and be referred to in glowing terms in the next morning's papers. But we never saw the foe'.[262] Twenty-seven years later he recalled with some amusement that 'We were stout, pompous-looking gentlemen, the majority of us, in frock coats and silk hats', and the drill sergeant hardly knew what to do with them.[263]

If he was not exactly making a name for himself in defence of his country, Jerome was doing rather better with plays. In February 1888 he wrote half-petulantly and half-cajolingly to Clement Scott:

> I know its very unprofessional but I am so disappointed at not finding any notice from you (even a bad one would be better than none) on my little piece "Sunset" that I am trying to believe it – a small matter – must have escaped your attention, especially as you have always been so kind and encouraging to all us young authors ...
> It doesn't seem as if the piece had been produced without a notice from you...[264]

The plot is based on Tennyson's poem 'The Sisters', and offers a display of feminine altruism as the unworldly Lois declares, 'There are so many wives of wealthy men.' Meanwhile, of course, she wants 'to be the wife of a great man!' and ends by renouncing her fiancé in favour of her unsuspecting sister, instead marrying the neighbourhood dullard.

Woodbarrow Farm was brought out by Gertrude Kingston at the Comedy

Theatre in June 1888. Writing from Salisbury Street, Jerome confided to Clement Scott that it was to have a trial run as a matinee, and if that was successful, it would be taken on. He admitted, 'I have no love for matinees myself & I yearn for a pit & gallery but managers are peculiar.'[265] All went well and soon Jerome was writing, again from the office, to thank Scott for his notice of the play. *My Life and Times* reports taking the play on tour with his own company, and it reappeared in London in 1891, with a run at the newly reopened Vaudeville.[266] 1888 also saw the production of *Fennel* and *Pity is Akin to Love*, as well as *Playwriting*, a handbook for novice dramatists.

On 21 June 1888,[267] less than a fortnight after her divorce became final, Jerome and Georgina (Ettie) Marris were married. Understandably, Jerome, the most reticent of men, makes no reference in his published work to the circumstances under which he met his wife, although he refers to her informally as 'the wife' in letters to friends. What is suggestive is his description of her daughter Elsie and his own daughter Rowena, born in 1890, as indiscriminately 'my girls'. In fact they were both half-sisters (on their mother's side) and second cousins through their respective fathers (Jerome and Marris being first cousins). In a rare public allusion to his marriage Jerome later implied that he was re-reading *David Copperfield* as he waited the result of Ettie's confinement. Even by the 1880s the death of David's mother as a result of labour would have been less than reassuring as a means of distraction. He told his readers in 1905 that even then, 'Poor, pretty little Mrs Copperfield at the gate, holding up her baby in her arms, is always associated in my memory with a child's cry, long listened for. I found the book, face downwards on a chair, weeks later, not moved from where I had hastily laid it.'[268]

Jerome's relationship with Elsie, too, was evidently a close one – she referred to him in her letters as 'my father'[269] and she and not Rowena supposedly penned an article in 1895 on 'How I bring up my parents', in which as a precocious eleven-year-old she confides to the readers of *The Idler* that:

> My parents have a good many different moods; at any rate they have three. The first is what I call the severe mood, in which they will not let me do anything I want; the second, I call the lazy mood, when they are too lazy to disturb themselves whatever I do; and the third is when they are thoroughly good-tempered, and let me do anything I like. … On the whole, I find my mother more difficult to manage

than my father; my mother has too many ideas of her own on the subject of bringing up children, so she and I sometimes differ.[270]

Very little is known about the Jeromes' marriage, certainly in the early years. Unusually for a middle-class Victorian family they had only two children, and only one of those together. Given the relatively prompt arrival of Rowena, the obvious inference is that they subsequently practised birth control, a supposition that gains possible confirmation through Jerome's later declared support for family planning.[271] Whether his wife was in favour of limiting their family is less certain – in later life she would develop a seemingly obsessive relationship with the daughter of one of her servants, treating her as her own in the teeth of the mother's objections. The evidence that exists points to Jerome as less likely to be enthusiastic about increasing their family. While he wrote about his daughters with deep affection, both in their childhood and in his later memoir, he had already suggested before his marriage that there was a conflict between the rights of babies and husbands. *Idle Thoughts* contains an essay on 'Babies' that warns the new mother in no uncertain terms, 'Do not, in your desire to be a good mother, forget to be a good wife. ... A house where there seems no room for him, and a wife too busy to think of him, have lost their hold on that so unreasonable husband of yours, and he has learnt to look elsewhere for comfort and companionship.'[272]

It was during these years, when the newly married couple were living up a steep flight of stairs in Chelsea, that Jerome first met two very different women, Marie Corelli the anti-suffragist and novelist, and Elizabeth Garrett Anderson, the first woman doctor to qualify in England. He remembered Corelli as 'a pretty, girlish little woman' but 'an erratic worker' and noted pointedly that, 'To keep friends with her continuously was difficult. You had to agree with all her opinions, which were many and varied.' It would be many years before he would countenance women's entry into public life and he is unlikely to have approved of women doctors. However, the parties (at Madame Marras' house in Prince's Gate) where he met Corelli and Anderson seem not to have been based on intellectual exchanges – Jerome recalled playing hunt the slipper, puss in the corner and musical chairs on these occasions.[273] Nonetheless, he may have had more of an influence on Corelli than he realised – it is tempting to think that she had his essay 'On being hard up' in mind when she wrote the opening lines of her novel *The Sorrows of Satan* (1895):

Do you know what it is to be poor? not poor with the arrogant poverty complained of by certain people who have five or six thousand a year to live upon, and who yet swear they can hardly manage to make both ends meet, but really poor, – downright, cruelly, hideously poor, with a poverty that is graceless, sordid and miserable? Poverty that compels you to dress in your one suit of clothes till it is worn threadbare, – that denies you clean linen on account of the ruinous charges of washerwomen – that robs you of your own self-respect and causes you to slink along the streets vaguely abashed, instead of walking erect among your fellow-men in independent ease – this is the sort of poverty I mean.[274]

By now Jerome had left Hodgson's and was working for another solicitor, James Anderson Rose of Rose and Thomas. By coincidence this firm represented Ouida,[275] a notoriously eccentric novelist of whom Jerome recalled:

Her books earned her a good income, but she had no sense of money. In the course of a morning's stroll she would, if in the mood, order a thousand pounds' worth of goods to be sent to her at the Langham Hotel. She never asked the price. She was like a child. Anything that caught her fancy she wanted. Fortunately for herself, she always gave us as a reference. I would have to go round and explain matters. One or two of the less expensive articles we would let her have. She would forget about the others.[276]

He describes Rose as a highly respectable collector of china and fine art, both facts confirmed by his obituary. Politically he was a Tory, 'one of those men who, little known to the public, exercise a considerable influence in political affairs'.[277] By his own account Jerome only left the firm on Rose's death in September 1890. More importantly, he also claims that after his death Rose turned out to be a fraudster on a grand scale, although this certainly does not appear in the press. Jerome suggested afterwards that he may have been the inspiration for *The Voysey Inheritance*, and he almost certainly sat for the loveable, but shady, solicitor who employs the hero in *Paul Kelver*.

Jerome himself continued to write humorous essays at this time, contributing at least two articles to *Novel Review* in 1889. Nonetheless, his decision to continue in paid employment until 1890 suggests, perhaps unsurprisingly, that he was more cautious now than he had been when he threw in his job at the North-Western Railway at eighteen. The impending addition to his family (Rowena would be born in December 1890), taken with his responsibility to Georgina and Elsie, are sufficient grounds for a less maverick approach to work than he had shown in the past, particularly as he had by this time written just one moderately successful play. *New Lamps for Old*, licensed in January 1890, was probably written at about this time. But journalism and plays aside, there had been a substantial change in his prospects in the last twelve months. 1889 was also the year in which Jerome, after twelve years of hard work and ambition, had finally made his name. To his constant irritation he would be associated for the rest of his life with one book, for which he is now primarily remembered, the timelessly hilarious *Three Men in a Boat*.

CHAPTER THREE

'I did not intend to write a funny book, at first' From *Three Men in a Boat* to *The Idler* and *TO-DAY*, 1889-1892

'A man can take no heavier burden upon himself than the reputation of a buffoon. … Nevermore, though the role of chief mourner would better become him – may he lay it down.'

Mona Caird, *The Wing of Azrael* (1889)

Ironically, given his recent marriage, his comic masterpiece celebrates bachelor friendship, as Jerome, under the thin disguise of 'J', takes to the river with George (Wingrave) and Harris (Carl Hentschel). Playing his usual games with the reader, Jerome would claim decisively in *My Life and Times* that, 'I did not have to imagine or invent. Boating up and down the Thames had been my favourite sport ever since I could afford it. I just put down the things that happened.' This seems plausible, and the admission that 'There wasn't any dog. I didn't possess a dog in those days'[278] only gives weight to the honesty of the teller. Until, that is, this paragraph is related back to the preface to *Three Men in a Boat*, in which Jerome claims with similar ingenuousness that, 'George and Harris and Montmorency are not poetic ideals, but things of flesh and blood – especially George, who weighs about twelve stone.'[279] Carl Hentschel, or Harris, later told a mutual friend that, 'It was roughing it in a manner that would hardly appeal to us now. … It says much for our general harmony that, during the years we spent together in such cramped confinement, we never fell out, metaphorically or literally.' Strangely, there was at least one real incident that he thought could have been invaluable in Jerome's hands, but was never used in the book:

We were on our way up the river, and late in the afternoon, as the sky looked threatening, we agreed to pull up and have our frugal meal, which generally consisted of a leg of Welsh mutton... with salad. We started preparing our meal on the bank, when the threatened storm burst. We hastily put up our canvas over the boat, and bundled all the food into it anyhow. It got pitch dark ... After a while we found the lamp, but it would not light; luckily we found two candle-ends, and by their feeble light began our meal. We had hardly begun our meal when I said after the first mouthful of salad, 'What's wrong with the salad?' George also thought it was queer, but Jerome thought there was nothing wrong. Jerome always did have a peculiar taste. ... It was not till the next day that we discovered that owing to our carelessness of using two medicine bottles of similar shape, one containing vinegar and the other Colza oil, the lamp and the salad were both a bit off.[280]

Why the incident never made it into the book is unclear, unless in this case truth was too much stranger than fiction for the public to be expected to swallow.

What Jerome could not have foreseen was the way in which he would still be defined by this one book nearly a century after his death. As he ruefully explained, 'I did not intend to write a funny book, at first. I did not know I was a humourist. I have never been sure about it.'[281] That Jerome knew he was a humourist is perfectly evident from some of his letters to *The Times*, and he had consolidated this position with *Idle Thoughts*, which went into its eighth edition the following year.[282] But equally he was a man of serious principles. The dilemma is epitomised perfectly in his satirical treatment of the serious side of his own character, 'In the Middle Ages I should probably have gone about preaching and got myself burnt or hanged.'[283] In this self-deprecating allusion to his own seriousness of purpose, there may well be an oblique reference to his own father, whose religious principles had so often placed him in a difficult position.

He told a friend that he had started his most famous book:

as a guide to the Thames. It occurred to us – George, Charles and myself – when we were pulling up and down, how interesting and improving it would be to know something about the history of the famous places through which we passed; a little botany might also be thrown in. I thought that other men in boats might also like information on this subject, and would willingly pay for it. So I read up Dugdale, and a vast number of local guides, together with a little poetry and some memoirs. I really knew quite a lot about the Thames by the time I had done, and with a pile of notes in front of me, I started. ... I thought George would ask questions, and Harry intersperse philosophical remarks. But George and Harry would not; I could not see them sitting there and doing it. So gradually they came to have their own way, and the book as a guide to the Thames is, I suppose, the least satisfactory work on the market.[284]

The unsatisfactory mapping of the Thames is ruefully noted in a twentieth-century historical whodunit, *Swing, Swing Together*, in which three men in a boat in the summer of 1889 follow Jerome's original itinerary. In this tribute, the men are actually murder suspects and Jerome's misrecording of a lock is bitterly resented by the pursuing force from Scotland Yard.

But in pitching *Three Men in a Boat* to a publisher Jerome knew exactly what he was doing. It had begun serialisation in *Home Chimes* and Jerome later confirmed that he had been trying to write a serious *Story of the Thames* interwoven with comic episodes for humorous relief. As if to underline the point, he instantly reverts to humour in the preface, even as he describes his difficulty in writing the serious parts:

About the 'humorous relief' I had no difficulty. I decided to write the 'humorous relief' first – get it off my chest, so to speak. After which, in sober frame of mind, I could tackle the scenery and history. I never got there. It seemed to be all 'humorous relief'. By grim determination I succeeded, before the end, in writing a dozen or so slabs of history and working them in, one to each chapter, and F. W. Robinson ... promptly slung them out, the most of them.'[285]

It was also Robinson who insisted on a change of title, and Jerome duly obliged with *Three Men in a Boat: to say nothing of the dog*.

Now seeking the status of volume publication Jerome penned a jaunty letter to the Bristol publisher Arrowsmith, 'You may recognise my name as author of *Idle Thoughts* a book of humorous essays now selling its 15th 1000 – I have also written my only other book – *On the Stage and Off* which sold splendidly.'[286] Notably the work is described not as a novel but as 'a series of entirely humorous papers'[287] and Jerome shows an astute knowledge of the market in pitching it as 'about size of *Vice Versa*' (Jerome knew F. Anstey, the author, through Bernard Partridge, but in placing his work in the same league as *Vice Versâ* he is suggesting that it can expect to sell around 1,000 copies a week).[288] Arrowsmith responded by return of post and was soon negotiating on technical points – he wanted, for instance, to divide some of the long paragraphs, to avoid 'frightening' the target audience. By this time Jerome was well able to hold out on the question of terms and persuaded the publisher to increase his original offer of 5d per copy up to 10,000 and 6d thereafter, to 7d per copy from the outset. He knew enough to point out that this was the price he could exact from a London firm, but he was clearly keen to see his book in print, and expressed himself as 'anxious to bring it out through you as I know yours is for energy and push – I suppose the leading firm now.'[289] As R. R. Bolland puts it, 'he was not averse to applying a little soft soap when negotiating with a publisher'.[290] A note in Arrowsmith's papers shows that these letters were the only documents relating to the publication agreement. That one of the best-selling books of the nineteenth century was published without any form of contract says much for the good faith of both parties, and their confidence in each other would prove to be justified in the course of the next decade.

The 'energy and push' Jerome approvingly cites is, of course, kept as far as possible from the narrative itself, as J, Harris and George undergo a series of comic disasters on the Thames (the mere mention of 'George's shirt' or 'the tinned pineapple' still gets a laugh from fans who may not actually have read the book in years), but the creative energy underlying the book is kept well out of sight as J insists on the laziness of his companions and, indirectly, of himself. His famous dictum 'I like work. It fascinates me. I can sit and look at it for hours'[291] has entertained generations of school pupils[292] and remains a staple of pub talk to this day. The novel also contains at least one personal joke intended for his friends alone. Harris / Hentschel is recognisably characterised as a natural organiser, as J teasingly puts it, 'so ready to take the burden of everything himself, and put it on the backs of other people'.[293] But much of the book is then taken up with Harris's love of pubs, causing the narrator to reflect that if he died Prime Minister, 'It would be the houses he had never entered that would become famous. "Only house in London that Harris never had a drink in!" The people would flock to it to see what could have been the matter with it.'[294] The real joke of course is that 'Harris' was the only one of the party to be completely teetotal.[295]

Likewise, Jerome contrives to get in some of his 'dreamy' response to the landscape by the simple process of sending up his own meditations. Generally speaking it is Harris who interrupts:

> If you were to stand at night by the seashore with Harris, and say:
>
> 'Hark! Do you not hear? Is it but the mermaids singing deep below the waving waters; or sad spirits, chanting dirges for white corpses, held by seaweed?'
>
> Harris would take you by the arm, and say:
>
> 'I know what it is,' old man; you've got a chill. Now, you come along with me. I know a place round the corner here, where you can get a drop of the finest Scotch whisky you ever tasted – put you right in less than no time.'
>
> Harris always does know a place round the corner where you can get something brilliant in the drinking line.[296]

One of the few entirely serious passages in the book concerns the suicide of a young woman. As J, Harris and George are in the middle of one of their many arguments about whose turn it is to row, George suddenly pulls back with a cry:

> It was the dead body of a woman. It lay very lightly on the water, and the face was sweet and calm. It was not a beautiful face; it was too prematurely aged-looking, too thin and drawn, to be that; but it was a gentle, lovable face, in spite of its stamp of pinch and poverty, and upon it was that look of restful peace that comes to the faces of the sick sometimes when at last the pain has left them.

J notes that, 'We found out the woman's story afterwards. Of course it was the old, old vulgar tragedy. She had loved and been deceived – or had deceived herself. Anyhow, she had sinned – some of us do now and then.' The tone is characteristically compassionate, which makes it all the more surprising that these two paragraphs are separated by the almost brutal lines: 'Fortunately for us – we having no desire to be kept hanging about coroners' courts – some men on the bank had seen the body too, and now took charge of it from us.'[297]

This incongruous aside makes uncomfortable reading, but it is enlightening for that very reason. In *Paul Kelver* some years later the ambiguous Dr Hal would defend a woman who showed no emotion at the thought of her husband's death. In a grimly comic account, he describes her telling him 'I think he's dead' before shouting in to the next room, 'Jim, are you there?' When Paul's sententious schoolmaster is shocked by the story and demands, 'you don't admire a woman for being indifferent to the death of her husband?', Hal answers, 'I don't admire her for that' ... 'and I don't blame her. I didn't make the world, and I'm not responsible for it. What I do admire her for is not pretending a grief she didn't feel.'[298] The narrative comment earlier in the novel, 'our feelings are not under our own control, and I have never been able to understand the use of pretending to emotions one has not'[299] suggests that this is Jerome's own view.

Regardless of appropriate response, the encounter with the dead body in *Three Men in a Boat* was almost certainly a real event. An inquest on 13 July 1887 on the body of a gaiety girl, Alice Douglas, shows that she had drowned herself in the Thames near Goring. R. R. Bolland, who first discovered the newspaper account of the case, points out that Jerome's account of the woman living on six shillings a week, and his knowledge of her circumstances previous to her suicide, are too accurate for coincidence.[300] His knowledge of the event does not prove that he and his friends actually saw the body as described in *Three Men in a Boat*. However, it is worth noting that from this time Jerome's fiction and journalism show a preoccupation with drowning for which there is no other obvious explanation.

The book was an instant success, and Arrowsmith became adept at capitalising in humorous vein on Jerome's marketability. In 1894 the New Woman writer Mary Cholmondeley was expressing amazement at seeing 'sixty fifth edition' on one of Jerome's books.[301] Several decades earlier, in 1858, Wilkie Collins had foreseen that the future of literature lay with an 'unknown public' and Jerome clearly agreed. Contesting the assumption that Art was morally educative, he insisted bluntly in 1903:

Watch the faces of the thin but conscientious crowd streaming wearily through our miles of picture galleries and art museums; gaping, with guide-book in hand, at ruined temple or cathedral tower; striving, with the spirit of the martyr, to feel enthusiasm for Old Masters at which, left to themselves, they would enjoy a good laugh – for chipped statues which, uninstructed, they would have mistaken for the damaged stock of a suburban tea-garden.[302]

This is the class behind the comic creation Pooter, in George and Weedon Grossmith's *The Diary of a Nobody*. The essential difference between the two books is that *The Diary of a Nobody* assumes a reader whose status is above that of the Pooters and who will therefore understand and smile at the suburban respectability on which the diarist prides himself. At one point Pooter is notably discomfited by a dinner guest, a wealthy American, who breaks the rules of hospitality by making a satirical commentary on his surroundings and on his fellow guests. Picking off the assembled company one by one, he criticises the wine and the serving of the meal, before winding up his remarks with a dismissive, 'We have no representative at Mr Franching's table ... of the unenlightened frivolous matron, who goes to a second-class dance at Bayswater and fancies she is in Society.'[303] On the contrary, Jerome positions himself directly among the middle class, making one of his characters a bank clerk not simply because it was true but as a statement of allegiance.

As Jeremy Lewis points out in an introduction to the Penguin edition of *Three Men in a Boat*:

> Many of these new readers were employed, like George or Mr Pooter, as clerks in banks, insurance offices, estate agents and the like; many of them lived in the new suburbs which – to the horror of the intelligentsia – were spreading out around London and the other great cities, addressed one another as 'Old Man', and employed a slang of their own, half-jocular and half-defiant. ... as Jerome would soon discover, they were looked down upon by writers and social commentators who had enjoyed the benefits of a university education, and regarded the upstart clerks and their spokesmen as bumptious philistines.[304]

Jerome deploys just such slang quite deliberately in *Three Men in a Boat* (his more Latinate expression in his 1880 letter to the British Museum shows an admittedly uneasy control of formal language, but his correspondence with *The Times* achieves a careful balance between humour and standard grammar).

In his fiction, however, more so than in his published correspondence, he exploits precisely this gap between educated and popular language, as only a skilled writer could. Fresh from his musings on Kingston, or Kyningestusn as he pedantically informs his reader it was once called, J. comments:

Caesar, like, in later years, Elizabeth, seems to have stopped everywhere: only he was more respectable than good Queen Bess; he didn't put up at the public houses.

She was nuts on public-houses, was England's virgin Queen.[305]

The humorous excesses of the novel are in fact subtly regulated by careful use of syntax and rhythm; by 1894 Jerome was himself complaining, with no trace of irony, that:

> the art of correct punctuation is not more taught in schools; without it, it is not possible to express one's meaning precisely, and yet – though the principal rules might be easily mastered in an hour – very few people can punctuate correctly. There are probably in England at the present time more women who speak French fluently than understand the punctuation of a relative sentence. At the same time, reforms are needed in the art. The comma is much overworked, even when it is employed legitimately.[306]

At least one commentator in his lifetime appreciated the careful use of slang and idiosyncratic speech to delineate class and character in the fiction. In 1911 Olef Bosson explained that, 'he shows a remarkable talent in rendering with perfect accuracy the characteristic talk of different classes of society. The persons he introduces to us need only utter a few words, before we are able to form a conception of their social position, their degree of culture, etc.'[307] While the subsequent glossary of terms such as 'mashed' for 'in love with' – this is used by an 'uncultivated young man' in *Novel Notes*[308] – suggest a growing distance between Jerome and his later readers, this very assumption that readers will fail to recognise certain terms allows Jerome to evade the kind of judgement made by Victorian highbrow critics, who had repeatedly identified him with his less educated characters. In those last years of the nineteenth century, of course, it was this very ability to create the voice of the urban lower-middle class that appealed to readers. It has also, as Hall Caine predicted, been a selling point to later readers curious for period detail. As Faurot approvingly comments, 'Jerome's voice at the turn of the century came as near as anyone's to a non-distorted echo of the masses who read him.'[309]

It was the success of *Three Men in a Boat* that ensured Jerome's lasting fame as a writer, even as it cast a trailing shadow over his later, more serious work.

As a 'New Humourist' he would receive negative treatment in a number of papers, including the *National Observer, Standard* and *Morning Post*. As Faurot perceptively suggests, 'The conscience of Jerome, developed in his Puritan upbringing, made him on the defensive about his humor.'[310] In any case, for someone as well versed as Jerome in the journalism of his time, it would have been impossible to avoid these reviews (as writers traditionally claim to do). Much of Jerome's later humour then is rooted in this abuse. It could be said that he caricatured himself as an idler and New Humourist much as the equally hard-working Oscar Wilde reinvented himself as a languorous aesthete at around the same time.

Not all critics concurred in their contempt for Jerome and his work. If he ever read *The Star* in St Peter Port he must have been cheered to find himself described in 1893 as 'undoubtedly a rising young man who has pushed his way to the front rank as a humourist with a force of character and a brilliancy of style which are sufficiently unique in these days of plagiarism to have obtained for him a certain amount of kudos'.[311]

Another article in the same year was less generous. That spring the *Glasgow Herald* launched a tirade against the restlessness of the current generation, blaming 'smartness' as represented by the 'booms' of Kipling, Haggard and Barrie, 'the New Journalism with its everlasting sensationalism and nauseating liveliness … the New Oratory with its strenuous pathos and its perpetual pyrotechnics, above all the New Humour with its "blow winds and crack your cheeks" appeals to the public to laugh at all hazards'.[312]

The pain of his reception never wholly left Jerome, however he may have claimed to find amusement in it. In the year before his death he still remembered with feeling, 'I think I may claim to have been, for the first twenty years of my career, the best abused author in England. *Punch* invariably referred to me as "'Arry K 'Arry", and would then proceed to solemnly lecture me on the sin of mistaking vulgarity for humour and impertinence for wit.'[313] An 'Arry or 'Arriet, in the slang of the time, was a stereotype approximating roughly to the twenty-first-century 'chav', a working-class figure with little education and a flashy style of dress. As late as 1897 *Punch* was still insisting that Jerome's fame was purely ephemeral, and even inventing an alcohol problem in its spoof interview in which he has 'a massive nose, in which the rich, red blood shows boldly and perpetually at the tip'.[314]

Faurot for one is understandably bewildered by the contempt shown by such periodicals as *Punch* for the New Humour, which to all intents and purposes it was practising in its own pages. Indeed, illustrators such as Phil

May worked for both *Punch* and *TO-DAY*. Nonetheless Philip Waller argues that the New Humour 'quickly became formularized. It was a social rung lower than *Punch* (established in 1841), which progressively shed its radical and bohemian character and, after 1880, was steered by a predominantly public-school, Cambridge clique'.[315]

Critical abuse notwithstanding, at this stage the instant popularity of Jerome's new book must have seemed providential. It did not, however, exempt him from office politics, and in January 1890 he was complaining that he was 'up to my eyes with work and worry this week'.[316] Nonetheless, it must have been some consolation to think that his market worth in the wake of such a success could not be in doubt. His employer James Anderson Rose died the year after its publication and, on the strength of his new marketability, Jerome was able to leave office work behind him. He had originally planned to train as a solicitor, 'Not that I had any intention of giving up writing' but 'I had just married. A new sense of prudence had come to me'.[317] Years later Jerome still remembered Rose with a degree of fondness mixed with a certain acerbic humour, 'He was a dear old gentleman. In the office we all loved him. And so did his clients, until soon after his death, when their feelings towards him began to change.' Either way, 'His death put an end to my dream of being a lawyer. ... I decided to burn my boats, and to devote all my time to writing. My wife encouraged me. She is half Irish, and has a strain of recklessness.'[318]

One of the advantages of being self-employed was that Jerome could now plan his own time and enjoy a freedom of movement that had not been possible since his days as a provincial actor. He enjoyed travel and in the spring of 1890 he set off for Germany with Walter Helmore to see the Oberammergau Passion Play. This religious play was inaugurated in 1633 when the plague was spreading throughout the region, and the inhabitants of the village vowed to put on a play every ten years if God would spare them. The village remained untouched by plague and to this day the play is performed according to promise. Taking roughly eight hours to perform, it covers the events following Jesus's entry into Jerusalem, finishing with the resurrection. A series of tableaux is interspersed with the main scenes, 'intended to aid theological analysis and serve as foci for meditation'.[319] Jerome noted that each of the tableaux lasted two or three minutes, and 'not even the most infantile of the two and three hundred living models sometimes needed, seeming to move so much as an eyelid'.[320] As Ludwig Mödl, the theological advisor in 2010, puts it, 'the play is not museum-like folk theater, it is a theater of the people for the people that reaches deep into life and seeks to convey hope.'[321]

The party was to have included the writer Eden Phillpotts – 'I had got the habit of going about in threes'[322] remarked Jerome later, suggesting that he found it every bit as difficult to break free of 'J' as did his readers. But Phillpotts fell ill before they were due to leave, putting paid to this arrangement. Like Jerome, Phillpotts was a humourist, although he would be remembered for his novels of Devon rural life. By this stage he was already earning £400 a year from writing, and became assistant editor to the weekly *Black and White* from 1890. If the resulting *Diary of a Pilgrimage* is to be believed, the journey was not a comfortable one, Jerome observing:

> Railway travellers, I have always noticed, regard fresh air as poison. They like to live on the refuse of each other's breath, and close up every window and ventilator tight. The sun pours down through glass and blind and scorches our limbs. Our heads and our bodies ache. The dust and soot drift in and settle on our clothes, and grime our hands and face. We all doze and wake up with a start, and fall to sleep again upon each other. I wake, and find my neighbour with his head upon my shoulder. It seems a shame to cast him off; he looks so trustful. But he is heavy.[323]

While a modern reader responds instantly to the humour of this account, the narrator reminds his original audience that European travel was not entirely safe at the time of this trip.

Over the next few years Jerome would express horror at the brutality of the Turkish regime and he writes in the fictional diary of how, half-asleep when the train stops in Berbesthal:

> I had a vague idea that we were travelling in Turkey, and had been stopped by brigands. When they told me to open my bag, I said, "Never!" and remarked that I was an Englishman, and that they had better be careful. I also told them that they could dismiss any idea of ransom from their minds at once, unless they were prepared to take I.O.U.'s as it was against the principles of our family to pay cash for anything – certainly not for relatives.[324]

That Jerome enjoyed the trip hugely is clear from *Diary of a Pilgrimage*. Inconvenience notwithstanding, he responded enthusiastically to the landscape and the people – it is not surprising that when he wanted to leave England a few years later, his thoughts should turn to Germany, and he would write nostalgically to Helmore, from Munich that, 'I always think of you as I recognise this spot & that I am reminded of the jolly time we had together.'[325]

The play itself was anything but jolly, but Jerome found it deeply moving in its intensity, commenting specifically on the strong role of Mary, whose 'cry is the cry of a mother parting from her child'[326] and noting approvingly that the tableau of Abel's murder by Cain was conducted *au naturel* – 'The Oberammergau peasants are not so dirty-minded as we English Pecksniffs. They see nothing evil in the form that God has created in his own image'.[327] This was of course a well worn theme for Jerome (a few years later he was wondering about the reaction of purists in the tradition of a British Matron, 'if any of them reach the heaven they always have upon their lips, and find the inhabitants clothed only, as we are told, in shining light').[328]

Most impressive of all was the crucifixion scene, in which the staging was so realistic that the actor appeared to be literally nailed to the cross, while actually wearing a crown of thorns and spurting blood from his side when pierced by the soldier's sword. Here, Jerome observed, was 'no shirking of the details'. Only a quick jibe at his habitual target the 'society woman' momentarily comes between the watcher and his awe in his retelling of this climax to the play:

> It is difficult to give an idea of this scene that will do it justice. It is a marvel of mechanism, skill, and stage management; but you forget to think of it as a thing being acted. A hushed awe pervades the audience, and even the society woman sits still and thinks – or tries to – for one moment in her life. The scene is enacted with such strong simple earnestness that there can be no thought of irreverence. The two thieves, bound upon their crosses, hang one to the right side and one to the left; while in the centre, twenty feet from the ground, is nailed the Christ upon the cross.[329]

Jerome would grumble in his semi-fictional account of their trip that every season 'sees the European tourist more and more pampered, and the difficulties and consequent pleasure and interest of his journey more and more curtailed and spoilt. In a few years time, he will be packed in cotton-wool in his own back-parlour, labelled for the place he wants to go to, and unpacked and taken out when he gets there'.[330] Toward the end of his life he insisted that since his own Spartan experiences, the lodging with village peasants had made way for the railway and great hotels, although he was honest enough to admit, 'Of course I had written a book about it … so perhaps I am hardly entitled to indulge in jeremiads.'[331] As he makes a point of telling his readers in the years after the war, 'I liked the people and their homely ways; and later some four years' residence in Germany confirmed my first impression.'[332]

Back in England the newly liberated and newly famous Jerome was in demand, directing a series of *tableaux vivants* at the Camden School of Art that December of 1890.[333] Willing as ever to vent his concerns as a British citizen, he took a cab driver to court a few months later for using 'language' to himself and his wife.[334] In literary terms he was set for an extraordinarily productive few years even by Victorian standards. In 1890 he published a short story, 'The Prince's Quest',[335] and in 1891 a collection of framed ghost stories, *Told After Supper* (he would later tell a correspondent that 'It is a book I have tried to suppress ever since it was written').[336] In the same year he would justify his recent holiday with the appearance of *A Diary of a Pilgrimage*. The 'diary' first appeared in the *Graphic* and Burgin's apocryphal anecdote about the substitution of 'flies' for 'fleas' is as good as anything in the book itself:

> I had known Jerome K. Jerome for some time and, consequently, was not at all shy with him, so called at his flat in Chelsea one afternoon and found him a little bit ruffled, for his copy of "The Diary of a Pilgrimage" had been altered to suit the fastidious taste of the more delicately minded readers of the Daily Graphic. They had objected to the frequent use of the word "fleas" in connection with foreign travel—as if one could ever indulge in foreign travel without meeting fleas! Jerome said that he had always considered fleas "such chummy little things." His protestations had due effect and it was arranged with the editor that "flies" were no longer to be substituted for "fleas" in the remainder of the Diary.[337]

Published only two years after his famous *Three Men in a Boat*, the 'diary' exploits the lessons Jerome had learned from having his lovingly composed descriptive passages 'slung out' of the earlier book. Now he wrote teasingly to the reader that he had planned to write lengthy passages on the scenery and history of the places he visited, 'I started with the idea of giving you a rapid but glowing and eloquent word-picture of the valley of the Rhine from Cologne to Mayence. For background, I thought I would sketch in the historical and legendary events connected with the district, and against this, for a foreground, I would draw, in vivid colours, the modern aspect of the scene, with remarks and observations thereon.'[338] Having promised that such lucubrations will not after all appear in the published version, he insists on including in any case what are ostensibly his working notes, such as, 'Talk about Albert Dürer. Criticise his style. Say it's flat. (If possible, find out if it *is* flat)'[339] and 'Quote Byron. Moralise about ruined castles generally, and describe the middle ages, with your views and opinions on same.'[340] This mockery of his own stylistic excesses deservedly creates one of the funniest passages in the book. It may also be a private joke to himself in a second sense. Jerome would later claim that the system of representation by agents who obtained payment for their authors by the thousand words had destroyed the integrity of literature. As he explained:

> It is a pernicious system, putting an unfair strain upon a family man. One's heroine is talking too much. It is not in keeping with her character. It does not go with her unfathomable eyes. Besides, she's said it all before in other words, the first time that she met him. From a literary point of view, it ought all to come out. The author seizes his blue pencil; but the husband and father stays his hand. "Don't stop her," he whispers, "let her rip. That passionate outpouring of her hidden soul that you think so unnecessary is going to pay my water-rate."[341]

On publication *Punch* pulled out all the stops with a more offensive review than it had accorded *Three Men in a Boat*: 'It is "'Arry Abroad," that's all. 'ARRY Abroad laughs and talks loudly in foreign churches, sneers and jeers at everything he does not understand – and this includes the greater portion of all he sees and hears ... this Cockney pilgrim goes too far, especially when giving us his valuable opinion on the Passion Play.'[342]

By 1891, when the *Diary of a Pilgrimage* was published, Jerome had secured the services of an agent (at this point his old friend Addison Bright), who was charging £10 per thousand words on his behalf. By 1892 he had transferred to A. P. Watt, a wise decision (on his death in 1906 it transpired that Bright had defrauded other old friends such as Barrie and Conan Doyle, whose interests he had represented). Nonetheless, Bright's business associate Elisabeth Marbury continued to represent Jerome's dramatic rights, later employing Bright's brother Golding to secure a deal for what would prove his most successful play *The Passing of the Third Floor Back*.[343]

Extraordinarily, however, given his recent success in fiction, his initial impulse was towards drama. Speaking at the Playgoers' Dinner in December 1891 on the purpose of the drama, he:

> remonstrated with the critics who wished the drama to take upon itself the work of the Church and of Parliament. There were people who wished the theatre to take upon itself the work of the County Council in revolutionising the universe. The drama was to do everything except interest and amuse. The theatre was not the place to expose social evils so long as there remained Parliament, the pulpit, the platform, and books. The theatre should not be turned into a hospital dissecting-room. They had no right to ask Art to step down from her temple to mingle with the factions of the day. The arts were the flowers of the garden, and had a right to exist even though they did not assist in the drainage of the house. The drama needed no apology if it brought bright moments to those who loved it.[344]

His own dramatic career continued to be productive. The year 1890 saw the production of no fewer than four plays, *New Lamps for Old*, *Ruth*, *What Women Will Do* and *Birth and Breeding*.

Notwithstanding his jokes about actors who felt they could only propose from the hearthrug, he was conscientious about stage directions - the MS copy of *New Lamps for Old* in the British Library contains several sketches showing the positioning of furniture onstage. Nonetheless he was promptly taken up by *The Times* for allowing his characters to speak 'stagese'[345] and A. B. Walkley likewise accused him of deploying stage cliché. Walkley began his assault by deriding the subheading to *New Lamps for Old*, 'A (comparatively speaking) New and Original Play', claiming that on the contrary it:

> reminds me very strongly of an old, old play by Marivaux, and a very recent one by Meilhac. Let not Mr. Jerome suppose that I accuse him of plagiarism. Heaven grant that I could! For the delicate marivaudage of Marivaux, the subtlety and elegance of Meilhac, happen to be more to my own taste than the literary graces of a playwright whose hero calls himself a "Juggins," whose heroines exclaim "What the devil!" and whose old men talk of "getting the

needle." These little Jeremiads betray a Muse too prone to flirtation with our old friend 'Arry. All that I mean is that Marivaux, Meilhac, and Mr. Jerome K. Jerome have all three been working with one and the same formula. That formula may be expressed algebraically. A and B love one another, so do C and D. But, for a reason which, being at present undetermined, I will call X, A "carries on" with D, and B with C. Then a general uneasiness (in Act ii.) shows A, B, C, and D that they have made a mistake. There is a resorting in Act iii; A recognizes that B is his only love, and D rushes into the arms of C.[346]

He was even more ruthless in his assault on *Woodbarrow Farm*, ironically matching scenes from the play to paragraphs from *Stage-Land* and suggesting that the author 'suffers from the idée fixe that the conventions of the stage are immutable. Or has Mr. Jerome produced his play as an object-lesson in the faults satirised by his book, so constituting himself his own Sparton Helot? If so, the joke is a dangerous one.'[347] More favourable was the *Penny Illustrated Paper and Illustrated Times*, which advised its readers 'to make haste' to see this 'admirable specimen' of Jerome's dramatic work.[348]

Ruth, co-authored with Addison Bright, offers an early portrait of the socially committed woman Jerome would explore more fully in Joan Allwood shortly after World War I. Despite being told that 'great ladies baked and brewed in the 9th century but it would be considered infra dig in the 19th',[349] Ruth longs for a life of social usefulness. With a low-key satire of the craze for horror in these years after Jack the Ripper, it is leavened with some irresistible lines – 'we British authors do not dabble in French-Frenchiness. Besides the English public would not tolerate anything improper. A plain wholesome murder is the only thing they ask for.'[350] Some of the best moments are provided by a writer of murder stories who persuades an admirer that he has conducted his research on actual victims. The main plot centres on the murder of a traveller in Australia, and the wrongful accusation of a doctor who had administered an untried antidote to his poisoned arrow wound before abruptly leaving – in fact the hapless victim was on the point of recovery when the inn landlord was found rifling through his belongings and precipitately smothered him. As this scene is enacted a second murderer rushes in and persuades the landlord to misidentify the dead man so that he can evade capture. Cut to Ruth's English home, where she falls in love with the doctor, only to be warned by her suitor Denning that he will turn in his rival unless she marries him instead. The twists come thick and fast, as Denning reminds himself that the supposedly dead man is in fact the heir to a fortune, which he is, of course, unable to claim and which will therefore descend to Ruth. Reproaches from the lover are followed by a nobly miserable marriage, until Ruth finally leaves her husband in time to turn up as a nurse in the last scene and rescue him from a dangerous illness. This final act of altruism performed, and a last attempt to betray the doctor lover having failed, Denning belatedly reveals himself as the Australian landlord and hence the real murderer.

Somewhere along the line Jerome found he had been trapped into apparently consenting to a radical rewrite by a man called Barrett. As he explained to the sympathetic Clement Scott, he had agreed by cable only to 'necessary alterations'. Having seen the result, he wanted Scott to take the matter up publicly on his behalf, demanding, 'Would any author who respected himself & his profession give permission to any other living human Being to "do what he thought best" with his work[?]'[351] This experience aside, Jerome was so pleased with the opening scene of his play that he used it again in 1894, as the first chapter of a chain story in his journal *The Idler*.

That Jerome was taking his dramatic work seriously is clear enough from his fury when he felt his plays were being misappropriated. But ironically he was not above acts of literary appropriation himself. *Birth and Breeding*, registered in September 1890, is actually 'adapted' from a German play by Hermann Ludermann, a decision that strongly suggests Jerome was fairly fluent in the language some years before he went to live there.

As if all this were not enough, it was around this time that the man who could sit and look at work for hours decided to embark on a new venture altogether. The original idea had come from Robert Barr, who was seeking a co-editor for a new monthly periodical, *The Idler*. Jerome excitedly told Arrowsmith, 'when I give you the details I am sure you will agree that if it is properly conducted – bound to be an immense go'.[352] Jerome proved a brilliant editor, as he had been an able journalist, and he clearly took a pride in the role. Advising a young correspondent in 1905, he warned him that success did not come easily, 'The good journalist is born – not made. Journalism consists of seeing into the essentials, of knowing instinctively what is interesting. He is an artist.'[353] Barr's requirements were less exalted – according to Jerome, 'He wanted a popular name and, at first, was undecided between Kipling and myself. He chose me – as, speaking somewhat bitterly, he later confessed to me – thinking I should be the easier to "manage". He had not liked the look of Kipling's jaw.'[354] Jerome in turn told a journalist in 1926 that 'he complimented himself on keeping friendly with a man of difficult temper'.[355]

In 1895 Jerome was able to buy Barr's shares in the journal, becoming sole editor and proprietor. Robert Dunkerley was appointed as the business manager and G. B. Burgin (described by Jerome as 'a glutton for punishment') as the subeditor.[356] Burgin was working as a freelance writer when the journal began, and by his own account leaped at the chance to get involved:

> I had met Jerome K. Jerome several times, and wrote to say that I wanted to interview him for a paper. He appointed an hour, and the interview progressed swimmingly until he asked me what paper it was to appear in and I had to confess that I did not know. Whereupon, he gently but firmly pointed out that such a proceeding would do him a great deal of harm and that nothing but my ignorance of journalistic etiquette could excuse my action. I agreed and tore up the interview with many apologies. "Stop a bit," he said, as I took up my hat. "How would you like to put in three days a week with me as my secretary? That will give you plenty of time to do other things." How would I like! I jumped at it. When, a few weeks later, I met Robert Barr and told him of this kindness on Jerome's part, he hauled me into his den at the Free Press office. "You're just the man I wanted to introduce me to Jerome. I'm thinking of starting a new monthly and if he'll go in with me you shall be the sub-editor." They met and arranged the whole affair in December, 1891.[357]

Initially borrowing a room from the Free Press,[358] in February 1892 the first issue of *The Idler* appeared, 'Edited by Jerome K. Jerome and Robert Barr'. It was an ambitious venture, but as Jerome told a journalist for *Cassell's* the following year, 'It is the big scheme now that wins. ... It only wants pluck.' At this moment his 'clever young wife' came in and said laughingly 'my husband doesn't want for pluck, does he?'[359]

Clearly he did not and the journal got off to a flying start, with the *Review of Reviews* calling it 'a formidable rival' to *The Strand*,[360] admittedly before changing its mind after the April issue, when it warned, '*The Idler* is in danger of becoming somewhat vulgar, with a vulgarity of the music hall.'[361] This barbed comment of course fed into a growing body of criticism of Jerome as an '"Arry" as well as questioning the serious intent of the journal. But as was the case for music hall entertainment, if the title was a natural one for the author of *Three Men in a Boat*, it was deceptive in concealing the sheer amount of work and the level of organisation that must have lain behind it. In his memoirs Jerome focused on the camaraderie and 'idleness' of the journal, recalling 'pleasant offices in Arundel Street, off the Strand' and 'tea parties every Friday.' Burgin likewise enjoyed reminiscing about these occasions:

> Once a week we gave afternoon tea to contributors, at that time a startling and new-humorous novelty. The refreshments consisted of tea and cake—cake in slabs—and bread and butter. Jimmy, the little office-boy who wanted to be a prize-fighter, handed round the tea, which was prepared in the back office by an elderly female with black-beetles in her bonnet. Someone said they were "bugles" but the majority inclined to the beetle theory.[362]

Despite the tone of cosy enjoyment, 'They were known as the "Idler at Homes,"' a secondary purpose of these tea parties peeps out in the throwaway phrase, 'and became a rendezvous for literary London'.[363] They also included actors and actresses such as Ian (Forbes) Robertson, brother of the J. Forbes-Robertson who would later star in *The Passing of the Third Floor Back*, Phyllis Broughton and George Hawtrey.[364] Jerome was quick to secure some big names , including a number of old contributors to *Home Chimes*. He kept a close eye on them, writing to Conan Doyle in June 1892 to urge him to 'try and keep out of your interview with the "Strand" as much as possible all the matter you have given us'.[365]

It must have been particularly gratifying to approach the eminent journalist George Augustus Sala, who, like Clement Scott, had turned down *On the Stage – and Off* only a few years earlier. Coulson Kernahan testified that if Jerome was a Columbus of the little world called the New Humour, 'It was a jolly little world in Jerome's time, for when he discovered and annexed those happy hunting grounds, he "discovered" also not a few humourists, Jacobs, Barry Pain, Zangwill, Burgin, Eden Phillpotts and others who rallied round his flag, and accepted him as the Chieftan of the clan of The New Humour.'[366] Of course it was Robinson rather than Jerome who had 'discovered' Phillpotts and Zangwill, but it was Jerome more than anyone whose name would come to stand for the 'New Humour.' Kernahan might also have included Pett Ridge, a frequent contributor to *The Idler* whose horror of managing women evidently equalled his editor's own. It was Ridge who would complain of the cost of fame in 1896 that:

As matters exist at present the only present that Mr Gifted Author receives is an occasional letter from a lady who has a stall at a bazaar and who likes Mr G. Author's books *so* much though (as she says candidly) he is a perfect stranger, and will he send her several complete sets with his autograph and an original thought on each fly-leaf. If Mr Author be a bachelor, this lady usually finishes her letter cheerily by hoping that Mrs Author and all the dear little bairns (she has a pleasant style, the bazaar lady) are going well and strong.[367]

The journal was initially published by Chatto, but by the spring of 1893 this arrangement had already run aground, with the *Idler* staff accusing the publisher of 'being too content with the present position of things. ... Words have naturally followed' and the upshot was that Chatto offered to take back his £600 investment and withdraw from the concern. Jerome was quick to take him at his word, suggesting that Arrowsmith should invest instead. The draft of Arrowsmith's response, written on Jerome's letter to him, shows that he was tempted but was not prepared to take the necessary capital from other successful ventures.[368]

Notwithstanding his newfound fame Jerome sustained his bohemian links, drawing on this network for literary contributions to the new journal. Many of these contributions were mock serious debates on the nature of marriage, often focused on the imaginary union of Edwin and Angelina, a couple of whom Jerome himself remained particularly fond for some years afterwards. Other contributors followed his lead, W. W. Jacobs (whose own marriage in 1900 would prove notoriously difficult) observing of the courtship period that:

There is generally a pleasant rivalry between engaged couples in the matter of presents. Edwin gives a brooch, and Angelina responds with a pair of hand-worked slippers, which he wears by stealth. He gives a jewel-case, and she returns with a patent pipe full of internal complications invented to prevent any smoke getting into his mouth, or cigars which have the same hygienic quality without any complications whatever. By these means they obtain a knowledge of each other's dispositions which enables them to marry with confidence.[369]

Despite his marriage, Jerome remained 'clubbable' during the 1890s and beyond, intermittently appearing in the press as being present or a speaker at various dinners. These clubs were a predominantly male environment, even the Playgoers' confining women mainly to lectures.[370]

He also continued to write for the stage, with *The Rise of Dick Halward* running for twenty-four performances at the Garrick[371] and a more successful run with *The Prude's Progress*, which made 117.[372] This was the play that came between Jerome and Bernard Partidge, who was originally cast as the knowing journalist – Jerome, much to his regret, was persuaded by George Hawtrey to replace him with another actor, and Partridge politely agreed to withdraw but apparently never forgave the incident.[373] Still musing on the question of the nude in art, Jerome provides his stage heroine Nelly with a skull for a confidant (her brother is an impoverished medical student). In conversation with the landlady of their lodgings she places a handkerchief over it, remarking, 'You are shocking the susceptibilities of the British Matron, Mr Tapley. You must be dressed.'[374] An exchange between Ted the student and his friend is telling in its emphasis on male bonding rituals – having finally been persuaded that Ted as an artist cannot find a more beautiful model than Nelly, whom he loves, the brother exclaims delightedly, 'We'll put Nelly between us, old man, and face the world together – and, damn it all, we'll win!'[375]

As in many of Jerome's plays, the heroine must pretend to choose riches over love (in this case so that her more wealthy suitor can help her brother) before the successful lover returns his 'property' to its rightful owner in the final act. Comedy is provided by a member of the National Vigilance Association who turns out to be a confidence trickster and bigamist (at one point he is photographed drunk in the Aquarium while trying to kiss an artiste called the Female Hercules). His second wife, a former denizen of the stage, ironically regrets having married him for his social status, complaining to a former colleague, 'That's not a respectable man. That's potted respectability. They must have boiled down a church to make that.'[376] There is also a gentle satire of the aesthetic movement in the shape of Theodore, a writer who makes notes for future use on his shirt cuffs and explains that he 'told my first lie before most children can lisp the truth. I posed before most children can stand'.[377]

In addition to chairing the Playgoers' Club dinner in 1890, Jerome was present at the Savage Club dinner in honour of F. H. M. Stanley in June of the same year[378] and at the Press Club annual dinner in April 1891;[379] he presided at the annual meeting of The Retail News Agents' and Booksellers' Union in May 1894.[380] In January 1898 he attended the Article Club dinner at the Hotel Cecil,[381] and turned out in support of his friend Hall Caine when he was the guest speaker at the New Vagabonds Club dinner, again at the

Hotel Cecil, in the Christmas of 1904.[382]

From the first, *The Idler* was given a cohesive identity with the creation of the Idlers' Club, including: W. L. Alden, Robert Barr, G. B. Burgin, Captain David Gray, Joseph Hatton, Jerome K. Jerome, H. A. Kennedy, Coulson Kernahan, Clement R. Markham, Admiral Markham, Barry Pain, Eden Phillpotts, G. R. Sims, J. F. Sullivan and I. Zangwill. As time went on this line-up would vary, including the 'unrivalled and inexhaustible store of the humours of Cockneydom'[383] Pett Ridge, and it would come to accommodate female contributors, even featuring occasional paragraphs from controversial feminist writers such as George Egerton and Sarah Grand. In fact, as Anne Humpherys notes, 'Ironically, the greatest number of contributions by women to the journal is to the most insistently masculine section, The Idler's Club.'[384] Notably it made space from an early stage for the redoubtable Eliza Lynn Linton. Linton famously had a horror of the modern woman, whom she had attacked mercilessly in her 'Girl of the Period' articles for the *Saturday Review* in the 1860s.

Despite her fearsome reputation, at least two of Jerome's other contributors were prepared to stick up for Linton in their post-Victorian memoirs. Burgin called her 'that dearest of friends and deadliest of enemies, the woman who would flay you alive in print if you quarrelled with her, and spend her last penny to help you when you needed help'.[385] Anthony Hope, who seemingly had nothing to say about his association with *The Idler*, said of his fellow contributor that, 'Nothing could have been less scathing or alarming than Mrs Lynn Linton herself. She was the gentlest old lady, and, however she may have expressed herself as to the girl of her own period, she had plenty of indulgence for the girl – and boy – of mine, and would listen, with a twinkle in her eyes, to any little stories illustrating the fashions and follies of the day; and to her juniors in the business of writing she showed a most appreciative generosity.'[386]

Pre-empting any possible assumptions about its status as an erudite journal, the first number began with the invention of the 'English Shakespeare'. The Mutual Depreciation Society, tiring of flattering each other in print and running each other down in private, find a new amusement in the creation of a fictional writer called Fladpick – as other countries are discovering the Belgian Shakespeare or the Cochin Chinese Shakespeare, they decide it is only fair that England should have an English Shakespeare. With some judicious reviews, Fladpick's style is soon a matter of discussion and inspires emulation among younger writers. In fact there was – or Jerome later claimed there was

— a serious purpose to this satire, namely to protest against:

> the assumption held by a certain school of critics that whatever is
> popular is bad; and that true literature can only be looked for among
> the worst sellers. Zangwill, some years ago, directed against them
> an amusing skit. It was at the time that Shakespeares were cropping
> up like mushrooms. A Russian Shakespeare had been discovered,
> followed a week later by a Dutch Shakespeare. And then there came
> an Irish Shakespeare. Zangwill, with the help of a few young and
> ardent journalistic spirits, discovered an English Shakespeare. Why
> should not England be in it? …

Of course Fladpick's actual writing was excerpted in the pages of *The
Idler*, but was not otherwise available to the public. 'Such greatness did not
condescend to make appeal to mere buyers. And then came his funeral, if I
remember rightly.'[387]

Zangwill's own writing habits were apparently even more eccentric than
Fladpick's. Burgin remembered that he would sit at one end of a table, inches
deep in paper and losing each page as he wrote it; meanwhile his brother Louis,
also a writer, would work at the other end, arranging his papers methodically
and vainly insisting that Israel should not encroach on his space. Like Jerome
himself, Zangwill must have been a man of extraordinary energy, but:

> He has adopted that most dangerous of all systems of writing, i.e.,
> of being absorbed in a book until it is finished, to the utter exclusion
> of everything else. It burns and holds and eats into him, and until
> it is on paper he knows no rest. People style him a humourist; but
> there is little humour in his method of work; it would kill most men
> in a very short time.

Burgin had a photograph of him which he had asked him to autograph,
'and he wrote under it; "Can this be I—Zangwill?"'[388]

Jerome's first contribution to the Idlers' Club was a sketch about trying,
at the vulnerable age of seventeen, to buy a valentine for a baby.[389] In a comic
reworking of the very real shyness he had felt at this age, he describes himself
as being thrown by the shop girl's asking, 'What sort of baby?' He answers
helplessly, 'You ought to know what a baby is like', innocently offending the
girl and incurring the hostile glares of everyone in the shop.[390]

The magazine's success did not depend wholly on such recognisably

Jeromian humour. Keeping a close watch on the aesthetic movement, that May it ran a spoof of Oscar Wilde, again by Zangwill, 'When you point out that Art is infinitely superior to Nature, I feel that you are cribbing from my unpublished poems, and I am quite at one with you in regarding the sunset as a plagiarism.'[391] But if the public responded to the humorous tone of the journal, Jerome's hard work and professionalism belied its name. Despite his periodic pen sketches of affably idle contributors, he would insist on standards being maintained. Burgin's anecdote about Phil May the *Punch* cartoonist (and therefore a dangerous person to offend) may of course be apocryphal, but either way, it makes the point. One morning:

> just as I reached the office, Phil May, the *Punch* artist, appeared. He looked very sad, for we had kept the magazine waiting for some sketches which he had promised to do and it had to appear at the last moment without them. Jerome had sent a red-hot letter to him on this breach of faith. Hence his call. "Is he about anywhere?" he asked, nervously shifting his portfolio from one hand to the other and preparing for instant flight.
>
> "Fortunately for you, he isn't."
>
> Phil May produced Jerome's letter and re-read it. Then he drew out a wonderful sketch from his portfolio—a sketch which represented an enormous-footed Jerome kicking him out of the office. "D'you think this would make some amends if I were to give it him?"
>
> "You can try if you like to come in later; it's a bit dangerous."
>
> He read the letter again—"shuffling, unreliable man who can't keep his word"—and became very indignant. "You like this sketch? Is it a good sketch?"
>
> "It's a very good sketch."
>
> "You're right. So it is. I'm d—d if I give a sketch like this to a man who wrote me a letter like that"; and he bolted out of the office.[392]

In the five years of his editorship Jerome managed to secure some of the most famous writers of the time. This was a world in which many of the contributors knew, or quite possibly recommended each other. The early numbers featured work by George Gissing, Rudyard Kipling and Robert Louis Stevenson; Anthony Hope (who published *The Prisoner of Zenda* in 1895), Stanley Weyman and Eden Phillpotts were all regular contributors.[393]

In 1892 Jerome himself published *Weeds: a Story in Seven Chapters*. Still one of his least known works, this was intended as a major piece of artistry, and marks a new departure in his thinking. Published three years after *Three Men in a Boat* made him a household name, this novella exists only in a handful of copies from the original edition, although it can now be read online and has recently been published in a Kindle edition by a member of the Jerome K. Jerome Society. While Jerome was keen to see the critical reaction to his new work, not a single review has yet come to light. One of the reasons for the critical neglect of *Weeds* is that Jerome's name does not appear on the title page, which gives the impression that he was not particularly proud of the book himself. In fact, the reason for remaining anonymous was quite the reverse. As he explained to Arrowsmith, 'I wd put my name to it after it had passed through the critics' hands. But if my name was on a serious work like this it would never get fair treatment. They would all say I had tried to be funny and failed.'[394] This was not a fate he could contemplate for his book, written 'at great cost of thought', not for the money it might bring but 'in hopes of gaining a reputation'.[395]

Just how seriously Jerome took it comes across in a series of letters to Arrowsmith, in which he tried to reassure his publisher that it was not too scurrilous for publication. The correspondence suggests that Arrowsmith had agreed to publish the book, before becoming nervous about a scene in which the anti-hero Dick sleeps with his wife's cousin in a downstairs room while she herself is ill in bed. Jerome was quick to reassure him that the reading public had advanced since the publication of *Tess of the d'Urbervilles* the year before, and 'I don't think the public who would be offended will read beyond the first few pages. The thing will not interest them. The thoughtful public will not be offended.' In any case it was unlikely that the average reader would draw the correct conclusion from his circumspect description. He had, he told Arrowsmith, tried it out on his wife and she 'never guessed the drift of it'. Without this hint, even a suspicious modern reader could be forgiven for thinking that the guilty pair are simply kissing when the wife comes in and sees her husband's face reflected in the mirror. In retrospect Arrowsmith was surely being over cautious, for as Jerome urged, it was unlikely that the phrase 'They are alone with Heaven',[396] as he originally wrote it, would convey much to the unsuspicious mind.

Jerome's letters to Arrowsmith are almost desperate in their attempts at persuasion, 'If I weaken my resolve the object of all my labour is gone.'[397] The offending passage describing the sexual encounter of the lovers 'will only convey itself to a very limited public indeed, to that public I am writing for. The general reader will never care for the book. You see in this I am not the business man I am the artist. The whole attempt is artistic.'[398] To prove the point, he suggested that Arrowsmith should read the scene to his wife. In a subsequent letter he suggested that the book should appear without publication details, and offered to replace what was certainly a fairly obvious phrase in which the lovers' 'quivering limbs entwine' with 'The room dissolves and fades. They are alone with nature'.[399] This suggestion was adopted in the published text.

Finally Jerome carried his point and the book was published by the end of the year, without any indication that he was the author. Certainly it was unlike anything his readers would have expected, or perhaps even accepted from him. The theme, as the title suggests, is sexual corruption, as Dick harbours thoughts of infidelity to the wife he loves. Disturbingly, as Alan R. Whitby points out, Dick and Daisy have been married for three years, the same period as Jerome and Ettie.[400] In the context of Jerome's increasing obsession with the dark side of sexual passion and his delineation in both journalism and fiction of marital fidelity as a perpetual struggle, it is possible that Dick is intended as an alter ego for the narrator himself.

More tangibly, the horror with which he views his own impurity casts an important light on late-nineteenth-century sexual politics and gender ideology. Social complacency about irregular male sexuality is often taken as just one more example of the oppressive double standard operating at the time. Of course this is true, but Dick's agony, even before he begins his flirtation with Jessie, stands as a reminder that male purity was also a widely respected ideal. The supposedly angelic purity of women was held up as a safeguard for men's morals, just as the idealised physical courage of men was used to justify conscription in World War I by a generation born in the Victorian era. In this formulation, female infidelity is harder to forgive, not because it is inherently worse, but because it is believed easier to resist.

In *Weeds* Jerome makes the point that female education, in shielding girls from all knowledge of the supposedly greater masculine propensity to indulge in destructive passion, does no favours to either sex. Both the wife Daisy and her 'luxurious' cousin are, as a result of their training, utterly incapable of foreseeing the probable result of Jessie's prolonged visit, in the course of which she and Dick pass rapidly from teasing to flirtation and ultimately sexual obsession. In this formulation, sexual desire is catastrophic in its probable effects, as the change from girlhood to womanhood creates 'a glorious creature of the sun. And our first natural instinct is to follow it, cap in hand, seeking to possess it, so that we may destroy it.'[401]

At various points Dick tries to justify his illicit desire to himself with the language of worldly wisdom – as the narrator comments acidly, 'Words are coloured spectacles, through which we look at facts.'[402] Throughout the book the emphasis is on the relationship between evil thoughts and their fulfilment, refusing the distinction between thought and action that Dick initially uses to console his conscience. But for the narrator, as for Dick in his more honest moments, this is sophistry. Crucially he regards himself as a fallen being, before setting eyes on Jessie in her grown-up condition; that he has the potential to commit adultery is sufficient to mark him, through a metaphor that Jerome would reuse again and again in later years, 'a man's heart is the link between the animalism from which we have sprung and the spiritualism towards which we tend.'[403] The link between mental and physical corruption is sustained throughout the book through the central metaphor of a weed-infested garden, and through the trope of animalism, 'Evil thought is a dangerous pet. It is safer to play with it from behind the iron bars of circumstance.'[404]

As important as the insistence on male culpability is the resolution in which the archetypal 'good' woman does not forgive her erring husband. In a radical conclusion that feminist writers would increasingly take up, she leaves her husband at the end, having offered only her cousin a momentary suggestion of forgiveness. Saying goodbye to Jessie for the last time, Daisy indulges in a moment's 'cruelty' as she implies that she must now marry the most persistent of her suitors, only to recall the affection she had formerly felt for her young relation, which causes a softening towards her. No such reconciliation is possible between Daisy and Dick, even though she knows it is she who will be more harshly judged as a woman separated from her husband.

Soon Jerome was asking anxiously, 'How does Weeds move? Do you think it would be useful in a month or so to let it leak out that it is mine? About how long does it take for a book by an unknown name to attract any attention?'[405] In Jerome's case it took over eighty years, until he was identified as the author in a letter sold at auction in 1968.

The year 1892 ended, as it had begun, with work. Jerome was not his father's son for nothing, and now he was keen to take up a new business opportunity. In addition to his role on *The Idler*, he had decided to begin a new publishing venture. There was some talk of Arrowsmith coming in with him, and Jerome told him that, 'If we could arrange it I would rather work with you than for comparative strangers' but this seems to have come to nothing. In the same letter in which he asks about the progress of *Weeds*, Jerome tactfully thanks him for his offer but says that after careful consideration he has decided to 'go it alone'.[406] In a subsequent letter he candidly admits that he has signed contracts with two authors who would otherwise have gone to Arrowsmith, a coup that he hopes will not damage their friendship. The effort to retain a personal relationship even in the midst of active rivalry shows Jerome in an attractive light, 'I write this as only with one practical idea. ... that you may not have any possible reason for feeling less friendly to me in the future. I am now getting this publishing scheme of mine into working order. ... I want to feel that my working against you instead of with you is a business accident... and that our personal friendship will not unduly suffer.'[407] The idea of Jerome running a publishing company raises all sorts of intriguing questions, but it is unclear what happened to it. Certainly it is not mentioned in 1897, when he was carefully weighing up his business assets.

It was probably in the same year that he moved with his family to 7 Alpha Place, Regent's Park on a twenty-one-year lease. This period also saw the first part of Jerome's *Novel Notes*, a twelve-part serial later published in one volume the following year. At one level *Novel Notes* is an entertaining satire on the process of novel writing, as the narrator and three friends make notes on a collaborative work that somehow never gets written. The narrator prefaces his publication of these notes with a defence against plagiarism, noting that in the case of Brown in particular:

> In thus taking a few of his bald ideas and shaping them into readable form, am I not doing him a kindness, and thereby returning good for evil? For has he not, slipping from the high ambition of his youth, sunk ever downward step by step, until he has become a critic, and, therefore, my natural enemy? Does he not, in the columns of a certain journal of large pretension but small circulation, call me ''Arry' (without an H, the satirical rogue), and is not his contempt for the English-speaking people based chiefly upon the fact that some of them read my books?[408]

Humour notwithstanding, it contains serious passages on the possible failure awaiting the young writer. The lack of encouragement offered to aspiring writers may even present an oblique comment on the bohemian world in which Jerome himself wrote his work. Zangwill was apparently notable for 'the stimulating acidity with which [he] was wont to season his discourse'[409] and one member of the Savage Club, of which Jerome was a member, explained:

> In the Savage Club, it must be admitted, there is as little mutual admiration – or, at any rate, as little inclination to express it – as is to be found among any assembly of mortal men. Rudeness, based on real friendship, and such as only a very real friendship can tolerate, are much more common than compliments. Instead of log-rolling, the Savages are somewhat given to baiting their brethren. It is all done in the way of good-fellowship, but with a frank understanding that it is not good Bohemian form to be thin-skinned.[410]

At one point in *Novel Notes* the narrator remembers exchanging criticism with a friend, when both were aspiring but, as yet, unpublished authors. He admits sadly that neither encouraged the other, rather thinking it more helpful to lash each other into greater efforts. Many years later he meets the friend, who has now become homeless, and reproaches him for his lack of confidence in his abilities. When the friend explains that with lack of encouragement he ultimately lost belief in himself the narrator bursts out with, 'I always believed in you, you know that. I –' only to remember his 'candid criticism' of many years before. '"Did you?" he replied quietly, 'I never heard you say so."'[411] The narrator knows that he will never meet his friend again, and wonders in quasi-religious language, 'whether Art, even with a capital A, is quite worth all the suffering that is inflicted in her behalf – whether she and we are better for all the scorning and the sneering, all the envying and the hating, that is done in her name.'[412]

But *Novel Notes* should not be seen purely as an answer to Jerome's critics. In posing the question of what is or is not acceptable to the reading public it also gestures towards some of his deepest anxieties. The theme of the double may be in part inspired by Jerome's admiration for his friend and *TO-DAY* contributor Stevenson's *Jekyll and Hyde*. Its most obvious expression in *Novel Notes* is the case of a clubbable man, Oxford-educated and deeply fastidious, named 'Joseph', who has a secret life as an 'Arry, and whose dilemma is caused by the dislike each self has for the other – the comic twist comes about through Joseph's unrequited passion for a tea shop waitress, while 'Arry falls for an aristocratic woman who barely acknowledges him when he holds her carriage for her, but attempts to attract him as Joseph. The relevance to Jerome's private self, his desire to be seen as a serious writer and the endless conflict with the press representation of him as 'Arry K. 'Arry is hard to miss.

A darker presentation of the double appears in dream sequences and narrative commentary elsewhere in the text. In chapter two the semi-fictional narrator questions the appropriateness of working a dream into a novel, and decides against it, before offering a detailed account to the reader after all. Significantly, the dream concerns the double face of a woman, who has potential for good or evil but is finally corrupted by the same mixed nature of the man who initially seems destined to save her:

> I dreamt I saw a woman's face among a throng. It is an evil face, but there is a strange beauty in it. The flickering gleams thrown by street lamps flash down upon it, showing the wonder of its evil fairness. Then the lights go out. I see it next in a place that is very far away, and it is even more beautiful than before, for the evil has gone out of it. Another face is looking down into it, a bright, pure face. ... I see the two faces again. ... I see the room in which they live. It is very poor. ... The woman sits by the open window. ... Then, very slowly, her face changes, and I see again the evil creature of the night.

In the dream, an indefinite time passes and then:

> Out of the dimness, there fashions itself a long, deserted street. ... A figure, dressed in gaudy rags, slinks by, keeping close against the wall. Its back is towards me, and I do not see its face. Another figure glides out from the shadows. I look upon its face, and I see it is the face that the woman's eyes gazed up into and worshipped   ... But the fairness and the purity are gone from it, and it is old and evil... They walk together in silence, till they come to where a flaring gas-lamp hangs before a tavern; and there the woman turns, and I see that it is the woman of my dream. And she and the man look into each other's eyes once more.[413]

This passage is disturbing in its intensity and in its recognition of men and women as equally corruptible. Specifically it suggests a deep cultural anxiety about sexuality and the impossibility of recognising the pure from the fallen.

In one of the inset stories this fear is dramatically explored through another of Jerome's recurring tropes, the drowning man. A beautiful but immoral woman pushes her husband into a lock where he almost drowns, only to be saved by the woman's lover. Only at the end of the story does the lover explain that his seemingly noble act was entirely selfish, in that he wanted to avoid being forced into marriage with the woman should she become free.

Jerome would return to the theme of cruelty in two further stories written for *The Idler* in 1893 and 1894. In 'The Woman of the Saeter' Jerome presents the reader with a newly married couple who take a house on a mountain in Norway. From the moment the male protagonist writes to a friend with stories of a ghost woman who was murdered by her lover's wife, the reader suspects that the idyllic interlude is over. Sure enough, the man is soon becoming obsessed with a strange female figure, and comes to hate his wife, writing to his friend that, 'here, amid these savage solitudes, I also am grown savage. The old primeval passions of love and hate stir within me, and they are fierce and cruel and strong, beyond what you men of the later ages could understand. The culture of the centuries has fallen from me as a flimsy garment whirled away by the mountain wind; the old savage instincts of the race lie bare.'[414] 'Two Extracts from a Diary' returns to the trope of the apparently noble but disingenuous lover, through the confessions of the disabled narrator, who holds a longstanding grudge against a beautiful but less wealthy schoolfellow, Jenny. Her revenge is first to accept a mercenary offer of marriage from the man who loves Jenny, while manipulating the man Jenny herself loves into falling in love with her instead; finally she tricks Jenny and the husband into eloping so that her rival will be disgraced. The main interest of the story lies in the diarist's claim that minds are formed by the bodies they inhabit, and her insistence on the cruelty of passion, as she explains that in marrying a man who does not return her love, 'I shall ... fawn upon him, as Gascoigne [the man Jenny loves] would marry and fawn upon me, and love me the better for my contempt and indifference. We are animals, we men and women, and we love our masters.'[415]

This preoccupation with the evil in human nature informs much of *Novel Notes*, both through stories of infidelity and also in the wider context of cruelty. Only a year or two earlier Jerome had insisted on 'the impossibility of getting away from "convention" (which after all is only another name for "facts")'. Like *Weeds*, *Novel Notes* insists on the dark side of the human psyche.

As much of his work from this time suggests, he was greatly interested in Tennyson's lines on the perfectibility of human nature in *In Memoriam*, in which mankind is urged to 'work out' the ape and the tiger,[416] deploying the trope of the tiger and the ape repeatedly in his own writing. In the ostensibly comic *Novel Notes* he warned his readers:

> Nature, whether human or otherwise, was not made to be reformed. You can develop, you can check, but you cannot alter it.
>
> You can take a small tiger and train it to sit on a hearthrug, and so long as you provide it with hearthrugs to lie on and sufficient milk to drink, it will purr and behave like an affectionate domestic pet. But it is a tiger, with all a tiger's instincts, and its progeny to the end of all time will be tigers.
>
> In the same way, you can take an ape and develop it through a few thousand generations until it loses its tail and becomes an altogether superior ape. You can go on developing it through still a few more thousands of generations until it gathers to itself out of the waste vapours of eternity an intellect and a soul, by the aid of which it is enabled to keep the original apish nature more or less under control.
>
> But the ape is still there…[417]

That Jerome took Darwinian notions of the animal very seriously is clear. But increasingly it would be the degeneration of the human race, rather than its perfectibility, that would haunt his most humorous work.

As *Novel Notes* neared the end of its run in the magazine, Jerome, who was by now himself being 'inundated' with offers from America,[418] turned to his friend Conan Doyle, urging him to produce six or eight stories to begin the following March (1893). Within a few years there would be division between them, as Conan Doyle's increasing obsession with spiritualism would prove too much for Jerome. Jerome had already satirised the *fin de siècle* spirit craze, questioning why 'a spirit, not compelled as we are by the exigencies of society, should care to spend its evenings carrying on a laboured and childish conversation with a room full of abnormally uninteresting people'.[419] In more serious vein he shared his contemporaries' anxiety that the séance, played on or created hysterical symptoms in women, 'Excitement, expectation, emotion, the darkened room – everything is done by the professional medium to vitiate the evidence of what takes place.'[420]

As it turned out, he himself now wanted 'something very strong to follow my "Novel Notes,"' and with an adroit layering of flattery and decision he now wrote to suggest, 'we could advertise this series, and make it the feature of the magazine. ... Let me know at once as to this, and if possible let us have a chat over it. I have been trying to get away, but have not been able to spare an hour.'[421]

He also approached Swinburne's friend Theodore Watts-Dunton, reminding him of an earlier request for a poem from each of them, and assuring him of the serious intent of the journal itself, 'I did not press you more at the time as I knew you had an idea that we were rather frivolous on the "Idler", & my arrangements were not complete to show you otherwise' but now 'we are striking a more serious note which will continue to sound louder through succeeding numbers'.[422] This assurance is clearly calculated to secure a heavyweight literary 'name'; nonetheless, Jerome was approaching Hall Caine in January 1894 with the idea that he should produce something on Ruskin:

> I do not mean an interview in the ordinary sense but a talk between you. For an interview I would of course send a journalist down who for £5 would give me a description of Ruskin's house & study & cat – the date of his birth & a catalogue of his works. I want Ruskin's thoughts & views – such thoughts & views as would come out of the man during an argument with yourself – his memory of the past & his insight into the future. ... I doubt if he would open himself to anyone as he would to you & you would paint the heart & the mind of the man & leave a picture of him in these his later years. Would you do this? I don't disguise the fact it is an article I should be entirely proud to publish. At this present time it would be of immense interest & of importance.[423]

No article on Ruskin appeared as a result of this suggestion, but Watts-Dunton agreed to be interviewed by Burgin for an article on the function of criticism.[424] Zangwill's comment in this issue that he would rather praise a good book written by a friend than review one that he could not honestly praise, gives some indication of the support Jerome could expect from his friends and contributors. *The Idler* posthumously published Philip Marston's poem 'Poet and Cobbler', featuring the lines, 'He brings his boots home to mend and polish; / I bring my books for a weekly journal / Poor books to abuse, to review, and demolish / For editors like their critics infernal.'[425] This was by no means the ethos of *The Idler*.

The idea of an Idlers' 'Club' provided Jerome with a much needed sense of shared identity at a time when many of the critics were being particularly brutal. In April 1892, for instance, the *Glasgow Herald* had described the New Humour as some kind of disease 'breaking out in a fresh place' and Jerome's work as 'a curious commentary on the literary taste of the reading public'. With familiar snobbery it assumed that:

All that is necessary is to write a slipshod sentence, which might mean almost anything, and then proceed to explain it. For example, supposing you write 'I kicked my uncle under the table' you have an opportunity of explaining that you didn't kick him so as to send him bodily under the table, but merely kicked whatever part of him was next you under the table. This is a very pretty style of wit, and may be applied in almost any direction.[426]

This critique is, of course, the more damning because it cleverly adopts the very mode of wit from which it yawningly distances itself. It would take a conscientious reader to resist the inference that this example had been thrown out at random rather than being carefully constructed.[427]

In October 1893 a satire on 'The Academy of New Humour' presents a concerned Literature counselling his friend the Reading World, whom he encounters 'in a shocking state' after 'taking a course of the New Humour'.[428]

In a characteristically light response to these attacks, Jerome demanded to know in particular why 'Cockney' was such a favourite term of opprobrium:

Whenever the superior book-reviewer, sampling a new work of mine, has expended on me all his stock epithets of cad, boor, blackguard, snob, liar, brute, bank-clerk, new humourist, thief, upstart, and such-like subtle thrusts characteristic of the new criticism, he invariably concludes his "notice" by calling me a "Cockney." The main portion of this abuse I have by long practice schooled myself to bear with equanimity. I even endeavour to derive from it some benefit, as one should from all criticism. But the "bank-clerk" and the "Cockney" do, I confess, rankle within my breast. I have never been a bank-clerk. I have served as clerk in most other offices, but never in a bank. To call me "Cockney" is even more unjust. Meaning from the beginning to be a writer, I took the precaution of selecting my birthplace in a dismal town in the centre of the Staffordshire coalfields, a hundred and fifty miles, at least, away from London.[429]

CHAPTER FOUR

'a real and useful influence'
Living *TO-DAY* 1893-1894

'I had a tie that hooked on — and why not? If these remarks were not personal they were rather careless...'

George and Weedon Grossmith, *The Diary of a Nobody*

Aside from his war with the critics, Jerome's mind was turning again towards more serious concerns than *The Idler* was really designed to carry. While he would continue with the journal until the end of 1897, his thoughts now turned to a different kind of publication. Towards the end of 1893 he started a weekly journal, *TO-DAY*, in which he would develop the editorial column as a platform for his political views and social campaigning, notably his crusade against the perpetrators of animal cruelty. With its weekly editorials, often written under pressure, the journal shows Jerome communicating more intimately and instinctively with his public than he ever did in the carefully revised manuscripts of his fiction.

The original idea was that Jerome himself would put in £500 and take a share of the profits in lieu of salary and fees. Again, he invited Arrowsmith to invest £500 in his latest scheme.[430] It seems that on this occasion Arrowsmith did seriously consider investing, but by the time he answered the invitation Jerome already had all the capital investment he needed. He did offer to split his own £500 worth of shares, giving the reason, slightly tactlessly, that his publishing business was growing faster than he had anticipated. Otherwise, he had four subscribers of £4,000, all 'of many years experience in the journalistic world', and an additional £500 from advertising agencies.[431] In a bizarre twist, the investors then decided to do without Jerome's capital altogether. As he explained to Arrowsmith, 'My capitalists have played me rare larks. First four were going in with any others I liked to bring. This was when I first wrote to you, then, as I explained they wanted to take the whole thing themselves, but agreed that I should put £500 in. Then three weeks ago they made up their minds to turn me out, & to put the whole of the money in themselves. They are sensitive birds, & I have had to humour them.'[432] In the end Jerome either invested capital after all or, at any rate, acquired shares, telling Conan Doyle in 1897 that he had £2,000 of debs, or debentures, in the journal.[433]

Cassell's Family Journal interviewed Jerome in December of this year and noticed both his 'quietly humorous way of putting before his listener the most ordinary incidents of human life' and his 'quite remarkable serious-mindedness ... nothing weak about it though'.[434]

It was in these years of his first fame that he first met Douglas Sladen, who had returned to London from America in 1891. Coulson Kernahan introduced them[435] and, after Jerome's death, Sladen would say that, 'Most of my literary friendships I owe to Jerome K. Jerome, who took me by the hand when I came back from America, introduced me to literary circles, gave me an editorship on one of his own papers, and showered hospitalities on us. As an author I owe more to him than anyone else.'[436]

While many of the *TO-DAY* articles were published anonymously, Sladen (who appeared as D. S. in the paper) later identified himself as its literary reviewer, in addition to dealing with correspondence. He was:

> at the time his chief and only book critic on *TO-DAY*. I believe I was called the literary editor... I believe also that it was I who suggested the name *TO-DAY*. At any rate, it was I who helped him to formulate the paper, and for the first year or so it was my duty to do all the book reviews in it, and my duty to receive all the ladies who came to see Jerome about the paper. Of course, they mostly came in search of work or fame... The only thing I could do for them was to write about them if they were sufficiently interesting, which frequently happened in that age of personal journalism. And, if they were quite harmless worshippers, without any ulterior designs, I occasionally induced Jerome to be worshipped for a minute or two. I made many lady friends at this period, especially from the Stage.[437]

Sladen's account is slightly misleading, in that a young Ernest Bramah was

employed in the office partly to deal with the constant flood of letters, and
G. B. Burgin was also on hand to help direct the reading public. His job was
to pose as 'a benevolent old bookseller who chatted to customers about the
books they ought to buy. So full of wisdom was I that people wrote to ask my
advice about their love affairs, and their husbands, and what they ought to do
if a gentleman asked a girl out to tea without an introduction. To my credit, I
always sternly insisted that an introduction was necessary.'

Barry Pain wrote the 'De Omnibus' column, in which he held forth in
what he assumed was phonetic cockney. Burgin said that he once asked an
omnibus driver if he had seen these articles. 'He had. "Well, what do you
think of them?" He gently drew his whip over the off horse's back. "The
man as wrote those things, sir, knows a b y lot about 'osses, but he can't
spell!"' was the response.

A series of celebrities, including George Bernard Shaw, found themselves
interviewed under the banner of 'ten minutes with', while such luminaries
as Mary Braddon, Conan Doyle and Gissing provided fiction for the early
numbers. By 1894 Jerome had 'discovered' W. W. Jacobs, who would become
a close friend but whose marriage in 1900 would have serious implications
for Jerome's own relationship with Ettie. It was Jacobs of whom Burgin
said that he 'looked as if he had had greatness thrust upon him and wished
someone would take it off again. He is the shyest and most retiring of men,
slight, thin, and rather delicate.'[438]

In a defence of the New Humour for which he, like Jerome, found
himself constantly attacked, Zangwill in one issue warned other writers
against taking themselves too seriously, 'For my part, I have been grieved to
see more than one of my fellow-authors morbidly anxious to cover up their
humorous past, in deference to the conventional opinion that the gravity
of the owl is a sign of wisdom. Too many writers hasten to assume the
statue in their own lifetime, and to compose their public features to a non-
human frigidity.'[439] He must have been as delighted as Jerome himself when a
joke predicting that some critic would discover the 'new pathos' was actually
fulfilled. In his editorial for the week Jerome wrote joyously:

> I thought they would do it; I said they would; I told everybody so
> weeks ago in these columns, and now they have done it. The young
> man who "does literature" for the *Pall Mall Gazette* has started it, and
> in a week or two they will all be doing it. I know them so well. Andew
> Lang will write long leaders about it, and Buchanan will write long

letters on the subject. Canon Ainger will lecture about it through the country, and Zangwill, in *The Star*, will explain what everybody else means. Mr Eden Phillpotts is the first victim. He has written a book called "Some Everyday Folks", and the *Pall Mall Gazette* girds at it as "the new pathos." For myself I am glad. It will give the new humour a rest.[440]

Humour notwithstanding, the scope of the paper was more ambitious than anything Jerome had attempted in *The Idler*, which had according to Sladen 'no equal then as a magazine of fiction, and had a sale of a hundred thousand copies a month'.[441] Now he wanted to start a more serious paper, 'not only to amuse, but to educate Public Opinion, when it had secured attention by its brightness, for he had very strong views which he was eager to preach'.[442] Yet again the shades of Dickens in that favourite word of his: 'brightness'. Clearly a perfectionist, Jerome was so incensed by the poor quality of the first issues that he sued the printers. He was awarded a farthing in damages and remarked bitterly, 'The worst I can wish any one of them [the jury] is that he may risk a small fortune on a paper, and find it turned out by the printers as Messrs. Speaight printed my early numbers.'[443] It is not known whose idea it was to send specimen copies to all the West End Theatres, placing a free copy of the first number on each seat in return for free advertising in the Entertainments section for thirteen weeks.[444] But it was a stroke of genius.

In the first few weeks Jerome evidently enjoyed his skirmish with the *Pall Mall Gazette*, which had taken an instant dislike to the new weekly. The *Pall Mall* got in first, jeering before an issue of *TO-DAY* could appear that the paper planned to 'deal with literature, art, and the drama as they have never been dealt with before. We quite believe it.'[445] On 11 November it returned to the charge, beginning the 'Literary Notes' column with 'Presuming to offer any advice to the conductors of the new twopenny magazine TO-DAY, it may be premature to make the most obvious recommendation – to discontinue it.' This sally was immediately followed up with a criticism of the illustrations, 'shockingly printed on bad paper'.[446] While Jerome must have winced over cheap hits at the printers' shortcomings, he lost no time in putting this particular critic in his place:

The very young gentleman from Cambridge who "does the literary column" for the *Pall Mall Gazette*, and who of late has been taking such a touching interest in me and my affairs, counsels me to discontinue this paper at once. I cannot complain that the advice comes too late, for I am told that a fortnight ago he solemnly protested against my starting it at all. In the bustle of work, however, I did not see his previous warning, and I am now, therefore, on the horns of a dilemma. Either I must reject his advice (which seems ungrateful), or ignore the apparent wishes of some two hundred thousand subscribers. Perhaps my young friend will see his way to allowing me a day or so to further consider the matter.[447]

Notwithstanding this ebullience, a glimpse of the daily work involved is offered by one of Jerome's letters from this time, to Coulson Kernahan. Admitting that he has not yet had time to read his friend's new book, he explains, 'This paper (*TO-DAY*) is costing on an average of 14 hours' work a day. On Sundays I have been at it 20 hours. It is getting a bit easier now.'[448] Not surprisingly, most of his extant letters from this period are addressed from Arundel Street, Strand, the headquarters of both journals. Sladen remembered that he very rarely answered letters addressed to him as the editor of *TO-DAY*.[449] In fact, the work does not seem ever to have got too much easier – one of his particular bugbears was the well-intentioned criticism of those around him, leading him to comment wryly in *The Idler* in April 1896 that, 'If the editor of a newspaper is under any delusion as to his capabilities, it is not the fault of his friends.'[450]

He could not know at the beginning that he was starting a new journal at such an apposite moment, but in its first two years of circulation Jerome would engage with some of the most important debates of the *fin de siècle*.

A certain amount of latitude was allowed to contributors, but while the new journal eschewed a homogenous stance on the issues it discussed, it did aim for a certain cohesion. A printed list of 'suggestions' for editorial paragraphs included:

Common sense to be their backbone.
The writer's views and opinions of the subjects to be the raison d'être, not the subjects themselves.
They should refer to great things reverentially; to good things sympathetically; to evil things sternly; to foolish things scornfully; and to hypocritical things angrily.
Style to be literary rather than journalistic.

It is desired that bias of all kind should be avoided.
They should represent the opinion of the plain man, free from
   prejudice. [451]

The suggestions end with the words, 'I wish to aim at a real and useful
influence. Use all the weapons of wit, sarcasm, humour, fancy, plain-speaking,
and, if necessary, abuse. But let us remember we are fighting a real battle,
not indulging in a mere display of skill.'[452] As in Dickens's journal, many
of the articles were anonymous, although the serial stories – an important
feature of *TO-DAY* – were attributed. While the suggestions for editorial
paragraphs, taken with the lack of attribution in many of the first numbers,
suggest an initial intention to rotate authorship of what became the 'TO-
DAY' (or editorial) column, in practice this column seems almost always to
have been written by the editor himself. Certainly it was very much Jerome's
paper. At this stage of his career he was a principled Conservative (although
he denied this initially, insisting in an early number, that, 'The only party I
desire to belong to is the party of common-sense'),[453] and devoted many
pages to abjuring socialism in particular.

Over the next few years he would also engage in a kind of guerrilla
warfare with the 'advanced woman' and her supporters. In December 1893
he came out firmly against the Parish Councils Bill on the grounds that
enfranchising a married woman was simply to give her husband a second
vote. For someone so well informed it is significant that he invokes the
obsolete language of coverture (i.e. the assumption that a woman ceased
to exist as an individual on her marriage) by way of protest against social
disorder, 'Unless we adopt the theories of the female on the rampage, and
maintain that woman is to compete with man throughout life, we must accept
the old principle that a woman on marriage merges her individual existence
with that of her husband.'[454] Many of his contributors were of similar views,
and between them they filled the pages of both *The Idler* and *TO-DAY* with
diatribes against the advanced woman. In February 1895 a poem on 'The
New Woman' made plain a belief in the moral difference between the sexes:

> The woman I would love must not be she
> Who vainly dreams a grandiose career,
>
> ...
>
> Whose moral voice is strident...
> She must be rather one whose kind tones break

In keen regret that some dear one must sin,
Whose timid eyes look down, and chastely make
An outlet for the gentle soul within[455]

Later in the year, in an edition of The Idlers' Club suggestively entitled 'Should Man be Woman's God?', the subeditor Burgin insisted that, 'The woman who is intellectually above the average of her sex is generally a law unto herself; what she gains in intellect she loses in femininity. There is quite enough masculine intellect wherewith to carry on the business of the world, but there is nothing to replace a good wife and mother.'[456] From time to time Jerome included strategic defences by such figures as the Girton girl – 'there still exist some cautious beings who regard a college young lady with a sort of nervous dread, as being stamped for life with the seal of learning and undesirability.'[457] These interventions nothwithstanding, his own stance and that of some of his closest collaborators remained conservative. If Jerome viewed the advanced woman with something like horror, he was equally wary of the 'frankly feminine' man, labelling both as 'that curious animal product of modern times' and claiming that he could ascribe a gender to neither of them with any certainty.[458] This troubled reaction to shifting gender roles and their expression would provide a focus for the paper over the next few years.

But while it distanced itself from *The Idler* in its openly political focus, the new paper made no secret of its populist aims. The weekly contents of *TO-DAY* indicates precisely why it was so popular with readers. The artful mix of humour, fiction and topics of the day is well calculated to appeal to an educated middle class wanting to keep abreast of social and political affairs without necessarily aspiring to the gentility of the class above them. Reassuringly, Jerome himself was disparaging about the writers for other journals who fed such insecurity in their readers, demanding:

Is not the literary critic working the adjectives "suburban" and "middle class" a little too much? ... A Brixton shopkeeper stints himself, and saves enough money to enable his eldest son to get an education on the foundation of a public school, and afterwards to send him to Oxford or Cambridge. He comes back with a smattering of Latin, and by the aid of some well-to-do college contemporaries, who feel they owe him some reparation for the snubbings they have always administered to him, gets a berth, bringing him in about two pounds a week on a paper, and from that day till he marries his landlady's daughter, and settles down to common sense in a four-roomed flat at Kilburn, he sets to work to show his supreme contempt for all classes but the aristocracy, and to try and persuade the few people who read his criticisms that he haunts the houses of the nobility, and does not know an omnibus when he sees one.[459]

Eschewing this type of snobbery *TO-DAY* itself deployed the 'New Humour' for which Jerome was reluctantly famous. Jerome himself, of course, knew all about the snobbery of literary critics, who had renamed him 'Arry K. 'Arry'. Unabashed, he gave a talk on humour at the Westbourne Park Institute on 9 October 1894.[460] A large audience came to see him and to speculate on his reputed shyness, but as a reporter for *Hearth and Home* observed, 'his matter and his manner were equally attractive, and his audience listened, entranced, to racy anecdotes, quaint phrases, and good, wholesome fun. ... Probably only a man or woman here or there realise that it was the truth and reality of Mr Jerome's own "humour" which appealed so strongly to them.'[461] He was subsequently reported in the Bristol press as lecturing on 'Humour New and Old' in the Merchant Venturers' Technical College in March 1895.[462]

Despite his political rhetoric, Jerome would remain famous for his humour rather than his politics. Capitalising on this reputation, the new journal would include eight 'characterscapes' in the first year. An early series 'If he had lived To-day' not only punned on the journal's title but parodied the literary and dramatic critics by imagining a young Shakespeare being dismissed by a manager – Hamlet's speeches, the man explains, are 'too long altogether, and rambling'. In an adroit appropriation, Dickens receives even worse treatment on the appearance of *The Pickwick Papers*, 'Mr "Charles Dickens" – the name is evidently a pseudonym – is apparently one of the New Humourists. We do not remember that we have ever heard his name before, and we only notice his book at length in the hope that by so doing we may save ourselves from ever hearing his name again.'[463]

Jerome himself was suffering criticism of his humorous creations at around the same time. He had by agreement sent his characterscapes to America for publication in *McClure's Magazine*. Evidently the sketches were not what McClure had expected, leading to an abrupt letter from Jerome across the water, 'I am extremely sorry you took them but having done so there must be an end of the matter[.] I think them good humour, you don't. The question resolves itself into who is the better judge of humour – or at all events of what the public considers humour – you or I.'[464] The question is a rhetorical one. Interestingly, while the British public at any rate clearly did consider them good humour, Jerome later attributed the circulation of the paper (just under 100,000 at its best) less to the humour than to the quality of literature serialised in its pages, 'In the magazine department "TO-DAY" stood for good class literature. We had some of the best work of Stevenson, Weyman, Doyle, Jacobs, Zangwill, Hope, Wells, and so on.'[465] Jerome famously said in *My Life and Times* that he took Jacobs's unsolicited work after hearing a prolonged sound of laughing when he knew himself to be alone.[466] Jacobs was diffident about providing further stories in case he failed to match this promising effect, but as Aubrey Wilson records, 'Jerome, the kindest of men and the best of mentors, recognising the latent possibilities of this pale, nervous young man, finally persuaded him to accept the contract and did all he could to encourage and re-assure him as well as guiding, with a gentle editorial hand.'[467] He remained a *TO-DAY* contributor until 1905. It may well have been Jacobs who in turn introduced Pett Ridge, a friend from Birkbeck College days.

Just as the Idlers' Club gave to the monthly periodical a sense of identity, so the weekly sold itself as a kind of club for its readers. Sladen later commented that it was 'not so much literary as a paper of personalities'.[468] One means of achieving this was through the weekly correspondence column, often so oversubscribed that letters were held over for another week. In this column Jerome took on the roles of everything from medical advisor (he had the sense to direct enquirers firmly to a responsible doctor), commentator on political and social affairs, and agony uncle to everyone from young girls in search of excitement to bank clerks aspiring to a literary career.[469] On occasion he would take his readers to task, telling one rejected contributor who had objected to being charged for the return of his MS, 'We don't expect genius, we don't expect literature, but we do expect stamps'[470] (the direct tone of the column would remain a feature for the duration of Jerome's editorship; in 1896 he would answer another hapless correspondent, 'No sir, I will not let you know through the columns of my paper the difference in height between the Earl Grey Monument at Newcastle and the Nelson Column in Trafalgar Square').[471]

To many, however, he came to represent a benevolent and avuncular figure – while he told one reader somewhat sternly, 'I must differ from you; my observation tells me that women's passions are not as strong as men's',[472] he could be trusted to give advice without judgement on such questions as whether a man should marry the mother of their illegitimate child[473] and other thorny questions of sexual relations. Just over a year after its inception, Jerome felt confident enough to proclaim, 'The dozens of letters that come in every day from subscribers give me great pleasure, for they show the close sympathy between TO-DAY and its readers. Indeed, I sometimes flatter myself by thinking that there can be few journals that have established so close and intimate a relationship with their readers.'[474] The echo of Dickens is unmistakeable, and is yet more obvious in Jerome's evocation of this time in later days. '"The Chief" they used to call me. "Is the Chief in?" they would ask of the young lady in the outer office. Just a convention, but always it gave me a little thrill of pride when I overheard it.'[475]

Jerome's editorial persona then was accessible and also instructive. In a weekly editorial he kept his readers au fait with developments in current affairs, what reviewers had to say about the latest books, and his own views on particular topics. Perhaps unsurprisingly, given his unmanageable workload, he occasionally used his editorial column to attack the creators of noise outside his windows. In particular, he showed an aversion to German street bands, and organ grinders, commenting irritably in 1895:

> Fifty years hence, Londoners will hardly believe that their forefathers allowed their health to be wrecked and their work interfered with by the hideous and distracting noises made by German bands and organ-grinders. We encourage all the riff-raff of Germany and Italy who choose to come over here, and we keep them for no other purpose than to annoy the majority of us, and to benefit only a few idle loafers with no ear for music. If they were confined to the slums they might, perhaps, afford a certain amount of pleasure, but two-thirds of their income is earned by blackmailing those they drive mad with their din.[476]

He never seems to have lost his sense of grievance against street musicians, describing gleefully in 1908 how he used to deal with them during this residence in St John's Wood:

> we used to keep an odd man who had a salary of about fifteen shillings a week, and was mostly occupied in listening for organs and going out to make them be quiet. You would hear a wandering musician start to grind out a melody on the other side of the square... A minute later that tune would break off abruptly in the

middle, and you would hear no more of it... I never inquired how he did it, and he never offered to take me into his confidence, but when I hear people wondering how it is organ-grinders have become so scarce I can't help thinking things.[477]

But by 1897 the problem still had not been resolved, and he claimed caustically that, 'The German traveller never hears a German band in London without thanking God that England has got it, and not his own country.'[478]

But one of the first editorial tasks was to record the demise of *Home Chimes*. Jerome paid tribute to it as:

> a magazine edited by that kindliest of men and best of friends to young authors, Mr F. W. Robinson, the novelist. *Home Chimes* was a little too sober and literary to catch on with the great public, but there are few of us younger writers who do not owe to it grateful remembrance. ... and it was in its pages that I first began to annoy the critics. [Robinson's] experience and advice were always at our service and our successes were his. I fear the new generation of writers will look in vain for another such editor.[479]

By his death in 1901 Robinson had been reduced to poverty and:

> Jerome and Kernahan and a few others put their heads together and persuaded him that they had obtained an order for him to write a play. A certain sum (they scraped it up among themselves) had been paid by the mythical commissioner of the play, and he must begin at once. Robinson was very grateful to them and unsuspiciously tried to write the play. But the hand of death was on him and he could not do it. On his death-bed he realised the truth. "You've made me very happy, you dear lads," he said, "although you humbugged me. But that money was useful—very useful.[480]

In these first few months of *TO-DAY* Jerome also campaigned tirelessly for a cycling match between his nephew Frank Shorland[481] and the French champion Auguste Stephane. In July of 1892 Stephane had taken the long distance record with 631 km in twenty-four hours, but Shorland capped this with 666 km later that month. In September Stephane upped the stakes by managing 673 km and the following July Shorland retook the record with 685. Meanwhile another French cyclist, Lucien Lesna, claimed to have beaten both of them with 696 km on French authority, although this victory was later thrown out. The 16 December issue carried a full page article on the refusal of the National Cyclists' Union to let Shorland compete in a French competition, on the grounds that a monetary prize would be involved, and would therefore jeopardise his amateur status. Ridiculing the decision as 'a crowning act in a long series of illogical follies', Jerome observed witheringly that, 'This General Committee is an annually elected body, whose term of office expires in March, and it is more than likely that new men may be elected upon it of more rational, more sportsmanlike, more representative views.'[482] On the opposite page a cartoon of a dejected Shorland is captioned 'Shorland: "Can I go out and have a run with Stephane and Lesna?" The N.C.U.: "Certainly not; I won't have you playing with those dirty little boys!"' *Cycling* was in full agreement with Jerome, carrying a spoof in March 1894 entitled 'Extract from "Electro-Cycling" of July 7th, 2075'. The 'extract' is an old epitaph in a country churchyard and the earnest visitor deciphers the initials NCU, which 'are supposed to refer in some way to a body of men which existed in those days for the nominal protection and purification of the amateur sport of cycling. ... Happily for us those days of tyrannical humbug no longer exist for our racing men'.[483]

Typically generous in his assessment of their relative positions, Jerome later said that at this time, 'In sporting circles I was always introduced as "Shorland's uncle." Close-cropped young men would gaze at me with rapture; and then inquire: "And do you do anything yourself, Mr Jerome?"'[484] Shorland himself may have been less concerned about his own success than was his yet more famous uncle. While he had been winning races since his late teens, and had begun his career at the age of fifteen on a 'bone shaker', he told a journalist in the spring of 1894 that he spent most of his time thinking about business (he was involved in a cycling business) rather than competitive sport itself, and gave 'the impression that there are few men, who have accomplished so much for a pastime, who display such a small amount of enthusiasm as does the English Long Distance Cycle Champion'.[485]

That July, Shorland broke the twelve hours' world record over the North Road course from Hitchin to Market Deeping, covering 211.5 miles just a fortnight after a rival cyclist had taken the record with 202.5 miles.[486] At the 24 Hours Path Race, later that month, where Shorland was defending his position as holder for two years in succession of the Challenge Cup,[487] Jerome was naturally on the sidelines. Again Shorland beat the world record, by two miles and 1,408 yards.[488] Insistently pro-war at this stage of his life (a position he would modify dramatically after 1916), Jerome proclaimed to his readers:

> Next to war, sport serves the useful purpose of bringing out all the virtue of a man – all the strength that is in him, both of body and mind, brain and heart. I watched young Shorland start and finish his great twenty-four hours' ride, and feel all the better myself for the emotions it stirred in me. ... I am sure that the twenty thousand young men standing round the track at Herne Hill on Saturday must have learned lasting good for life, from watching the look of dogged resolution slowly settling down into young Shorland's face as the last hour drew on.[489]

All of this was sufficient to attract the attention of the journal *Cycling*, who duly interviewed Jerome in October. As the uncle of the 'irrepressible devil-may-care' Shorland,[490] he was of interest in any case, but the paper was particularly appreciative of his inflammatory editorials attacking the NCU. The journalist sent to interview him clearly found Jerome amenable, joking that, 'Mr Jerome has recently removed his moustache, and, for a moment, we presumed he was undergoing a course of strict training, and was reducing all superfluous weight to a minimum. We were assured however, that it was not so, but was merely for lecturing purposes.' Jerome himself had recently learned to ride a bicycle, but asked whether he had yet ventured out with his nephew, 'Mr Jerome shifted somewhat uneasily in his chair, and fixing his eyes ceilingwards, murmured, "four-hundred and sixty miles in the day – marvellous boy!" then addressing us, remarked, emphatically, "No, my enthusiasm for the sport has scarcely reached that point just yet."'[491]

In his own paper the subject matter was sometimes more controversial. Never afraid to speak his mind, Jerome would more than once find himself sued for libel, although he would always insist that *TO-DAY* acted responsibly in checking the facts before publishing any detrimental comment. In some cases the charges and counter-charges risked descending into farce, as in the case of 'G. W. Moore v Jerome K. Jerome and Another' in 1895. The question of libel centred on whether Moore had introduced a 'music hall element' into his stage entertainments. Cross-examined by Mr Carson, QC, one of the girls said that, 'She wore a long skirt and sang songs à la Betty Lind.' Under cross-examination by Mr Danckwerts, a Miss Queenie Lawrence 'was quite sure that no clergyman left while she was on the stage (Laughter). She saw no one leave, in fact. Her dances were quiet and not violent in character. Her skirts were rather long than otherwise.'[492] In the event *TO-DAY* lost the case on a technicality. Determinedly bearing up under the inevitable £300-400 cost of the case, Jerome insisted, 'TO-DAY has no wish to act the part of the light-hearted libeller. When we make charges against a man, they are charges that we have carefully investigated, and that we consider it our duty to publish. Having made them, we do not, and shall not, ever shirk our responsibility for them, or thwart any man fancying himself libelled by us from having our accusations sifted in open court.'[493]

In the event it was just such a case, centring round a series of articles published as part of the 'In the City' section of the paper, that would finally bring the paper down. The first article on Samson Fox's 'water gas' company appeared on 12 May 1894. The 'In the City' column was lambasting Fox in connection with the opening of the Royal College of Music, when he had 'posed as a public benefactor'; it went on to provide figures for his and his associates' recent enterprises showing that £1,130,000 had recently been promised or passed over to Fox by shareholders 'And for what? The public were induced to subscribe the huge capital of the Leeds Forge Company by gross and deliberate misrepresentation as to the value of the patents and processes sold. As for the Water Gas Companies, for whose patents the public gave over half a million, and were asked to give more when the Notts and Derby was brought out, they have all passed into liquidation without returning a single stiver in the way of dividend.' The article went on, 'When a man like Passmore Edwards builds a library, or an hospital, or a light-house, the money it costs comes from the savings of thrift, and the Heir Apparent does well to honour the donor in any way he may, but the £46,000 given by Samson Fox to the College of Music was drawn from the pockets of the public by very gross misrepresentations, and the Prince of Wales was ill-advised when he condoned the methods by which Samson Fox made his money in consideration of the purpose to which a portion of the spoil has been applied.'[494]

By 19 May the paper was able to publish two letters in support of its claims.[495] On 23 June a full page was devoted to attacking Fox, 'Taking advantage of the speculative madness of 1889, Fox was able to persuade the public to subscribe over a million, and to offer over eight millions sterling, for patents that were not worth as many farthings.' Particularly unfortunate in the event was the repeated challenge in this article, 'Will Mr Samson Fox go into the box and deny it?' Finally the writer claimed (with something of a flourish) that, 'Next week this record of deliberate, shameless, utterly unscrupulous misrepresentation, for the purpose of fleecing the public, will be continued and concluded.'[496] In fact the 'final' article of 30 June was quickly followed by a further burst of indignation on 7 July. After almost a page of accusations, the 'In the City' correspondent notes that a telegram from Fox has arrived to the effect that he has written a letter to the paper for publication in that issue. It is not hard to see the smile behind the laconic addendum, as Fox's own fury is used to promote the circulation of the paper attacking him, 'TO-DAY regrets that Mr Fox's letter cannot appear in the present issue. It shall have prominence in the next.'[497] Insisting meanwhile on the integrity of TO-DAY's investigations, Jerome himself declares in his weekly editorial:

> Having taken the matter up, we have gone into it most carefully and thoroughly. Hearsay evidence has been put aside. The talk of those who have suffered in pocket through Mr Fox's schemes has been carefully sifted, lest bitterness of feeling should unconsciously vent itself in exaggeration. Every statement we have made has been enquired into, and nothing put down that we are not prepared to prove up to the hilt. Every witness from whom we have obtained information has been personally examined, and our chief reliance rests upon sworn statements and documentary evidence; indeed, our evidence goes far beyond what we have thought it necessary for present purposes to set forth, our object being, in a grave matter of this kind, to avoid the slightest suggestion of vindictiveness, and to confine ourselves to a bare statement of facts.[498]

The 14 July issue duly printed Fox's letter in its 'In the City' column, but followed it with a further attack about four times the length of the missive itself.[499] And there the matter apparently ended.

Mercifully, Jerome could have no idea in 1894 just what he had unleashed. In these months he was busy setting up what would be known indiscriminately as the 'Pluck Fund' or 'Gallantry Fund'. Always wary of charitable societies, Jerome had already adjured readers that, 'There are too many excellent societies. They rob us of our individual energy and close our consciences. We open our purses to this gushing appeal and that, and think we have squared our account with our brother. We have converted our Christianity into a limited liability company, and the system doesn't work. God's work never was done by societies; it is done by men and women.'[500]

The Pluck Fund, however, was different. Practical in scope, the idea was, as Jerome made very clear, not to reward heroism per se; rather he wished to recompense people who had acted to save others, and in the process suffered financial loss. Acutely aware himself of the significance of small amounts to the poor, he pointed out that a man rescuing a stranger from drowning in a pond might not be risking his life, but the ruin of his clothes might be a more serious issue than a middle-class reader could easily understand. Writing to explain that his involvement with a number of local projects prevented any immediate contribution, Thomas Hardy nonetheless praised the idea and the paper itself, 'I give your scheme my blessing but no money – at any rate now. It is excellent, but between ourselves I have so many local irons in the fire requiring odd guineas that I am prevented from doing much in a general way. We like "TO-DAY" very much, (if you care to know it)'.[501]

Elsewhere *TO-DAY* rallied subscribers, including old friends such as Hentschel and Thomas Wingrave (George's brother and Jerome's doctor), along with Conan Doyle, Kipling and numerous others, and sent out various sums of money to benefit valiant acts of rescue, many of them by small boys and almost all, for some reason, involving rescue from drowning. While the aim of the fund was purely practical (and Jerome assured his readers that all cases were carefully investigated), it eventually started sending medals in recognition of 'pluck'. On 2 May 1895 Jerome wrote to Hall Caine reminding him of an earlier promise to serve on the committee, although he made it clear that he was taking on most of the work himself, 'I shall, as in the past, make careful enquiry into each case, to make sure that we are not imposed on in any way, and that everything is as stated; and at the end of the year, I propose sending a statement to the members of the Committee showing exactly how the fund stands, and what has been done.'[502]

Despite its generally buoyant tone, Jerome was determined that *TO-DAY* would provide a platform for his opinions and also a much needed means of fighting oppression and injustice at home and abroad. He kept a close eye on the foreign press and by January 1894 he was already protesting in unsparing detail against the lynching of black Americans on trumped up charges, mainly for supposedly molesting white women.[503] While his own racism, in keeping with the attitude of many of his contemporaries, is impossible to explain away, he was horrified by the sadistic torture of 'negro' men by crowds of white vigilantes, a stance he would maintain during his own visits to the US many years later. Just as he protested against animal cruelty, he expresses horror at the crimes he relates, rather than a sense of identification with the victims. In his accounts of men mutilated and hanged from trees, or even skinned alive, it is the cruelty of the tormentors, even more than the suffering of the victims, that haunts him. He was always fascinated and repelled by what he saw as the innate cruelty of the average human being, a trait that he insisted had to be kept in check or it would break out in these very ways. It is this pessimism about human instincts (quite possibly a remnant of his early religious training) that led him to highlight the state of mind of the torturer – as he explained, at least the victim's sufferings had ended by the time the story came to light, but the evil of the mob was an unquenched force:

> I am no believer in the equality of man, and I can quite credit that the negro is an exceedingly low type, governed by animalism; but civilisation exists for the control of mere animalism by law. ... Justice for wrong by all means; stern, swift justice; vengeance if necessary where justice fails. But cruelty is of hell; it comes from hell; it is hell's work.[504]

Closer to home he spoke out against any case of cruelty that he came across, indeed correspondents soon took to reporting cases for broadcast in the journal. Notably he protested against the comparatively light punishments meted out to fathers in child cruelty cases, where the mother was treated with the full rigour of the law. Always practical in his social campaigning, he wrote repeatedly against the system of child insurance, pointing out the temptation for a poor family to neglect a child in order to cash in on its death.

He was harder yet on the middle classes who exploited vulnerable children. Jerome is careful to denounce the behaviour of the abusers without appearing to sensationalise – apart from anything else he was aware of the unlicensed thrill many readers felt in the minutiae of sadistic practices. As an experienced writer and journalist, however, it was also his instinct to involve a reader emotionally in the circumstances. In the case of one thirteen-year-old victim, he notably details the crime itself with a certain briskness, allowing far more space to the context in which such attacks are made possible. One Ella Spooner of Liverpool had apparently tortured her young servant, applying a hot poker to her tongue and lips. Having got himself and his readers through the basics, Jerome turns to the familiar trope of the middle-class home as a threatening place of imprisonment, undetectable because of its very respectability:

… in the case of the servant-girl the story always presents an added horror to me. I seem to see a door opened for a moment and closed quickly. In lonely country-houses, in quiet suburban streets, behind the respectable venetian blinds there must be many thousands of poor, overworked, overdriven, bullied and starved little sluts, whose lives are made to them one long hell by the tyranny of their mistresses. No one knows what these little drudges suffer. They are taken from their home or from the workhouse when they are mere children; they know nothing of the world; they cannot defend themselves; they have no one to appeal to. Month after month they hardly ever leave the house to speak a word into a sympathetic ear.[505]

As well as reporting on such cases as these, Jerome also campaigned tirelessly for the better treatment of animals. In particular he attacked Londoners (women, especially, he held to be key offenders) who would not wait for an omnibus at the appointed stop, but hailed it and forced the horse to keep stopping on hills and slippery roads. He hailed the advent of the electric tram in 1897 with relief, as an effective means of relieving overworked cab horses, whose plight Anna Sewell had famously protested against in *Black Beauty* in 1877. Notably, Sewell had acknowledged the dilemma of the men who drove them, faced with long hours waiting in cold weather and the persistent spectre of poverty if they did not sometimes overwork their horses. Cases of cruelty to horses took up so much space in the pages of *TO-DAY* that by the end of 1895 one reader wrote in to complain, incurring the stinging response, 'I am sorry to say that your letter only makes me feel contemptuous towards you. … You are kind enough to warn me that my "cruelty crank" may do harm to the paper. Good Heavens, man! do you think that we none of us have any opinions that are not to be bought and sold by the promise or loss of a few twopences?'[506] Between January 1894 and October 1897 he wrote weekly editorials on cases that had come to his notice, making full use of the chance to 'name and shame' individuals, or even to publish their addresses. On occasion his appeal to readers seems dangerously like a call for a body of vigilantes. Thus, 'Will any readers in the neighbourhood of Thomas Treadwell's stables, 11, Hambly Wharf, Harrow Road, kindly keep an eye upon this person and the unfortunate animals that get into his hands? I should welcome gladly the chance of prosecuting him myself for cruelty.'[507]

It was also in 1894 that he published 'John Ingerfield', which, he told a correspondent, 'I consider one of the best things I have written.'[508] The eponymous hero is a type for which Jerome had particular affection, a hard-working merchant who marries purely for status and to display his wealth, but belatedly realises his social responsibilities. He dies of typhoid as he and his wife fight to save his workers from an epidemic, in the course of which they finally come to know and love each other. Of at least equal interest are the 'and other stories' of the volume title, including 'The Woman of the Saeter' and two fictionalised accounts of Jerome's early life, including his illicit visit to a music hall when he is believed by his parents to be visiting a more respectable venue. Whether or not this story is based on fact, and it certainly has an authentic feel to it, it is significant that it was *intended* to be read as true. As he would later do in *Paul Kelver*, Jerome takes issue in this story with his parents' disapproval of music halls and the stage, a serious enough issue given his own professional interests. In the second story, the abrupt ending comes with the father telling 'Maggie' that he is ruined, a clear enough indication that Jerome was still haunted by the financial disaster that had overtaken his family in 1862.

Of course in this first year *TO-DAY* also engaged with *the* topic of 1894, the explosion into the public consciousness of the 'New Woman'. The Woman Question had been a source of debate since mid-century, with the realisation after the 1851 census that the number of 'superfluous' women meant they could not possibly all hope to marry and that many of them must therefore emigrate, enter the workforce or starve. From the 1860s a new feminist movement had been calling for greater economic opportunities and for the female suffrage (finally attained in 1918). In the 1880s and '90s a new generation of women novelists, including Olive Schreiner, Mona Caird, Sarah Grand and George Egerton had begun to publish radical and unsettling fiction focused on women's experience and, in many cases, demanding change.

The second half of 1892 had seen the launch of the Pioneer Club, a female-only club based on teetotal and feminist principles. The founder, Mrs Bernard Massingberd, came from one of the oldest families in Lincolnshire but, as she explained to a journalist in 1893, 'Here we have no social distinctions, we all meet together on the common ground of sisterhood.'[509] With the distance of someone recalling long-past events, Jerome wrote satirically in *My Life and Times* of how, 'A women's club was launched called the Pioneers. All the most desperate women in London enrolled themselves as members. … It was the typewriter that led to the discovery of woman.'[510]

At around the same time, female-authored articles began to appear in the press debating the social position of women. Famously, Mona Caird's 'Marriage' had sparked a long running series in the correspondence column of the *Daily Telegraph* in the autumn of 1888, 'Is Marriage a Failure?' At the time Jerome himself had responded with comic impatience to this fracas, writing in *Home Chimes*:

> I vote we all give it up, and play at something else. I've had three columns of it with breakfast every morning, and a few articles later on in the evening papers, and an essay every now and then in a magazine, and three 'bus drivers have given me their views of the subject, and I have discussed it with seventeen men whose names I shall never know; and everybody that has come to our house has talked about it. My youngest nephew, aged twelve, has very decided views about the matter, and our charwoman has given me her experiences – which I hope are exceptional – four times over.[511]

But society seemed disinclined to 'give it up, and play at something else.' Over the next few years Charlotte Perkins Gilman published the psychological 'The Yellow Wallpaper' about a woman driven to madness by following the orders of her doctor husband; Mona Caird continued to campaign against women's position in marriage in her chilling gothic novel *The Wing of Azrael*; and in 1893 Sarah Grand shocked a number of readers with her controversial discussion of syphilis in *The Heavenly Twins*. In January 1894 came B. A. Crackenthorpe's 'The Revolt of the Daughters', calling for greater freedom for unmarried women in their twenties.

Jerome expostulated in February 1894, with something suspiciously close to anxiety:

> It is now definitely time that the journal and magazine talk about the Revolting Daughters should cease. I say this because the revolt has no existence of any importance. I do not deny that in a small London set there is something of the kind, and that the daughters there desire, in the ignorance of innocence, to disregard their mothers' advice in a variety of ways – most of which they would afterwards repent. But to treat the movement as if it were national is perfectly absurd.

Interestingly, given the persistent equation of the New Woman with all things decadent that would become a marked feature of conservative protest,

Jerome is already linking the figure of the emancipated woman with the experiments of Oscar Wilde himself:

> It was much the same thing with the aesthetic movement of 1881. It was Mr Whistler, if I remember rightly, who wanted to know whether Mr Du Maurier had invented Mr Oscar Wilde or *vice versa*. The movement was killed and trampled upon so frequently and so brilliantly that ultimately it came into actual existence, and there are still penny Japanese fans in Bloomsbury back parlours to witness if I lie. If we only keep on persistently with a discussion of the revolting daughters, and with frequent incursions of wild women into print on the subject, we may ultimately actually bring the thing into being. [512]

Over the next few years Jerome would alternately expostulate and have fun with the New Woman, who became the heroine of *Biarritz* in 1896 and *The MacHaggis,* co-written with Eden Phillpotts in 1897. In the earlier comedy one Jenkins Jnr is sent to manage his father's hotel and becomes embroiled in a plot laid by by the head waiter and his girlfriend, who want to sabotage the hotel and buy it themselves. In one scene a female character disguises herself and sells false noses – 'Will Madame buy ze New Woman nose? It knows all that a man's nose knows.'[513] Some excuse is then found to bring on a chorus singing 'The New Athletic Woman up to Date', who is shameless enough to play football among other sports:

> We do not care what anybody says
> Yes, you'll see us all as kickers,
> In our jerseys and our knickers,
> If you're curious enough to pay a shilling gate!

In *The MacHaggis* a newly-engaged man, James Grant, tries desperately to evade the attentions of a young woman on a bicycle, only to discover that she is his missing ward Ewretta Gordon. When he is then informed that he is the new Laird of the MacHaggis clan, he disappears to Scotland where much comic business ensues, involving clan traditions and near misses in the marriage market. These culture clashes, between English and Scottish and between the conservative Englishman and his emancipated ward, are hilariously developed, and the increasing confusion of all parties is cleverly worked out in the extant typescript.

Like all successful journalists, Jerome shows a talent for making a talking point of the very subjects he supposedly wishes to quash, but in this case his words must have seemed almost prophetic. A month after his editorial, in March 1894 came the notorious exchange between Sarah Grand and Ouida that popularised the term 'New Woman' and helped to define a cultural and publishing phenomenon. Sarah Grand published 'The New Aspect of the Woman Question' in the *North American Review* in March, arguing that women's influence was vital to the regeneration of the social system; in response Ouida brought into play all the available stereotypes of the advanced woman as humourless and 'unsexed'.

While Jerome was not necessarily in sympathy with Ouida despite their previous acquaintance (he would later note caustically that 'Ouida is a lady who exaggerates a good deal...')[514] he had no time at all for Grand.

Occasionally Jerome allowed practicality to override conservative horror, advising a female correspondent who had been jilted and was now seeking a new direction, that:

> If there is no material reason against it, I certainly think you would be well-advised in working for your next B.A. degree. What you want is some strong interest that will take your thoughts away from yourself. ... The callings that a woman can enter into are somewhat limited, but the boundaries are extending every day. I can quite understand your dislike to settling down to an idle existence, where you would only brood over your trouble; and in work of some sort lies your best hope.[515]

This does, of course, need to be set against his comment, picked up by other newspapers, that an unhappy marriage was better for a woman than no marriage at all.

That Jerome's own response to the New Woman was inconsistent is only confirmed by Douglas Sladen's comment, about twenty years later, that 'if Suffragism had been a burning question then, the paper [*TO-DAY*] would have been full of it, and enjoying a circulation of a million, or whatever number the adult woman suffragists run to. I can picture Jerome, a man famous for his hospitalities, being reduced to a hunger-strike by the ardour with which he would have espoused the idea.'[516] Sladen is evidently forgetting a number of scathing editorials, but his misremembering of Jerome's attitude is a timely reminder of both his reputation for espousing good causes and his good relationship with many of the women (professional or otherwise) whom he knew.

It is not clear how his female contributors responded to Jerome's attack on the New Woman and what he deemed her particular brand of fiction. But among the largely masculine staff of *The Idler* and *TO-DAY* he was far from alone in his suspicious observation of women authors' supposed obsession with analysing sex. In an interview for *The Idler* in 1894 Phillpotts 'laments the tendency of latter-day fiction. He finds it too introspective, and thinks it a matter for regret that women novelists in particular seek to abolish the mystery of their own sex and human nature generally. ... Further he holds the co-called Realists to be more untrue, more unreal, than any.'[517] Barry Pain, seemingly unlike Phillpotts, was hanging on to his sense of humour, but in his comic *TO-DAY* series 'Men I have murdered' he includes among his victims a reader of salacious literature. 'William Gorlsford said he called a spade a spade. What he really meant was that he frequently used in full the words which are only printed in the form of blanks with initials. In fact, when he said that he called a spade a spade he meant that he did not call a blank a blank. He was muddy and metropolitan. His idea in literature was The Pretty Hot.' [518]

Returning to the attack himself in 1895, Jerome commented that he would rather read a penny dreadful than a New Woman novel.[519]

By 1895 Jerome had been able to buy Robert Barr out of *The Idler*, and was enthusiastically revamping it, as he explained to his readers in an open letter in August. By this time he was describing it in far more serious terms than he had ventured in 1892, 'It will never be my aim to make it a magazine for what is generally termed "the masses," but to appeal to that growing public which possesses literary tastes and artistic sympathies. I wish to make it a magazine that will be almost a need to thinking men and women.'[520] Abandoning the carefully crafted image of bachelor idleness, Jerome now exhorted his readers to derive an almost moral benefit from the paper, as he did himself:

> To me, THE IDLER is almost a part of myself – my own life has become bound up in it; nor does it seem to me a small or unimportant task. To launch out monthly a magazine that speaks to hundreds of thousands of men and women throughout the world, appears to me a great work – a work full of responsibility, of delight – a work full of unknown possibilities – a work worth living for.[521]

This avowed seriousness brings *The Idler* more into line with *TO-DAY*, a relationship Jerome had already begun in soliciting contributions from the same writers (Anthony Hope, G. B. Burgin, Zangwill, Barry Pain among them). Hope provided a number of stories for *The Idler* in this year, and his name was a particular draw, following publication of *The Prisoner of Zenda* with Jerome's publisher Arrowsmith the year before. This unashamedly swash-buckling romance was nonetheless a serious commentary on statesmanship and personal responsibility, with an oblique critique of urban poverty in the narrator's first impressions of Ruritania, the fictional kingdom he briefly rules. Like London itself:

> The city of Strelsau is partly old and partly new. Spacious modern boulevards and residential quarters surround and embrace the narrow, tortuous and picturesque streets of the original town. In the outer circles the upper classes live; in the inner the shops are situated; and, behind their prosperous fronts, lie hidden populous but wretched lanes and alleys, filled with a poverty-stricken, turbulent, and (in large measure) criminal class.[522]

The theme of the double was important in the wake of Stevenson's 1888 *Jekyll and Hyde*, and would have particularly appealed to Jerome.

Of course, Jerome's ability to attract like-minded contributors to both his papers contributed substantially to their reputation, a point he implicitly acknowledged in his generous payments, even while he doubted the effect of 'names' on actual circulation:

> In magazines and newspapers no work is ever worth the price asked by the leading men. I can put a story in TO-DAY, the mere serial rights of which cost me £100, and it does not sell one extra copy of the paper. The truth is that any paper or magazine with a circulation of anything over fifty thousand is immovable by any mere name. Its readers already number the whole of the public to whom authors' names convey any meaning. The big name is only useful to a new venture.[523]

Another point of contact already established by 1895 was, of course, the continuing controversy over the New Woman, and *The Idler* now took a firm line, with Burgin commenting sententiously that, 'The ordinary French novel became stale and insipid when the salacious muck-rake of the Unwomanly

Woman revealed the inexpressible nastiness of a world she had entered only to make nastier.'[524] All of which makes it more surprising that Jerome routinely stuck up for women who smoked (cigarettes were supposedly the hallmark of the New Woman).

An apparent inconsistency also appears in his response to the question of women's dress in these years. He was notably in favour of the then controversial woman cyclist, despite the notorious innovation of 'bloomers' (which caused much the same uproar as the fad for visible underwear a century later). As he explained thirty years later, much of the problem was resolved with the invention of the step-through frame. Until then women had found it virtually impossible to ride a bicycle in long skirts (in the twenty-first century no woman in her senses would attempt it) and were obliged to wear rational dress for practical reasons. As Jerome pithily expressed the controversy, 'Ladies have taken to bicycling, and other ladies are very indignant with them, not for bicycling so much as for bicycling in the only possible costume in which any-one can bicycle.'[525] He was outraged to read of two ladies having been refused service in an inn because of their bloomers,[526] and he later mused fondly that, 'Very fetching they looked in them, too, the few who dared', but by the 1920s he had had plenty of time to acclimatise. What he actually said at the time was, 'Let women exchange their skirts for knickerbockers if they like, but, at any rate, let them produce something a little prettier than the rational cycling costume that the advanced woman adopts at present. Woman has pleaded frequently of late for permission to be rational. By all means, but she can surely be rational without also becoming grotesque and ungraceful.'[527]

Understandably, all of this caught the attention of the Anti-Corset League. In order to understand Jerome's stance it is important to remember the politicised status of this famous undergarment. Firstly the repudiation of the corset implied a particular set of values, as Christine Bayles Kortsch has argued, 'Although many commentators criticized the corseted figure, few acceptable alternatives existed for women. Those who chose not to wear a corset were typically associated with one of two movements, Rational (or Hygienic or Reform) Dress or Aesthetic (or Artistic) Dress.'[528] Notably:

> The dress-reform societies emphasized comfort, health, rationality, and beauty in dress. In England, they were heavily influenced by the aesthetic movement. Their particular strength was reform underwear. … By the mid-1880s, many Victorians seemed to accept elements of

rational dress, perhaps because the style had become associated with increasingly popular women's athletics. Some mainstream Victorians found alternative dress styles refreshingly modern. But many others still found them offensive, unattractive, and dangerous.[529]

Jerome had approached this subject twice in 1894, although his remarks were hardly promising. Despite his belief in healthy exercise, he deliberately distanced himself from this debate as yet another media fad, asking wearily:

> Cannot, for instance, the faddist allow one year – one little year, with only 365 days in it – to go past without an anti-corset demonstration in some newspaper? It is not that I want to plead the cause of the corset; I don't want to argue about it; I am not even sure that it would not be indelicate to argue about it. I only ask for a little variety. …There must surely be many other subjects about which it would be just as easy to lose one's sense of proportion.[530]

Jerome's agenda comes sharply into focus in a third editorial, responding to the League's invitation to come and actually see for himself what the fuss was about:

> I have refrained from availing myself of [their invitation], not knowing what the exhibition may be, and fearing that perhaps my sense of modesty might be shocked. With the object of the society I have, however, some sympathy. I quite agree with them that the wearing of tightly-laced corsets conduces to the moral and physical degradation of women, and I would propose that there be a male branch of this league, formed to promote legislation on the subject. We husbands, fathers, and brothers have a right to be heard on this subject. Our homes are being ruined, our children's future is being endangered, and crime is being engendered by this growing vice. When the ladies are waiting upon the Home Secretary to insist that we should not be allowed to drink a glass of beer, to put half-a-crown on a horse, or play a game of nap, it is time we had our little deputation, our association, and our league to reform and improve them.[531]

In this rejection of the League's overtures Jerome attempts to have it not 'both' but three or four ways at once. In his formulation the corset itself is pernicious but its female opponents are instantly identified as subjects for mockery – women cannot appropriately invite men's involvement in the campaign, the details of which will supposedly 'shock' them. By the end of the paragraph all women are implicated in the 'growing vice' of tight lacing, while by extension the comically treated 'little deputation' of men undermines women's interference in masculine concerns.

His stance on corsetry must be seen, however, in the wider context of his policy of non-interference, an attitude that had significant implications for his social and, indeed, sexual politics. Throughout these years he strenuously opposed the attempted eradication of prostitution, fanatical licensing laws, the regulation of drugs (getting it slightly wrong, he saw the taking of opium as less injurious than excessive tea drinking), or the reform of women's underwear, in much the same terms. But if responsible human beings could take care of themselves, animals clearly could not. On this one issue he was prepared to work indefatigably with women, even New ones.

Chapter Five

————— ❦ —————

'One monkey examining another for fleas'
1895 – 1900

'...sometimes when I read literary recollections of "London in the Nineties," or references to that period in the newspapers, my first petulant impulse is to protest that all London did not live in Chelsea, all London did not read *The Yellow Book*. ... And "Fin-de-siècle"? A catchword that soon became a joke! We actually ended the century still beset by the miseries of the Boer War.'

Anthony Hope, 1927

Predictably, vivisection became a regular topic in the pages of *TO-DAY*. Interestingly Jerome's initial opposition to animal experiments was based not on the alleged cruelty of scientists, which he denied at this stage; rather his eugenicist thinking saw both prolonged life expectancy and the changing role of women as deeply threatening:

Man has reversed the order of Nature, and compelled her to rescind her edict; but if we think that Nature will not have her revenge in the end, we are much mistaken.

It is useless and absurd to say that vivisection has led to nothing; it is reasonable to fear that it will lead to too much. As one disease after another is taken in hand and rendered incapable of doing its proper work, men will live who would have been better dead, and the result will be a deterioriation of the human race. Other causes, besides the advance of medical science, seem to be working towards the same end; the change now at work in the position of women is one of them; the want of change in our method with the criminal is another. But it is in the advance of medical knowledge that the chief danger lies; we have nothing to fear from the cruelty of science, but we may well dread its mercy.[532]

To those who know him primarily as a humorous author, his illiberal response on particular issues somehow comes as a shock.

However, within a few months of his declaration that vivisection was only too effective as a means of research, Jerome had completely reversed the terms of his argument, claiming now that it *was* practised by brutal scientists for their own enjoyment, and had done little to advance medical knowledge. At around the same time he was obliquely aligning medical vivisection with the unsanctioned torture of animals, as a kind of sexual practice (very much as he would later link corporal punishment to perversity). Reporting on a case in April 1896, in which a man had been found guilty of torturing cats in his leisure hours, he noted, 'There is a side to this question of cruelty that would only be discussed with freedom in a medical journal. ... There are thousands upon thousands of men so constituted that the infliction of cruelty excites in them all the emotions of the sexual instincts.'[533]

The turning point seems to have been Louis Pasteur's experiments relating to hydrophobia. Jerome's argument, put forward in a series of editorials, was that hydrophobia was not proved to be a real condition, and could certainly not be understood by the torture of animals. In answer to a medical correspondent, he further explained that he had no objection to vivisection under chloroform, but wished to protest against the infliction of pain. Greatly as he felt for the suffering of animals, his central concern was, characteristically, the mental state of the scientist. Just as he had focused on the mentality of the American lynch mob rather than the suffering of its black victims, he now wrote, 'When I attack vivisection I am thinking as much of the torturer as I am of the tortured. The man who inflicts cruelty of any kind takes a terrible responsibility upon himself. He puts himself outside the sympathy of God and man.'[534] A few months later, in July 1896 he picked up on a suggestion that human vivisection was the logical conclusion to such experiments, commenting grimly:

The vivisection of animals has led us wrong in many instances, and, considered as anything more than surgical practice, it has always been useless ... surely, if the whole of the human race is to be benefited to all time, a certain amount of agony inflicted upon a few individuals is not to be taken into consideration. ... There must, among the crowd of people who defend vivisection, be one or two who would be willing victims to this sacred cause, for which they profess so much affection.[535]

After Pasteur's death in September 1895, Jerome managed a tactful allusion to his achievements, overshadowed though they were by his methods with hydrophobia (in fact Pasteur is remembered not least for having developed the rabies vaccine).[536] But when he heard of plans to build a Pasteur Institute in Chelsea, he immediately denounced the methods of Pasteur's followers as an 'unredeemed evil', calling on women to exercise their voice, 'Women have a good deal of power in their hands. They might make a list of the men connected with this precious Pasteur Institute, and determine that never, under any circumstances, should any man whose name is on that list pass their doors.'[537] Notably, Jerome is quick to call on women as a powerful voice in the social realm, but he maintains that their influence should be exerted in traditional ways. Importantly, many New Women took a public stance on the vivisection issue. Thus far, and thus far only, he was even prepared to forget his antipathy to Mona Caird, who had written to protest against the Prince of Wales's Hospital Scheme to give more power to the governing body and doctors. Adding his voice to hers on this particular issue, he observed, 'Mrs Caird cannot forget that a Bill to vivisect criminals was actually laid before the Legislature of an American State a little while ago, and she fears, and not without reason, that to give the medical profession a completely free hand would be to multiply enormously even the present debauch of cruelty.'[538] Women in his formulation should be socially responsible beings, but not political activists. How society hostesses responded to this appeal is unclear, but in June he was complaining that, 'Vivisection is practically licensed, not by Act of Parliament, but by the apathy of the public.'[539]

A second point of contact between Jerome and many New Women was of course his eugenicist ideas (although ironically this led him to repudiate calls for female emancipation in the 1890s and beyond). Entering the environment versus heredity arena with his gloves very much off, he argued that:

if we gave children moral as well as intellectual training, saw to it that the conditions under which they lived were compatible with health and decency, and that they started life fairly, without exceptional temptations and evil company, we should do a great deal towards the lessening of our habitual criminals. But we should not have done all that is possible. These remedies touch environment alone, and it is not only environment that makes the criminal. There is also heredity. I do not know whether it is too much to ask that some restriction should be placed upon the freedom with which habitual criminals people the world with more habitual criminals. ... But, at any rate, criminal parents might be refused some of the ordinary parental rights – briefly, they should not be allowed to bring their children up themselves.[540]

His ideas at this time effectively allied him with some unlikely voices and, even after Oscar Wilde's fall from grace, Jerome was ready to quote his writing on criminality, to the effect that if criminality is rightly associated with the city slums, it is also to found among the apparently respectable:

Probably a good deal of genuine criminality escapes notice or censure because it does not conflict with the letter of the law. Every callously selfish person, even though he may contrive to live in the odour of sanctity, is *in posse* a criminal, all that is wanted to make him one *in esse* being a little bad luck or a certain lack of judgement in the pursuit of his ends. Before illustrating the thesis in his own person, Oscar Wilde wrote an essay to prove that culture and criminality were not necessarily antagonistic, taking the case of Wainwright as his text, and he was quite right.[541]

This was one of the few occasions on which Jerome was likely to quote Wilde with approval as, apart from his opposition to women's rights, he was deeply opposed to the homosexual culture of late-nineteenth-century aestheticism. The first rumours of this kind of work appearing in *The Chameleon*, carrying the later famous poem by Wilde's lover Bosie, 'The Two Loves' drew instant and damning reprimand from the editorial pages of *TO-DAY*:

I do not think I shall be mistaken for a prude on the prowl, but I am anxious for further information concerning a publication that has just come under my notice, called "The Chameleon." It is issued from Oxford, and published by a West-end firm. As far as I can judge, it can be purchased by anyone who likes to pay the subscription. If I am wrong – if it is a private publication, intended only to circulate among a limited and known *clientele* – there is an end of the matter. A hundred gentlemen or so have as much right to circulate indecency among themselves, by means of the printing press, as they have to tell each other dirty stories in the club smoking-room. Each to his taste. But if "The Chameleon" is issued broadcast, and any immature youth, or fooling New Young Woman, can obtain it, then it is certainly a case for the police. The publication appears to be nothing more nor less than an advocacy for indulgence in the cravings of an unnatural disease.[542]

He noted with relief on 5 January 1895 that *The Chameleon* had been withdrawn from circulation, and explained his motives for speaking out:

Many a young man into whose hands this publication may have fallen would have gone upon his way with the impression merely that he was reading broad-minded literature, free from the narrowing trammels of conventional prudery. It is the duty of those who know to see that poison is labelled poison, so that those alone may touch it who are determined on moral suicide. Silence is only useful where a thing of this sort is likely to die if unnoticed. Here was a filthy, soul-destroying publication, offered for sale throughout England, thrust under the nose of every young man studying at Oxford and Cambridge, advertised as an organ of the intellectual and the advanced, and bearing world-wide names in its contents list. The only way to stop it was to make these people ashamed of their connection with such a thing.[543]

The close connections between the groups of writers makes such accusations potentially explosive – only the year before *TO-DAY* had been describing Aubrey Beardsley as 'the new master of art'.[544]

Jerome's conservative attitude leads him here to conflate decadent literature quite directly with sexual malpractice. After his exposé of *The Chameleon* he apparently received a deluge of letters accusing him of 'advertising an evil', to which he retorted that, 'Evil loves silence; it flourishes in silence and darkness'[545] and warned 'dear Mr Podsnap and dear Mrs Grundy' again that a boy or girl could never recover from the 'poisoned wound' once inflicted.[546] Interestingly, Jerome is himself willing to distinguish between a publication as privately circulated and therefore permissible, and a public journal – only in the latter case does the offence become one for the police. This attitude confirms Trevor Fisher's claim that, despite increasing levels of homophobia from mid-century onwards, known homosexuals were not in any immediate danger before the Wilde trials in 1895. As he puts it, 'In order to trigger the growing homophobia of late Victorian Britain, an almost conscious effort was required. Tragically for Wilde and homosexual subculture, Wilde's behaviour provided exactly such a trigger.'[547] As I have argued elsewhere,[548] intense male friendships had long been upheld as an ideal only through the steady rejection of erotic elements (notably in *David Copperfield*, where Steerforth's insistence on calling his friend 'Daisy' as much as his seduction of Emily necessitates his final expulsion from the text). In a powerful and moving invocation of male love at his trial, Wilde unintentionally highlighted precisely why homosexuality could not be generally tolerated by the 1890s. In drawing attention to the erotic potential of male friendship as inculcated by the public schools, he effectively undermined the credibility of an institution that existed largely to establish co-operation and deep feeling between men in later life. While the then popular writer Howard Sturgis was openly homosexual, drawing no worse reaction than affectionate jokes about his love of knitting, Wilde's spectacularly well-documented trial made him a test case, forcing other members of literary London either to side with him or denounce him. It is to Jerome's credit that he at least refused to increase *TO-DAY*'s circulation by covering the trial.

This issue was not the only one to activate Jerome's conservative protest. Elsewhere he expressed equally reactionary views on the literary movements of his day. He made it clear that he was no fan of the New Woman novel, but as a pioneer of the 'New Humour', he was equally wary of 'psychological literature', perhaps surprisingly, given his stance that, 'Truth is the only thing worth fighting for; good and evil, right and wrong, they are merely relative terms.' Jerome's response was the more innocuous comedy *The Rise of Dick Halward* (1895). Following a review in *The Times* he could not resist returning to the habits of his youth and penning a letter in return. Thanking the paper for its 'courteous and sympathetic notice' he pointed out that the device of a microscope revealing the contents of a letter photographed to a small size was not impossible, but had in fact been used during the siege of Paris.[549] In *Novel Notes* a few years earlier he had accorded to one of his characters the memorable line that psychological literature was simply 'One monkey examining another monkey for fleas'[550] and had publicly opined that 'the subjects treated by Ibsen were unfit for the stage'.[551]

In this context it may be surprising to find him, only a few years later in 1897, expressing an admiration for Ibsen as 'the one living dramatist who allows me to think.' Indeed, he satirised the play-going public for failing to appreciate this most psychological of dramatists, 'Open confession is good for the soul, and I may as well admit that I belong to that immoral minority who are not only willing that Dr Ibsen should be allowed to continue to breathe God's air, but who are even prepared to descend to such further depths of infamy as to be willing that he should be allowed to write plays.' Having ruthlessly despatched a philistine public, he then allies them by implication with the second-rate dramatists they presumably admire:

> I do not think our present dramatists need stand much in fear of the rivalry of Ibsen. People do not go to the theatre to think. ... Ibsen can only appeal to a very small circle. A generation or two after he is dead he is pretty sure to be popular, but that is not for many years to come. I suppose I have seen most London productions during the last fifteen years. To sit out a play like *The Wild Duck* makes me feel young again.[552]

It was in this year that Jerome brought out his own very different assault on the sensibilities of conservative opinion, in the shape of *The MacHaggis*, which had a run of fifty-seven performances at the Globe.[553]

Weedon Grossmith, co-author of *The Diary of a Nobody*, took the lead and, in what is perhaps remarkably one of only two references to Clement Scott, Jerome recalled cheerfully that 'Our heroine shocked the critics. She rode a bicycle. ... She smoked a cigarette. The Devil must have been in us. ... In the last act, she said "damn". She said it twice. Poor Clement Scott nearly fell out of the *Daily Telegraph*.'[554]

In fact, Jerome was attacking advanced literature in 1895 not so much because he was conservative as because he feared that such overt disregard of public morals would only give the Mrs Grundys cause for complaint. Ten years earlier, George Moore had already attacked Mudie's library in his pamphlet 'Literature at Nurse, or Circulating Morals', for its prudish censorship – such was the buying power of the circulating library that by refusing to stock particular works it could spell disaster for the author. As Jerome now explained to his readers, in the year when Marie Corelli's bestselling *The Sorrows of Satan* bypassed the library altogether and Mudie's demise effectively ended this type of censorship, 'We want liberty – not license. We do not want literature to be controlled by either the bookstall clerk or the parson, by the unread old woman or the unread young girl. But we do want it controlled by the man and woman of sense and education.'[555]

For his own part, Jerome had a predilection for adventure stories, as instanced by his admiration of authors such as Anthony Hope and Stanley Weyman, whose historical romance *The Red Cockade* ran in *TO-DAY* in 1895. What would have particularly appealed to Jerome is its linking of battle to social protest, as the hero comes to terms with the horrors of the French Revolution, 'Alone, with time to think; and to think some grim thoughts. Where now was the sweet union of which half the nation had been dreaming...?'[556]

Specifically, he set his face against decadence; while he was ready to accept Wilde's literary excesses on the grounds of his genius, he attacked his imitators very much as mid-century critics had denigrated the purveyors of sensation fiction, 'Mr Oscar Wilde himself one could tolerate, for whatever else he may be he was undoubtedly an artist, and a brilliantly clever man, but he founded a school of scribbling apes; and, after the manner of schools, they exaggerated all his faults, and utterly failed to reproduce his merit. What has been called the "decadent" school has inflicted a severe blow on letters. It has given a handle to the prudes who would eliminate thought and truth from art.'[557] Interestingly, Jerome would claim in *My Life and Times* that he did not know Wilde personally, although he would presumably have met him through the Playgoers' Club, of which Wilde was also a member. It is in any case unlikely that they could have avoided each other altogether.

In his protest against the censors of 'truth and art' Jerome probably had in mind the reception of such recent realist novels as George Moore's *Esther Waters*; discussing Moore's achievement in glowing terms the year before, he had come closer than he might have acknowledged to the aesthetic dictum 'art for art's sake' that Wilde and his circle also embraced:

> Mr George Moore, like Mr Thomas Hardy, has had trouble with the Young Person. I have always thought that the novelist's attitude towards the Young Person should be one of complete disregard. A novel which is tied and bound by the supposed intellectual and moral needs of the Young Person, must, of course, be an artistic failure; so also, though this is frequently forgotten, must any novel be an artistic failure which is merely written to show the writer's independence of the Young Person. What is really essential is complete indifference to the Young Person and every other person, and complete concentration on art itself. Such canons of Art are easy enough to enunciate, but to follow them, fully and unconsciously, means genius.[558]

Despite his professed dislike of advanced literature, Jerome was sympathetic towards Wilde himself during his trial and refused to include salacious details of the proceedings in TO-DAY, just as he had earlier refrained from including sensational details when reporting on cases of child neglect. Indeed, he reserved a fair portion of his moral indignation for the society figures who had feted Wilde with a full knowledge of his homosexuality. 'It has never, I believe, interfered with Mr Wilde's reception at any house. Men and women to whom the tale must have been a good deal more than a rumour, have never hesitated to shake him by the hand.' More threateningly, he gestures cryptically to the homosexual subculture of London, believed to include a number of prominent public and aristocratic men:

> The only thing we ask of a man is that he shall not be found out, and here Mr Wilde has sinned. Perhaps it is as well that it is so. Were Mr Wilde surrounded by those who have no right to say a single word in condemnation of him, the dock at the Old Bailey would have to be enlarged to accommodate a good many hundreds of people, and the classes, up to the very highest, would find themselves well represented.[559]

There would be little enough in the drama to incur his anger, and he was honest enough to acknowledge the worth of Wilde's work, irrespective of his personal vagaries. Noting that a number of people were still capitalising on the plays by the simple expedient of removing the author's name, he expostulated:

> Do these excellent managers and the excellent people who form their audiences really imagine that they are doing anything beyond making themselves ridiculous by this piece of thoughtless nonsense? The plays are good plays, and there is no getting over the fact that they are written by Mr Oscar Wilde, which only goes to show that man is a complex animal, and can contain within his soul a good many personalities. Because we condemn the bad that is within a man, there is no need to condemn the good that is in him, and were this new morality to be applied to all art, I fear very much that some of the earlier classics might have to disappear from our libraries.[560]

That this defence of Wilde's work did not equate to anything like sympathy with his lifestyle should have been obvious to any regular reader of *TO-DAY*. Nonetheless readers did begin to write in to the paper seeking Jerome's advice on their own sexual struggles. Quite how many of them relate to homosexuality is impossible to prove, not least because only one side of the correspondence is printed. But in this context Jerome's reference to 'recent court trials' is surely suggestive. In answer to 'Resistance' in 1896, he thundered:

> With every effort to be broad-minded, I find it difficult to entertain any other feeling with regard to you than a desire to avoid thinking of you. Towards ordinary human failings and frailties, few of us, God knows, can stand in an attitude of virtuous superiority; but you and those like you — for, unfortunately, you are not unique; would to heaven you were! — are quite outside my power of sympathy. I do not understand such. It is as if some creature, with whose nature I had no connection, had asked me for advice. I feel myself powerless. Speaking personally, were the strange passion you speak of to assail me, and I found myself unable to combat it, I think I should cut my throat. But I quite admit that human nature is apt to be severe upon the vices of others, and somewhat forgiveful towards its own. There is no doubt in my mind that recent court trials, together with the stream of talk upon this matter that in consequence crept through the public press, have influenced you, and that is why some of us think it better to leave evil to take its own secret courses undisturbed than drag it to the light of day, even to punish it.[561]

More temperately, he wrote to a Welsh correspondent in 1897, 'I have read and replied to many letters similar to yours. There is always hope for a man whose conscience has not been silenced. Many men who have at last obtained mastery over themselves were once little better than you, by your own confession, are now. Evil is a thing to be fought daily with dogged determination. Despair is her greatest ally.'[562] Again, this letter could in theory refer to almost anything, but notably there is no reference to supposed evil being done to another party.

Sexual politics aside, the huge achievement of running two journals simultaneously is particularly impressive given the creative output Jerome managed to maintain at the same period (four plays and a volume of reprinted sketches between 1895 and 1897). The strain of this perpetual production, and of his continued fame, is evident in a *TO-DAY* editorial of 1896, in which he wistfully looked back on a Bohemia supposedly conquered by Mrs Grundy:

> When a man wrote for a few shillings, he felt he might as well enjoy the expression of his own thoughts, for it would not make too much difference to him. But when he writes for large cheques, he thinks a little bit too much, perhaps, of the public from whom those large cheques come, and does not care to risk offending or surprising. Besides, it is necessary to be interviewed once a week, and one's house must be in order for the interviewer to sympathetically describe it. ... I fear we must make up our minds to treat Bohemia as a vanished land, and let us hope that our modern artists, living their well-ordered lives, work with as much love at their art as did the sad old dogs who lived and loved – loved a little too much and too often, perhaps – struggled and misbehaved themselves generally in that forsaken country.[563]

In the month that he wrote this, his musical comedy *Biarritz* was beginning its career at the Prince of Wales's Theatre, eventually clocking up seventy-one performances. Despite this evidence of success, not everyone expressed themselves as satisfied with the production. Bernard Shaw, whose relationship with Jerome was often somewhat tense, had nothing good to say, telling his readers, 'What Mr Jerome K. Jerome was thinking of when he wrote it is hard to imagine; but he has written to the papers promising to explain everything when the worst is over.'[564] He personally feared that the musical would run for years because it was so bad as to necessitate the constant updating of its effects, but for himself he thought that, 'Two minutes of Biarritz would reconcile a Trappist to his monastery for life.'[565]

No one could have been more severe on the production than Jerome himself. Once again his script had been tampered with and, a week after its final performance on 20 June, he let rip with an extraordinary outburst in *TO-DAY*:

> Speaking personally, I cannot say I am sorry that *Biarritz* has failed to attract any large section of the public to the Prince of Wales' Theatre. ... What the play, *Biarritz*, or *John Jenkins*, or whatever it was called, may have been in the original script, will never be known. The authors and their friends, no doubt, considered it very fine;

others may have considered it very poor. That is of no concern to the public, because it is certain that the play, as presented, was not the play as it was written. I should doubt if fifty lines of the original dialogue were ever spoken, or any sequence of scenes maintained.
...

If Mr Arthur Roberts and his company are capable of writing their own plays, they might as well do this in the first instance; thereby avoiding insult to the librettist, together also with the payment of his fees. But the fate of *Biarritz* would seem to prove that Mr Arthur Roberts is not quite so clever as he imagines himself, and he will do better in the future to allow his author to do the author's share of the work, and confine his own attention to his own business. The audiences attracted by this class of play are not very critical, but there is a limit even to their want of intelligence; and a hotch-potch of disconnected gag, spiced with the impromptu wit of ballet girls, hardly makes an evening's entertainment at present West-end prices.[566]

As well as all this catering to the literary taste of a demanding public, and attacking the perversion of his plays to suit an uneducated audience, his correspondence refers to a prolonged lecturing tour he undertook in the early part of 1895.[567] At the same period he was campaigning for a monument to be raised to his friend Philip Marston, who had died in 1887.

It was the expansion of the railways that forced yet another change of address. Revisiting the incident nearly three decades later, Jerome was both laconic and characteristically inaccurate in his comment that 'The Great Central Railway turned me out of Alpha Place to make way for their new line to London. A chasm yawns where it once stood; a pleasant house with a long dining-room and a big drawing-room looking out upon a quiet garden.'[568] In fact, it was the Manchester, Sheffield, and Lincolnshire Railway Co., who unceremoniously dispossessed the Jeromes as a result of running their new line to London in 1892, leaving him justifiably incensed. As he ruefully explained in *TO-DAY*, 'It was in a quiet by-road through which no traffic passed; it was surrounded by big houses standing in their own grounds; it was quite detached, with a garden all round it.'[569] It had been chosen specifically for its quiet and picturesque location, and Jerome had spent £800 on renovations and refurbishment. Understandably, when the railway company offered £750 for a compulsory purchase he took them to court. As one newspaper summarised it, 'Plaintiff's case was that his house, which he rented at £90 a year, with option of purchase, was very secluded, enabling him to carry on his literary work with absolute privacy. Several well-known writers were called to vouch for the desirability of the residence.'[570] An article in the *London Standard* lists these witnesses as Hall Caine, Zangwill, Frankfort Moore, W. S. Gilbert and Sydney Grundy.[571] But, as ill luck would have it, the judge in the case appears to have been less than impartial. 'Throughout the hearing I watched the attitude of the jury with some amazement. ... Whenever Mr Littler, Q.C., winked – and he winked frequently – the jury leaned over, nodded back at him, and tittered. When he made a joke they roared; when he sneered they tossed their heads contemptuously.'[572] To add further insult to injury the court decided on a figure of £500 for the house and made him pay the costs of the case (some six or seven hundred pounds), meaning in effect that he had been 'fined' £200 for being turfed out of his home,[573] less than two years after the huge commitment of setting up a new journal. It is little wonder that when further financial trouble came he was not prepared to meet it.

But now, on the advice of the actor manager George Alexander, the Jeromes moved to 5 Park Row, Albert Gate, overlooking Hyde Park. It was here that Jerome had his one significant meeting with Mark Twain. Their daughters had met at a gymnasium, and Twain accordingly came to call. His guest remembered, 'We sat talking, looking out upon the silent park, till pretty late; and it struck me as curious, turning back into the house after having seen him and his daughter into the cab, that neither of us had made a single joke nor told a funny story.'[574] While they met again in public, this was the only time the two writers would meet alone.

Jerome seems never to have settled in the West End. As he said of himself, 'They say a man always returns to his first love. I never cared for the West End: well-fed, well-dressed, uninteresting. The East, with its narrow silent streets, where mystery lurks, its noisome thoroughfares, teeming with fierce varied life, became again my varied haunt.'[575] But even as he relocated to a new London address, he seemed to be falling out of love with the metropolis. In an editorial of 28 December he was responding to a Scottish paper who had questioned his description of Highland cattle as 'small, fierce animals'. He retorted, 'I have got a cow of my own in a field in Oxfordshire. Any Scottish journalist who cares can come and call it savage. He can say it is ferocious. He can abuse it up and down a whole column if he likes. It won't trouble me, and if we keep the paper away from the cow no harm will be done...'[576] The cow in question was part of a farm in Ewelme, near Bensington (Benson, as it is now known) in Oxfordshire, and the Jeromes had just taken out a twenty-one-year lease. For £82 a year they were now possessed of the 'dwelling house with gardens, stables and domestic offices belonging to Gould's Grove; also cottage with garden and appurtenances on north side of Beggar Bush Hill in Bensington and also all game on Gould's Farm containing three hundred and fifty acres and four perches or thereabouts'.[577] It was therefore above the main thoroughfare from Oxford to Henley, in a sequestered position just off the road, and with excellent views of the surrounding countryside. Tramps would sometimes stop to rest under the hayricks. It was here that Jerome first read Wells's *The Island of Dr Moreau* in MS, writing later, 'It had come into the office just as I was leaving; and I had slipped it into my bag. I wished I had not begun it; but I could not put it down. The wind was howling like the seven furies; but above it I could hear the shrieking of the tortured beasts. I was glad when the dawn came.'[578]

In his public capacity, Jerome was greatly concerned at this time with the Turkey-Armenia conflict. Like Edna Lyall, whose *The Autobiography of a Truth* was published in this year, with all profits being donated to the Armenia Relief Fund, Jerome repeatedly spoke out against the massacre of Amernians under Turkish rule. So outspoken was he, he almost found himself facing prosecution by Sultan Abdul Hamid. In an editorial in *TO-DAY* in June 1896, Jerome had stated baldly that 'Abdul Hamid has forfeited his right to live',[579] apparently with no idea that his remarks would reach as far as Turkey. At the insistence of the Turkish Ambassador, Jerome was summoned to the Foreign Office for what must have been an awkward meeting with Lord Salisbury (whom he had been vilifying fairly regularly in his editorials over the last few months). He was informed that he was likely to be charged with plotting the assassination of the Sultan, and his only hope lay in the penning of a highly contrite apology. As Jerome gleefully informed his readers that October, he no longer risked placing himself in contempt of court by discussing the whole affair, and he had flatly refused to write any such letter. While he was at it, he placed on record that, while he would welcome the assassination of the Sultan, he personally had made no plans in that direction.[580]

In the event, this confrontation with the ministry would be the least of his problems in the last years of the century. At the start of 1897 he found himself fighting 'a cantankerous artist ... bringing what is practically a blackmailing case against me, claiming goodness knows what, for my putting a picture of his into the Idler, though he really invited me to do so.' He appealed to Clement Shorter as a fellow editor to back him up in the witness box.[581] He had already lost £200 in 1895, in the case against the Manchester, Sheffield, and Lincolnshire Railway Co. (not counting the £800 he had spent on the house or the initial cost of the lease). This in the same year that he had bought out Robert Barr from *The Idler*. The very last thing he needed was yet another law suit.

But following the scathing series of articles on the 'water-gas bubble' in the spring and summer of 1894, he suddenly found himself defending a libel suit against the powerful Samson Fox in 1897. From this distance, an editorial in the previous year takes on a horribly prophetic shade. Discussing a case involving the *Railway Times*, he had sympathised with the paper, complaining that:

> the verdict [the paper would have to pay about £2000] is one that makes a newspaper dealing with financial affairs stop and consider its position. Judges and jury seem to have made up their minds that no word of criticism is ever to be passed by a newspaper upon a financier, and really it becomes a question whether journals should not refuse to expose themselves to enormous loss, perhaps ruin, merely with the idea of serving a public, who only laugh at them for their pains.[582]

Jerome was now forced to appeal to Arrowsmith for help, writing in March 1897:

> I don't want you to do anything unbusiness like but for the 1st time in my life I am in a tight place & if you can help me for friendships sake do.
>
> I have before the 20 March to find £1500 to meet a law case. It has come quite unexpectedly[.] Everyone thought it was settled & done with. It has come like a bolt from the blue. ...to climb down to such a rogue wd kill TO-DAY & I'll fight him if I have to pawn the coat off my back.
>
> Would you lend me say £500. I could give you 6% in *Today* and *Today* is a sound paying property making from £25 to £60 a week & going up. I would also add my own personal security to you and take a change on the copyrights of the books of mine you publish & I could add a Life Policy.[583]

He was still confident at this stage that 'when Fox sees I'm really for him there will be an end of the matter', although he felt some anxiety about not getting back his costs.[584] Arrowsmith obliged with the necessary £500 as a mortgage on future royalties.

As was usual in their business arrangements, the whole affair seems to have been conducted in a spirit of trust, backed up in this case by a clause never meant to be invoked. On seeing it, Jerome wrote first, 'The suggested document will do all right. I suppose you will take it as collateral security with the £500 debs on TO-DAY' (paying 6% and redeemable in 1906).' He thought that if Arrowsmith were satisfied with the soundness of *TO-DAY* as a concern he would take his interest from it. However, he would sign the deed and also send the debs, leaving it up to Arrowsmith as to whether he would let them remain or himself start paying royalties on them.[585] At one point he wrote to the publisher asking for a receipt and saying that he had sent the deed – as Arrowsmith had agreed to take payment each March and September if need be, Jerome assumed he wouldn't insist on the stipulation that the full amount must be repaid by September of that year (presumably 1897). The important point to note here is that he signed the paper first and questioned its terms afterwards.[586] It must have been a few months later that he told Arrowsmith of a chance to invest £3,000 in *The Idler*, remarking that he would put in the money himself had all his capital not gone to the lawyers.[587]

In the event, the costs of the Samson Fox case came to considerably more than this estimated £1,500. It was, Jerome later claimed, the most protracted case of its kind on record and involved travel over England and Germany to secure evidence, not to mention months of preparation. Both judge and jury were plainly in his favour, but as Jerome wearily explained in *TO-DAY*, he was finally defeated by a (by his own admission) well-known legal technicality, stipulating that each and every point in a libel case must be separately proved. Specifically, he also needed to prove that Fox himself had set out to deceive the public in his transactions, something that, as Jerome pointed out, he was hardly likely to admit.[588] In his summing up, the judge, Baron Pollock, made his sympathy with the defendant quite explicit:

> It is the case of a man's whole position among the persons among whom he moves and carries on his business being put in issue; and the jury say, 'True, we cannot give you, the defendant, the verdict, because you transgressed the law by asserting that which in some one

point or another is not true, and we cannot therefore give you the verdict; we must, therefore, give a verdict for the plaintiff, logically; but when you come to ask us what is the effect of that verdict to be, and say that you are a man who has been a righteous man, and a man who has been injured, we say, No; we say the result is that your conduct is such that, although you have been attacked, and in some one case attacked untruly, taking the whole of the case as a whole, you have been attacked, and that attack has been justified, and we are bound to find a verdict for the plaintiff, but when we weigh your character we put it at one farthing.'[589]

Buoyed up by a sense of having exposed this longstanding enemy, Jerome declared in *TO-DAY* that such work was essential, be the risk what it might, 'At present there is no protection between the public and its would-be fleecers other than the newspaper. There is no legal servant to watch financial transactions on the public's behalf. They are outside the range of parliamentary supervision.'[590] He summoned up sufficient bravado to thank his readers for sending in farthings to meet the fine incurred in his crusade.[591] But this defiant mood could not last, and he was soon remarking bitterly that the public, in the shape of judge and jury, had sat by and watched his destruction even as he had tried to help them. One correspondent, who rather tactlessly chose this moment to urge the paper to denounce every fraud it came across, was told tersely that, 'I have lately parted with £6,000 for speaking in the public interest, and I confess to feeling, at the present moment, a little cynical concerning the public interest.'[592] As an editor Jerome had expressed himself strongly before on the subject of would be contributors who provided neither genius nor stamps. Little wonder that American autograph hunters, who could not send in English stamps for return correspondence, were now reminded, 'Were I a rich man, I should be only too pleased to lavish my income upon postage stamps for this purpose, but I have a wife and family to support, and I must think of them first.'[593]

He may have written bitterly about the court case, but even as financial disaster was coming upon him, Jerome was keeping up with public engagements (a few days before this editorial appeared he and Ettie had attended a lunch for Mrs Keeley hosted by Dowager Lady Freake).[594] He also took the time to instigate a loneliness column in the correspondence section of the paper. The misery of feeling isolated in the city was, of course, one to which he responded instinctively and, for his own part, he responded warmly to the gestures of friendship made to him by readers, writing in 1896, 'I can hardly tell those who have written to me how much I value their friendship, or how closely I feel drawn to them.'[595]

The idea was that lonely people would write in to him outlining their circumstances and interests, in order to be put in touch with others in a similar situation. As his later fiction confirms, he had never forgotten his own sense of unbearable isolation after the death of his mother in 1875. The columns' numerous correspondents suggest the great need for the scheme, as well as occasionally registering its success.

By now Jerome had finally acknowledged that if women were to live in London lodgings, they too would benefit from the provision of appropriate entertainments and social networks. His commissioning of Mrs Humphreys early in 1896 to write a series of columns on domestic matters underscores his awareness of a female readership. The scope of this column, targeting 'inexperienced young wives whose husband's incomes are about £300 a year'[596] highlights Jerome's practicality, overtly addressing a lower-middle-class readership with a limited income. It also makes it perfectly clear that advanced women were not part of this target readership. Nonetheless, he retained his sympathy (from a safe distance) with some of their aims, notably the overthrow of the fashion for tight lacing. In August he wrote with the faintest discernible touch of seriousness:

> News comes from Paris which is almost too good to be true. We are told that the wasp waist is to disappear, or, rather, that it is to increase towards natural proportions. ...
>
> ...I have never been able to conceive what charm was supposed to exist in a fashion that made a woman look like a peg-top stuck upon a croquet ball. The poor woman could never breathe properly, she could never take exercise with any comfort, and could never eat a square meal.[597]

For reasons quite unconnected with corsets, Jerome was once again finding himself the target of abuse in the London journals, and pointed out satirically that, while this long-standing form of entertainment might help circulation, he could hardly keep these publications afloat by himself. With admirable restraint he now said, 'I have become somewhat hardened to abuse, and abuse is, to a certain extent, a compliment. Without being unduly conceited, I think I may flatter myself that, from my earliest entry into public life, I have been one of the best and most conscientiously abused men in London.' In fact he claimed now, 'abuse has whistled round my head till, in its absence, I feel a strange restlessness, a sense of something wanting'.[598]

Despite this cool response, the pressure was mounting on all sides. This spring saw the Thirty Days' War between Greece and Turkey, and following the defeat of Greece in May, Jerome decided the time had come to speak out about his experience of party politics. He was incensed to hear the case of a Haileybury College schoolboy being bullied literally to suicide by his peers, because he would not support the Turkish Sultan,[599] but insisted that he would not have died in vain if the scandal brought attention to bear on the system that fostered cruelty among boys in other public schools. For his own part, he claimed that:

> The personal persecution that has been brought to bear upon myself
> to induce me to abandon my position upon this matter affords me
> a remarkable insight into political life. I have been threatened with
> ruin, both of myself personally and of the paper, and I have only
> been able to stave this off by sacrifices of no small moment. I hope
> I possess a sense of proportion, and the question I ask myself is,
> if these extraordinary means have been taken to silence TO-DAY,
> what has happened in the case of still more important organs of
> public opinion?[600]

While he kept up such editorial crossfire in these stressful months of 1897, he must have known that there was only one way in which he could now meet his obligations. In September he was at Gould's Grove, giving a harvest dinner to the 'peasant neighbours' as the *Oxford Chronicle and Berks and Bucks Gazette* loftily termed them. After the toasts, two of them were heard arguing as to what exactly he was famous *for*, one guest asserting that he wrote books and the other apparently retorting, 'He rowed three men in a boat, and then won the race; that's what he's noted for.'[601]

Although the final editorials of 1897 contain no formal leave-taking to his readers, the editorial of 23 October was jointly written with Barry Pain, and it was Pain who wrote the 'TO-DAY notes', as they were called, for the succeeding issues until the end of the year. Jerome confined himself to the correspondence column before finally disappearing altogether in mid-November. One last, carefully-worded satire appeared on Samson Fox in the 'In the City' column to say that, at a forthcoming meeting of the

Amalgamated Water Gas shareholders, Fox planned to resign the chair to 'a man whose name will command a following. Whether this gentleman knows anything about the business is another matter.' Notably this appeared in the first week not to feature Jerome's name anywhere in the contents of the issue.[602]

The cost of the Samson Fox case meant not only the loss of *TO-DAY*, in which the articles had appeared; in order to meet the debts of one paper Jerome was forced to sell out his interest in the other. As he told Conan Doyle, in repaying a loan of £500 most probably connected with the case, 'After 4 years work I go out … poorer than I went in leaving the paper a fine property for others to reap the profit. In England in the 19th Century it does not pay to hold opinions not agreeable to our new King Capital.'[603] He wrote to Arrowsmith in the same vein, citing his politics rather than his temerity in taking on Fox as the cause of his misfortunes, 'It is a terrible story 3 years ago TO-DAY was a fine property I have been turned out of it. & perhaps ruined mainly because of my politics. It doesn't pay to be anything but high Tory just now.'[604] That the business 'broke up in anger' is hardly surprising. What is not clear is why, in 1914, the date of this description, it is Jerome and not the major investors who seems to have been still troubled with paying off the journal's creditors.[605]

At what point Jerome had changed his politics is unclear, but this comment offers some tentative means of dating his abandonment of conservative principles in favour of the socialism with which he was later associated. In 1927 he commented, somewhat bitterly:

> I commenced as a Radical. It was your Radical who was then the bogey of respectable society. The comic papers generally represented him as something between a fifth of November Guy Fawkes and a gorilla. I reformed. I became a true blue Conservative. I forget what converted me. It may have been the Liberal press. And from Toryism I passed on, naturally, to Socialism and joined the Fabians: in company with Wells and Shaw. Mr Wells is now an ardent supporter of capitalism, and Mr Shaw a humble follower of Mussolini; and I was saved only by a miracle from becoming a Liberal Member of Parliament.[606]

This last remark is presumably connected to his appearance as a canvasser for the Liberals in 1909, when he addressed the working men in Marlow just before the election.[607]

Press articles on JKJ often commented on his moustache, joking when he shaved it off in the 1890s that he was trying to get his weight down for a race with his nephew Shorland, the amateur bicycling champion. This photograph with thanks to Mark Richards.

Jerome Clapp [Jerome], the tragicomic 'man in grey' of *Paul Kelver*, took his family to live in London's East End, while in Walsall 'fortunes were being made all round him, even by quite good men'. By permission of the Bodleian Library.

Jerome K. Jerome's publisher, J. W. Arrowsmith (1840-1913); to say nothing of the dog. With thanks to Victoria Arrowsmith-Brown.

New Lamps for Old, Terry's Theatre 1890. The inserted card can be pulled up, to reveal an illustration of 'Mr. Penley in the lift' with the caption: 'Oh! I've sat in a pie'. By permission of the British Library.

Robina in Search of a Husband with Rowena Jerome (far right) as Robina. With thanks to Mark Richards.

The Passing of the Third Floor Back starring Johnston Forbes-Robertson (1853-1937) as the Stranger. With thanks to Mark Richards.

The industrialist Samson Fox (1838-1903). With thanks to Leeds Industrial Museum.

JKJ as an ambulance driver with Section Sanitaire No. 10 de la Croix Rouge Française in 1916. By permission of the Bodleian Library.

L-R Rowena Jerome, Elsie Jerome (neé Marris), Ettie Jerome in Germany at the turn of the century. By permission of the Bodleian Library.

JKJ and Ettie on a tandem outside Gould's Grove.

The original Three Men in a Boat. L-R Carl Hentschel, George Wingrave, Jerome K. Jerome. By permission of the Bodleian Library.

If his politics never seemed to square with the fashion of the day, neither, of course, did his writing please the most prominent critics. So pleased was he by one positive notice that he wrote to thank the author for 'the only courteous reference to myself I can remember having seen in any literary paper during 97'.[608] He may well have had in mind the downright offensive assaults made in the last year by the *Saturday Review*, which ran articles such as 'Words of Consolation and of Caution to Mr Jerome', supposedly in deprecation of previous attacks on his 'cockneyism', only to assure him that 'The narrowness of his outlook, the vulgarity and fatuousness of his jokes, his bad grammar, are not things which excite my anger. … One wonders that experience has not taught the author of "Dick Halward's Rise" and other plays that three or four acts of twaddling dialogue and threadbare episodes do not necessarily command success.'[609]

Little wonder that Jerome wrote of the lack of courtesy among his reviewers. But, by the end of 1897, he had more serious worries with which to contend. It must have been at this time that he wrote to Douglas Sladen in response to a query, 'I am sick of the Idler. I should advise you to sue them[.] I have nothing more to do with it.'[610] It may have been in response to a second letter that he wrote more peaceably to thank him for his sympathy and assured him that the demise of the paper had come at the right time, 'It has brought me little but cares and worry.'[611]

A Christmas card from a Russian friend, Madam Jarintzoff[612] provided a small boost. The card was framed by 111 visiting cards from his Russian admirers with the comment, 'You can see from all this how right we were to tell you in the summer that the moral success of your books is enormous here.' As Jerome confided to Douglas Sladen, 'I get so little honour now from a certain class of critic in my own country that I may be forgiven some gratification for my recognition abroad.'[613] At Jerome's request Sladen duly published the news in *The Academy*, taking the opportunity while he was at it to deny that his friend was in any way associated with a new journal, as had been rumoured.[614] It was doubtless this acclamation that persuaded Jerome to visit the country for himself in 1899. During this visit Jerome seems to have been lionised, and one writer recorded in his diary that he had asked the famous visitor to sign a photograph for Chekhov, only to have it snatched from under his nose by a female fan.[615]

By the middle of the month, he was hoping to be abroad, away from his worries.[616] It is not clear whether he left England as soon as he had planned – the theatre remained one source of solace and in the spring he was writing to Bram Stoker at the Lyceum to ask for seats for a production.[617] Certainly by October 1898 he had left for Dresden, from whence he wrote to Coulson Kernahan, 'Can you tell me if *TO-DAY* is dead yet? If not, will you send me over a copy? The *TO-DAY*'s creditors are coming down on us. I do not expect to be free from this business till I die...'[618] *Hearth and Home* duly reported in March that the Jeromes had taken an apartment after an initial stay at the Hotel Continental, and that they were often spotted out on their tandem bicycle.[619] At just around the time he penned this weary question to Kernahan, back in England his *Second Thoughts of an Idle Fellow* was going into its third printing. Generally perceived as a more sombre book than its predecessor, this collection of essays provides the kind of humour Jerome's readers expected, laced with questions on whether human beings were meant for happiness, and whether it really mattered either way. In October 1899 Jerome reassigned his lease of Gould's Grove to his solicitor Edward Ward for £150,[620] and that winter was spent in Munich,[621] partly to save expense.

Predictably, Jerome took to life in Germany from the first and made the most of the winter sports. He wrote later, 'There was good skating in Dresden in the winter. ... In the afternoon a military band would play, and there was a comfortable restaurant in which one took one's tea and cakes.'[622] On a more cultural note, the town was also steeped in history, 'Taking one consideration with another, Dresden, perhaps, is the most attractive town in Germany; but it is a place to be lived in for a while rather than visited. Its museums and galleries, its palaces and gardens, its beautiful and historically rich environment, provide pleasure for a winter, but bewilder for a week.'[623] A further consolation for his exile must have been the improved quality of 'German band' he had so frequently deplored in the pages of *TO-DAY*. As he had wryly noted in *Diary of a Pilgrimage* a few years earlier, 'The German bands that come to London are bands that have fled from Germany in order to save their lives. In Germany, these bands would be slaughtered at the public expense and their bodies given to the poor for sausages. The bands that the Germans keep for themselves are magnificent bands.'[624]

Depressed though he may otherwise have been, he set to work in Dresden to write two stories for Clement Shorter's new periodical *The Sphere*. Both were to be ready at least in time for Easter 1900, and Jerome wrote to Shorter in optimistic mood, inviting him to lunch at his hotel during a visit to England in May.[625] Nonetheless, the burden of money worries is apparent: on hearing that the stories would not appear until later in the year, he reminds him politely of their agreement to pay on delivery.[626] In a subsequent letter he fell back on the convenient assumption that a cheque for £30 might have gone missing in the post.[627] In the event, only one story appeared in the journal, in June. 'The Probation of James Wrench'.

He did manage to bring out a new play in 1899. *Miss Hobbs*, in which the feminist heroine comes between one woman and her husband and persuades another to break off her engagement, only to change her ways when she herself falls in love, ran from 18 December 1899 to 13 July 1900, with 210 performances.[628] Some time during this period, probably in the summer of 1899, his old friends 'George' and 'Harris' managed to come over for a holiday (it is possible that they returned with him after his flying visit to England in May).[629] It is, perhaps, inevitable that their way of cheering him up was to embark on a 'three men' holiday, and that Jerome should immediately set to work immortalising their adventures, not this time in a boat, but on the new and still perilous bicycles. *Three Men on the Bummel* sets the expected incompetence of the three travellers against German efficiency, in a landscape where nature herself is brought strictly under control:

> In a German park I have seen a gardener step gingerly with felt boots on to a grass-plot, and removing therefrom a beetle, place it gravely but firmly on the gravel; which done, he stood sternly watching the beetle, to see that it did not try to get back on the grass; and the beetle, looking utterly ashamed of itself, walked hurriedly down the gutter, and turned up the path marked 'Ausgang'.

Jerome would explain in his autobiography that, while a child might easily learn to cope with the mechanics of a bicycle, for an adult it was much more difficult and the inevitable falls much more painful, 'Providence is helpful to youth. To the middle-aged it can be spiteful. The bicycle took my generation unprepared.'[630] Jerome had previously had great fun in his *TO-DAY* editorials, describing encounters in the London parks between inexperienced cyclists and innocent-looking dogs. Now he found scope for this highly topical strain of humour, attacking the billboard advertisements for new models with merciless enjoyment:

> You tired young man, sitting dejectedly on milestones, too spent to heed the steady rain that soaks you through; you weary maidens, with the straight, damp hair, anxious about the time, longing to swear, not knowing how; you stout bald men, vanishing visibly as you pant and grunt along the endless road; you purple, dejected matrons, playing

with pain the slow, unwilling wheel; why did you not see to it that you bought a 'Britain's Best' or a 'Camberwell Eureka'? Why are these bicycles of inferior make so prevalent throughout the land?[631]

In fact, the holiday appears to have been far more idyllic and considerably less bothersome than the novel would suggest. While he was – ever the writer – mentally collecting copy all the time, Jerome was able to write reassuringly to Coulson Kernahan:

> At present I am not worrying about anything, but am holidaying through the Black Forest with two old friends, and forgetting everything but sleeping, resting and laughing. What a good life it would be, I sometimes think, if Art and Culture had never come to trouble us. They missed much of good and evil, the old folks. Probably in November we go to Munich. It is cheaper than Davos, and there is music, which I am coming to love deeply. Music takes one up in a lift, where thought toils up the stairs...'[632]

It is interesting to note in passing that notwithstanding the fame of George and Harris as J's companions on the Thames, Kernahan is addressed as if he did not know Wingrave and Hentschel personally, nor indeed does Jerome specifically identify them here. This is particularly surprising given that Jerome and Kernahan had first met through Tom Wingrave, George's brother. But what all Jerome's friends seem to have agreed on is that he was a deeply private man, and nothing suggests this idea more evocatively than his keeping the friendships of his days in London lodgings slightly separate (if only on paper) from the more recent relationships he had formed in the literary and dramatic worlds. Not only this, but just as he himself appears as 'Jerome', 'JKJ' or simply 'J' in different contexts, so too Wingrave and Hentschel are 'George' and 'Harris' when they appear in fictional form, but simply 'two old friends', even in correspondence with another close friend, before the book is written and it is time for them to reassume their comic guises.

In the novel itself, Jerome once again wryly acknowledges the tension between the 'high culture' he always wanted to write and the more successful humour for which he was famous:

> I could describe the Black Forest to you at great length. I could translate to you Hebel, the poet of the Black Forest. I could write

pages concerning its rocky gorges and its smiling valleys, its pineclad slopes, its rock-crowned summits, its foaming rivulets (where the tidy German has not condemned them to flow respectably through wooden troughs or drainpipes), its white villages, its lonely farmsteads.

But I am haunted by the suspicion you might skip all this.[633]

While he cannot resist several passages on the landscape and the social environment, Jerome is at his best in mock disquisitions on the German love of order as extended to the natural world, 'For in Germany there is no nonsense talked about untrammelled nature. In Germany nature has got to behave itself, and not set a bad example to the children.'[634] But if he plays the Englishman abroad in this commentary on foreign culture, he is equally ready to mock his own countrymen: 'I turned my head and saw what, I suppose, few living Englishmen have ever seen before – the travelling Britisher according to the Continental idea, accompanied by his daughter.'[635] The details are complete, down to the regulation guide book and the walking stick, useless in this part of the country where there are no mountains:

> The gentleman had an open Baedeker in his hand, and the lady carried a phrase-book. They talked French that nobody could understand, and German that they could not translate themselves! The man poked at officials with his alpenstock to attract their attention, and the lady, her eye catching sight of an advertisement of somebody's cocoa, said 'Shocking!' and turned the other way.[636]

But if he was happy to mock the English tourist, Jerome also acknowledged familiar anxieties about the innate brutality such apparent 'civilisation' was designed to conceal. Several pages of *Three Men on the Bummel* are devoted to an account of the German Mensur, a longstanding tradition in which students would fight almost to the death, disfiguring themselves and causing permanent injury in the process. As in his protests against vivisection in the pages of *TO-DAY*, Jerome's most palpable horror is provoked not by the idea of the young men's obvious suffering, but by the brutalising effects of the spectacle on the large audience who gathered to encourage the fighters:

> I wanted more. I looked from face to face surrounding me, and in most of them I found undoubtedly reflected my own sensations. If it be a good thing to arouse this blood thirst in the modern man,

then the Mensur is a useful institution. But is it a good thing? We prate about our civilisation and humanity, but those of us who do not carry hypocrisy to the length of self-deception know that underneath our starched shirts there lurks the savage, with all his savage instincts untouched. Occasionally he may be wanted, but we never need fear his dying out. On the other hand, it seems unwise to over-nourish him.[637]

He would later use this encounter as an analogy for the bloodlust of World War I, admitting in 1920 that he had been quickly drawn in by the sight of human suffering:

I regard myself as a humane man, more troubled at the sight of suffering than is usual. At first every splash of blood, every bleeding cheek laid bare, gave to me disgust and pain. It was sheer cowardice that kept me in my chair. At the end of half an hour I was watching each duel with lively interest, and a secret hope that something even more exciting might take place. I had heard that very often the combatants, either through clumsiness or rage, inflicted fatal wounds on one another. But luck was against me, and I had to be content with merely the sight of gushing blood and slashed and mangled flesh. It was with difficulty that during the next few weeks I restrained myself from seeking another invitation.[638]

By the winter of 1899 Jerome was back in Munich with Rowena, Elsie and their governess. Presumably the music rather than the weather was the attraction, as he later confessed, 'Munich is a fine town, but its climate is atrocious. I used to think that only we English were justified in grumbling at the weather. Travel soon convinced me that, taking it all round, English weather is the best in Europe. In Germany, I have known it to rain six weeks without intermission.'[639] Making the best of his situation he claimed in a letter home that 'I find it better for work and it is good education for the children.'[640] Certainly they seem to have increased their life experience in various ways. It may have been in these early days of living in Bavaria that he somehow, in the absence of his wife, who was visiting a sick friend in England, managed to get them all drunk in a beer garden.[641] As he explained in *My Life and Times* there was a famous beer garden near Munich that brewed for a year and opened to a large crowd for just one week in the spring:

They told me it was strong – '*heftig*'. But they did not say how *heftig*. Our governess, who was from Dresden, said, 'Be careful.' She had heard about this beer. I claim that I was careful. The girls had each one mug. I explained to them that this was not the ordinary beer that they were used to; and that anyhow they were not going to have any more. It was a warm afternoon. They answered haughtily, and drank if off. Our governess, a sweet, high-minded lady... had one and part of another. I myself... had decided to limit myself to three. I was toying with the third, when my eldest girl, saying she wanted to go home, suddenly got up, turned round and sat down again. The younger swept a glass from the table to make room for her head, gave a sigh of contentment and went to sleep.

In the end they all had to be helped back to the carriage by a man 'of powerful physique' evidently appointed for this purpose.[642]

Despite what he knew to be a brooding temperament, Jerome generally did manage to make the best of things, and he wrote in Christmas of this year that he was 'keeping to the sunshine – after all it is as true as the shadows'.[643]

CHAPTER SIX

'The mood was gone then' 1901-1913

'The country is too dull, and town too lively for work. The ideal place is still to be discovered. In the meantime it is as well to have an excuse.'

W. W. Jacobs, 1908

In January 1901 Jerome was writing from Dresden to his agent A. P. Watt in (partly) facetious vein, 'I am very satisfied not to be my own business man. It is not, that I do not appreciate the value of my own work. It is that I am never able to convince editors, publishers, of its value. <u>You</u> it is, who often open their eyes to the truth concerning me, much to my advantage. May you live long and prosper me.'[644]

Meanwhile, Ward must have decided against living in his newly leased property himself, because that spring the Jeromes returned to Gould's Grove, although they would continue to decamp to Brussels for the next two winters.[645] It seems possible that Blandina Jerome may have been living either with or near them at around this time, and that the attempts to escape the inclement conditions of an English winter were on her account.[646] However, Jerome's private letters confirm that he was in Lausanne in the winter of 1907-8, presumably enjoying the winter sports. Back in England for now, however, Jerome seems to have replaced his punishing editorial routine with an equally demanding schedule of fiction writing. He was able to write to Clement Shorter in response to a request for new material, 'It would not be worth your while. To turn aside from the mountain of work before me I should want fifteen guineas.'[647] Evidently A. P. Watt was indeed prospering him, as per supplication. In any event, it is not surprising to find him referring to a 'mountain of work' at this time. In 1901 Arrowsmith published *The Observations of Henry*, a series of mainly comic sketches held together by the frame narrative of a waiter - an equivalent figure to our modern taxi driver, who garners anecdotes while being treated by passengers as temporarily deaf.

It must have been around this time that Jerome met Nell Jacobs, the suffragette and new wife of W. W. Jacobs. What they made of each other is not known, and Jerome's one passage in *My Life and Times* is simply a comic rendition of a later episode, in which she was arrested for breaking a window in a suffragette protest. Her husband tried to bail her out by insisting that she was a good wife and mother who would suffer from the poor prison diet and general regime. In Jerome's hands this becomes an anecdote about the prison governor assuring Jacobs that she had put on weight since her imprisonment. But this was in 1911. In the early years of the century Jacobs's biographers concur that while the two families rarely met, Nell responded powerfully and emotionally to her husband's friend. In a private paper found after her death she made no secret of the fact that she had been in love with him, 'my whole being cried out for help, the comfort, the illumination, the wide, deep sympathies of JKJ – for his ugly face, his big presence, his forcible ideas (how he hated Dictators!) – for his great love of freedom – chivalry, his deep disturbance because of poverty.'[648] While Jacobs dedicated his 1903 collection of short stories *Odd Craft* to Jerome, Aubrey Wilson's unpublished biography suggests that the families had severed ties by 1904. Despite the potential tension, the two men themselves did remain friends. Just as interesting as Jerome's response to Nell Jacobs is, of course, the question of what Ettie thought of her and her ideas on female suffrage. But here again Mrs Jerome remains an unknown quantity. Even if she did approve of the women's movement, her reluctance to smash windows in its support would have kept her out of the papers. It is equally possible that she quietly assumed her husband's more conservative position.

Jerome himself was, characteristically, anything but silent. The year 1903 would see the publication by Hutchinson of a series of sketches, *Tea-Table Talk*, in which the Woman of the World, the Philosopher, the Girton Girl, the Old Maid, the Minor Poet and an unnamed narrator, a former journal editor, discuss topical questions such as the moral influence of Art and the position of women. Each of these figures talks over the others, and anecdotes begun by one figure are resumed after a break of several pages in which others are arguing related questions, creating a multi-voiced, contested series of questions unlike anything in Jerome's other work. At one point the Woman of the World is allowed to complain that 'Home to us women is our place of business that we never get away from,'[649] while the narrator finally manages to break in with his anecdote about a story he has read in which a renowned poet marries a practical but dull woman, only to find a carefully revised series of manuscripts in her desk after her death:

> All these years he had been living with a fellow poet! They should have been comrades, and they had never spoken. ... Years ago, when they were first married – he remembers now – she had slipped little blue-bound copy-books into his pocket, laughing, blushing, asking him to read them. How could he have guessed? Of course, he had forgotten them. Later, they had disappeared again... [650]

As Faurot observes, 'The topics of *Tea Table Talk* might have been the subject of editorials or of serious articles. ... In this conversational, colloquial discussion, Jerome catches, however, a larger reading public than he would have had he written in the formal manner of a serious thinker.'[651]

The following year Hutchinson brought out a series of linked stories that continued the theme of the advanced woman in another guise entirely. This was the mildly fantastic *Tommy & Co.*, in which the central protagonist thinks she is probably a boy, although no one can be sure until a pretext can be found for calling in a doctor, at which point she turns out be a girl. Despite his reservations about female employment, Jerome allows Tommy to work for her adopted father Peter Hope as a printer's devil (a gofer), before rising to eminence as a woman of letters, formally named Jane but known to her inner circle for the rest of her life as Tommy.

In between these largely comic works came the novel that would finally alter the critics' attitude towards the author of *Three Men in a Boat*. Jerome later told Alfred Moss that *Paul Kelver*, published by Hutchinson in 1902, had been written mainly in Germany, suggesting that more time was spent on this novel than probably any other. An intriguing but undated letter to Coulson Kernahan possibly refers to the germ of the idea. Writing affectionately in response to what was presumably a request to publish personal details, Jerome assured his friend that he should:

> Say what you like. All I say is that you must not puff me up too much. That anyone could be tried by you, old fellow, would be impossible – but I do want you to see your generous wish fulfilled. When you give your friends help, you give your whole self away, and can see no faults. I know you often make me feel a terrible fraud, and that two-thirds of the pleasant things you say and think of me are the result

of friendliness, and not of any merit. Your praise always makes me feel more ashamed of myself and my work than columns of abuse could do, because I know how little I deserve it, and I feel as though I had stolen something. There is one way in which it helps me. It makes me feel that I must try and do something a little worthier…

He goes on to say that, 'My work for some time to come will be of a much more serious kind. The old longing *to say something* – which has not troubled me for the last few years – is growing on me again; but, of course, in this road I shall have the fight all over again.'[652] This work, his 'first and only serious novel' as he termed it in 1913, 'gave me personally much pleasure', as well as having a galvanizing effect on the critics. 'Prior to that event, I was often abused as a sort of literary hooligan, and my works were occasionally spoken of as insults to literature.'[653] In particular, Jerome remained grateful for the praise of his fellow author and *Idler* contributor Francis Gribble, whom he told at the time, 'The aid you have given to me & to my whole future work is immeasurable.'[654] *The Bookman* was another of the many periodicals that leapt to his defence. In an article aptly titled 'The New Jerome', A. St. John Adcock admonished the public, complaining that it 'cannot easily persuade itself to accept any one man in more than once capacity, and if he has once won its suffrages as a jester it labels him accordingly, and expects him ever after to live up to his label.' He insisted, however, *Paul Kelver* was set to change this 'unwarrantable doctrine'. While he notes the humorous scenes with approval, the reviewer also praises the realism of the writing, 'Though Paul's story may, in some measure, reflect the early personal experiences of Mr Jerome himself, it does more than literally record such experiences, it lays bare and interprets their inner significance and shows their effect upon Paul's character and career.'[655]

Adcock was not the only reviewer to know or surmise the personal element in *Paul Kelver*. While even Jerome's non-fiction always needs to be treated with caution, the novel is obviously autobiographical in its treatment of the hero's early life. The son of a decayed middle-class family from a mining district reduced to poverty in the East End of London, Paul is virtually destroyed by the city after his mother's death, but works his way through provincial theatricals and vagrancy to ultimate success as a writer. Gratifyingly and inevitably, the critics discussed it as a successor to one of Jerome's favourite books, the semi-autobiographical classic *David Copperfield*, a point reiterated by Coulson Kernahan in his preface to Moss's 1927 biography.

Possibly to avoid implicating his sisters, the hero of Jerome's novel has no siblings – certainly the reader's intense response to Paul is enabled by his presentation of himself as not a youngest but an only child. Like Jerome, he is born in May to a Welsh mother (Maggie) who almost immediately has to face the news that her husband's mining venture has failed after a jammed pump allows it to flood, and that he will be moving to London in a bid to repair the family fortunes. Aunt Fan, who lives with the family, both during their time in an unnamed village in the Midlands and later when Maggie rejoins her husband in Poplar, is one of the least agreeable characters in the book, caustically greeting her brother-in-law in London with a taunt about not dropping his child down a mine.

Despite – or indeed because of – these very obvious parallels with his own life, the narrator of *Paul Kelver* evinces notable unease about the telling of his story. The Prologue itself is subtitled 'In which the author seeks to cast the responsibility of this story upon another' and the chapter headings invariably describe Paul in the third person, although he is ostensibly a first person narrator. In *My Life and Times* Jerome himself admitted to being drawn back to the house in Poplar where he had lived with his parents. Paul likewise feels compelled to keep revisiting the house where he grew up, beginning the novel:

> At the corner of a long, straight, brick-built street in the far East End of London – one of those lifeless streets, made of two drab walls upon which the level lines, formed by the precisely even window-sills and doorsteps, stretch in weary perspective from end to end, suggesting petrified diagrams proving dead problems – stands a house that ever draws me to it; so that often, when least conscious of my footsteps, I awake to find myself hurrying through noisy, crowded thoroughfares, where flaring naptha lamps illumine fierce, patient, leaden-coloured faces; through dim-lit, empty streets, where monstrous shadows come and go upon the close-drawn blinds; through narrow, noisome streets, where the gutters swarm with children, and each ever-open doorway vomits riot; past reeking corners, and across waste places, till at last I reach the dreary goal of my memory-driven desire; and, coming to a halt beside the broken railings, find rest.[656]

Throughout the novel Paul appears as both a haunted and a haunting figure;

the adult narrator is almost obsessively preoccupied with his own past, and even as he presents a version of his child self, he makes it clear that this earlier self has the power to confront and judge him in the writing present.

Many of the young Paul's experiences tally with Jerome's account, in *My Life and Times*, of his own childhood and, like his memoir, it is inseparable from his experience of the city. As Faurot notes, 'Jerome has a strong sense of place; for like the reader of a Dickens novel, we can go from section to section of the London mentioned in *Paul Kelver*, sure that the streets are accurately named and placed in the fiction.' [657] It is impossible to know how far Paul's parents are based on their real life counterparts, but the narrator of the novel feels a palpable anxiety in presenting them to the reader at all. At one point the child Paul gets out of bed and discovers his parents sitting together in their best clothes, enjoying sherry and biscuits and discussing Byron and the Crystal Palace, three hours after he had last seen them cleaning the windows with the lights off, so that the neighbours would not realise that (like the Jeromes) they had no servant. Immediately after this passage Paul asks, 'I wonder am I disloyal setting this down? Maybe to others it shows but a foolish man and woman, and that is far from my intention.'[658] In a later passage the narrating Paul goes on:

> The larder, I fancy, was very often bare, but the port and sherry with the sweet biscuits stood always on the sideboard...
>
> But I would not have you sneer at them, thinking all pretence must spring from snobbishness and never from mistaken self-respect. Some fine gentlemen writers there be – men whose world is bounded on the east by Bond Street – who see in the struggles of poverty to hide its darns only matter for jest. But myself, I cannot laugh at them. I know the long hopes and fears that centre round the hired waiter; the long cost of the cream and the iced jelly ordered the week before from the confectioner's. But to me it is pathetic, not ridiculous.[659]

Paul's own experience of poverty is largely defined through his encounters with street boys, most of whom mock and chase him. But in one of the most haunting scenes in the book, Jerome uses the familiar trope of drowning to indicate the stolid and hopeless heroism of the poor. The young Paul hears a cry coming from behind a curtained window and a few minutes later a boy comes out of the house and sits next to him, asking what happens when people die. Paul confidently responds, 'If you're good, you go to heaven; if you're bad, you go to hell.'[660] Evidently missing the theological point, the boy wants to know if both places are far enough off to prevent his being brought back. On hearing that they are, he gives Paul the local sign of friendship, a punch in the chest, and swears him to secrecy before giving him an old knife and running into the mud bordering the Thames. Paul calls to him but he does not look back and eventually sinks in the mud, where the slime closes over his head. This unnamed character literally drowns in excrement.[661] The adult Paul comments, 'I did not tell anyone what I had seen, having sworn not to; and as time went on the incident haunted me less and less until it became subservient to my will. But of my fancy for those silent, lifeless streets it cured me for the time.'[662]

Like Jerome, Paul ultimately rejects his parents' stern religious teaching, although he insists to the reader that it has its value:

> That Puritan blood flowed in their veins that throughout our land has drowned much harmless joyousness; yet those who know of it only from hearsay do foolishly to speak but ill of it. If ever earnest times should come again, not how to enjoy but how to live being the question, Fate demanding of us to show not what we have, but what we are, we may regret that they are fewer among us than formerly...
> No graceful growth, this Puritanism, for its roots are in the hard, stern facts of life; but it is strong, and from it has sprung all that is worth preserving in the Anglo-Saxon character. Its men feared and its women loved God, and if their words were harsh their hearts were tender.[663]

At the age of ten Paul goes to school where, quite possibly like Jerome, he feels isolated from the other boys. Desperate for popularity, he suffers the almost unbearable humiliation of being chosen as a hare for 'hare and hounds', only to lose his chance when one of the boys says that nobody wants him. The leader impatiently chooses a replacement when Paul hesitates on the order to run. Inevitably, he finally becomes popular through his sense of humour, and when he learns the reason for this sudden acceptance by the other boys:

> It struck me like a slap in the face. I had thought to reach popularity upon the ladder of heroic qualities. In all the school books I had read, Leonard or Marmaduke (we had a Marmaduke in the Lower Fifth –

they called him Marmalade; in the school books these disasters are not contemplated), won love and admiration by reason of integrity of character, nobility of sentiment, goodness of heart, brilliance of intellect, combined, maybe, with a certain amount of agility, instinct in the direction of bowling, or aptitude for jumping; but such only by the way. Not one of them had ever said a funny thing, either consciously or unconsciously.[664]

The young Paul, of course, dreams of being a serious writer, and it is around this time that he meets an unnamed author one evening in the park. Just as Jerome himself had done, the child confides to this strange man that he wants to be a famous writer, and that his mother finds parts of Dickens a trifle vulgar. Jerome insisted in later accounts that the man really did say 'Damn Mr Pickwick!' as he is made to do in the novel. The young Paul fails to ask his new friend's name, and 'after that he would not tell me',[665] suggesting that maybe next time he will tell him who he is. They never meet again. What makes the story particularly convincing is the response of the adult writer, who asks the child what he thinks of Dickens's work but appears to take little interest in the answer – Dickens himself (in fact the touchiest of men) observed that he routinely ignored public praise, deliberately giving the impression that he was impervious to either admiration or criticism.

Like Jerome himself, Paul will not find immediate success. At this stage of his life his father is involved with the businessman Noel Hasluck, whose residence in the north-east London suburb of Stoke Newington may well suggest the influence of Mr Wood on the character. Finding that he has involved himself in some dubious practices, Luke Kelver withdraws from the business, and dies not long afterwards, leaving Maggie and Paul virtually destitute. Still an adolescent, Paul goes to work for the solicitors' firm of Stillwood, Waterhead, and Royal, where the kindly Mr Stillwood takes him under his wing. It is only after Stillwood's death that his systematic frauds on his clients come to light, including the defalcation of money owed to Paul's parents. As Paul half-admiringly puts it, 'As a piece of organisation it was magnificent. No one but a financial genius could have picked a dozen steps through such a network of chicanery. For half a lifetime he had moved among it, dignified, respected, and secure.'[666] It was only with the publication of *My Life and Times* in 1926 that this story would have been recognisable as a comment on Jerome's own experience.

Some of the most moving passages in the novel relate to Paul's loneliness after his mother's death, as he moves from one Spartan lodging to another. As the narrator laconically puts it, 'My first lodging was an attic in a square the other side of Blackfriars Bridge. The rent of the room, if I remember rightly, was three shillings a week with cooking, half-a-crown without. I purchased a methylated spirit stove with kettle and frying-pan, and took it without.'[667] From here the young Paul goes daily to the Ludgate News Rooms to seek employment, observing, 'We were a seedy company that every morning crowded into these rooms – clerks, shopmen, superior artisans, travellers, warehousemen – all of us out of work. Most of us were young, but with us was mingled a sprinkling of elder men, and these latter were always the saddest and most silent of this little whispering army of the down-at-heel.'[668]

While the autobiographical sources are unmissable, particularly in the early chapters, the plot is driven more by Jerome's obsession with sexual darkness than by his own verifiable experience. Somewhat extraordinarily, given the obvious identification of 'the man in grey' with Jerome Clapp, the early chapters of the novel had allowed Luke to come close to sexual infidelity with the wife of a business associate. The rumours of Clapp's sexual lapse in Appledore predated his younger son's birth by several years, and there is no evidence to suggest either that the younger Jerome knew anything of the affair or that similar rumours arose at a later date. The theme of masculine frailty may indeed derive from some knowledge of his parents' marriage, or equally from a sense that he himself needed to guard against attraction to other women. With a somewhat remarkable lack of sensitivity he had told the readers of *The Idler* in 1895 that, 'It is one of the tragedies of civilisation that a man has to pretend to care only for one woman, and his life, in consequence, is generally a prolonged struggle to avoid thinking of the might-have-beens. In fact, the attitude of a man towards the table of the world spread with feminine dainties is that of the schoolboy at the banquet: there are so many good things spread upon the board that he bursts into tears; he cannot make up his mind where to begin.'[669] All that is certain, as becomes disturbingly clear in the dream passage of *Novel Notes*, is that Jerome felt threatened throughout his adult life by the destructive potential of sexual desire.

In the prologue to the novel the adult Paul asks the house whether there was any truth in 'the story' and the house snaps at him 'just truth enough to plant a lie upon; and, Lord knows, not much ground is needed for that weed. ... Your mother had a good man, and your father a true wife, but it was the old story: a man's way is not a woman's way, and a woman's way is not a man's way, so there lives ever doubt between them.'[670] This sense of sexual difference, presented somewhat complacently here, becomes the catalyst for disaster later in the novel and tests Paul's understanding of himself and of those around him.

From the beginning the narrator shows ambivalence towards the half-angel, half-beast figure Dr Hal, who works tirelessly in the East End rather than build up a successful practice among the more respectable classes. A passionate defender of the poor and disadvantaged, in one scene he is described as assaulting a drunken man who has been battering his wife; the young Paul watches fascinated, but later admits:

> I have no desire to see again the sight I saw that quiet, still evening, framed by those high, windowless walls, from behind which sounded with ceaseless regularity the gentle swish of the incoming tide. All sense of retribution was drowned in the sight of Hal's evident enjoyment of his sport. The judge had disappeared, leaving the work to be accomplished by a savage animal loosened for the purpose.[671]

The animalistic side of Hal is confirmed when he elopes with Barbara, the daughter of Noel Hasluck and now wife of a European Count. Perhaps deliberately evoking *Great Expectations*, Paul has long been in love with Barbara but, when he meets her again after her four years of 'finishing' abroad, describes himself as worshipping her without even the desire for consummation. He recollects after her fall that she had wanted his love for her 'to save me … from the apish voices whispering ever to the beast within us'.[672] It is Hal who enacts the 'apish' voice in his illicit passion, and who shrewdly interrogates this division between pure and tainted when he figures Barbara's marriage as worldly and sordid, and her elopement as a courageous act of integrity, 'I did not even know I was the villain till I heard the booing of the gallery. I even thought I was the hero, full of noble sentiment.'[673] In telling Paul on his deathbed of how the Count subsequently tricked him into leaving Barbara, only to divorce her immediately afterwards, he makes their connection explicit, commenting, 'What a pity you and I could not have rolled ourselves into one, Paul – you the saint, and I the satyr! Together we should have made her perfect lover.'[674]

While the familiar trope of the ape confirms that sexuality is potentially destructive, the bohemian chapters of the novel show a far greater tolerance for irregular unions. The relationship between the married O'Kelly and a trapeze artist known to her friends simply as the Señora is fondly detailed by Paul, while the long-suffering Mrs O'Kelly is presented as obstinately perverse in her refusal to divorce her husband. Meanwhile, Paul's own attempt to become a Lothario later in the novel is largely comic. Having disentangled himself from an ill-considered engagement with a London barmaid, he takes up with a touring theatrical company and tries to persuade himself that he is in love with one of the married actresses. His plan to run off with her is thwarted at the last moment, to his obvious relief, by the announcement that the manager has absconded with the week's takings, leaving Paul to take the blame.

At the end of the novel, of course, Paul becomes a successful writer and marries the right girl. Unlike his most obvious precursor David Copperfield, however, he remains dissatisfied with his work. Like his actor friend 'Goggles', who yearns for tragic roles but brings the house down simply by appearing in front of the audience, Paul is frustrated by the relative failure of his serious writing in comparison to his comic successes. He is consoled by his friend Dan, who reminds him of the serious work done by humour in a troubled world, 'Aren't there ten thousand penny-a-liners, poets, tragedians, tub-thumpers, long-eared philosophers, boring [the world] to death? Who are you to turn your nose up at your work and tell the Almighty His own business? You are here to make us laugh. Get on with your work, you confounded young idiot!'[675] Jerome himself was prepared to acknowledge the social value of comedy, commenting in 1905 that 'Passion creates prejudice. Humour dispels it.'[676]

Nonetheless, Paul's very success as a humourist registers his failure as a profound thinker or 'tub-thumper'. As Jerome himself said rather bitterly:

It is not difficult to maintain the reputation of a humourist in these days. If a man once write a book that makes people laugh, the public, for ever afterwards — or, at all events, a certain portion of them — will go into fits of merriment over his every utterance. As a young man, I occasionally made remarks that were supposed to be witty. I remember one friend of mine greatly appreciated them; but my difficulty was that he thought everything I said was funny. If I said it was going to be a fine day, he exploded with laughter. If I came and told him that my favourite cat was dead, he would fall into paroxysms of enjoyment. I often found it difficult to refrain from observations that might have weakened our friendship. Possibly I might have done so with impunity. Had I called him a blithering ass, the chances are that he would have regarded it as a gem of humour, and have repeated it to everybody he came across.[677]

Goggles transparently speaks for Jerome when he complains that, 'If I were to enter a room full of people ... and tell them that my mother had been run over by an omnibus, they would think it the funniest story they had heard in years.'[678] More wistfully, Paul narrates his own first visit to the theatre as a magical evening, concluding:

> ...it happened to be before that very same curtain that many years later I myself stepped forth to make my first bow as a playwright. I saw the house but dimly, for on such occasions one's vision is apt to be clouded. All that I clearly saw was in the front row of the second circle – a sweet face laughing, though the tears were in her eyes; and she waved to me a handkerchief. And on one side of her stood a gallant gentleman with merry eyes, who shouted 'Bravo!' and on the other a dreamy-looking lad, but he appeared disappointed, having expected better work from me.[679]

A few years earlier, in *The Second Idle Thoughts of An Idle Fellow*, Jerome had taken his reader into his confidence in similar terms. Characteristically slipping a serious passage into the middle of a supposedly humorous discussion on 'things we meant to do', he allegorises his own perceived failure through the inset story of a boy whose complicated firework display only works after the audience has given up and gone home. In the same way, he wishes the reader 'could hear the stories that I meant to tell you. You judge me, of course, by the stories of mine that you have read – by this sort of thing, perhaps; but that is not just to me. The stories I have *not* told you, that I am going to tell you one day, I would that you judge me by those.'[680] In another essay he imprecates the ghost of his youthful self:

> You, dull old fellow, looking out at me from the glass at which I shave, why do you haunt me? You are the ghost of a bright lad I once knew well. He might have done much, had he lived. I always had faith in him. Why do you haunt me? I would rather think of him as I remember him. I never imagined he would make such a poor ghost.[681]

Ironically, the achievement of *Paul Kelver* lies precisely in this register of frustration and failure. In Jerome's greatest serious novel, he finally achieved the subtle vein of tragedy he was aiming for by acknowledging the hero's inability to write profoundly without sliding into bathos.

In his discussion of *Paul Kelver* in *My Life and Times* Jerome gives no clue as to what his surviving sister thought of the novel, or indeed of his treatment of their parents' marriage as vulnerable to attractive and predatory women. That he remained close to Blandina is suggested by her presence in Wallingford when she died at his house in 1904. The following year Jerome resumed his connection with *TO-DAY*, after an absence of over six years.

Jerome's return to the paper was heralded by an interview billed as 'A talk on the young man's journal', in which his founding of *TO-DAY* was duly celebrated. The interviewer commented that, 'Mr Jerome K. Jerome and the late W. E. Henley are generally looked upon nowadays as having been the two most brilliant editors of weekly papers seen in recent years'[682] before sharing his impressions of Jerome in the flesh. At forty-five he was now 'Of the middle height, with the first grey flecking his thin, reddish hair, he presents a figure in which shyness and sincerity are the most immediately striking characteristics. ... one has only to hear him speak in his somewhat tired voice to feel that he is, above all things, retiring, and keeps his strength in reserve.' [683] This was a perceptive account, backed up by others who knew Jerome well.

In other respects his interests would have been recognisable to his readers of the 1890s. While he had always objected to any apparent prurience in literature, he conceded that, 'There are two subjects which will always interest humanity – sex and religion.'[684] Personally, he was just as interested, as he had long been, in overthrowing the tyrannous fashion that confined men to uncomfortable black clothes. In *Idle Thoughts* he had expressed a desire for 'lavender-coloured tights, with red velvet breeches and a green doublet, slashed with yellow', a somewhat startling suggestion but, as he said, 'Why should we all try to look like ants, crawling over a dust-heap?'[685]

A number of Jerome's fictional narrators hanker after brightly coloured waistcoats at the very least, and now he suggested a fashion column aimed at men, demanding, 'Why should not the thoughtful man's trousers crease at the right place – his collar be correct? The thoughtful young man must live as well as think – go courting, visiting. It was the mistake the woman made when she began to think: she dressed like a guy and the world looked at her and said that thinking must be harmful for woman. Let the thoughtful young man be good to look at, and then the world may listen to him.'[686]

The following week Jerome was back in a more official capacity, with a correspondence column modelled on the original *TO-DAY*. He was quick to resume his role as a social commentator, telling one correspondent that:

> The future of the working classes lies with the working classes themselves. It lies in their ability to organise themselves, to choose their leaders, and having chosen them, to follow them loyally, to decline to shout and vote for any and every man who will stand them drinks. ... The working classes have got to think, and to think with advantage they will have to drink a little less beer. You evidently are one of the men who do think, but in your own workshop how many of your fellows would listen to you? ... All this sounds preaching. I don't care what you call it. ... The middle classes have got their rights. They can afford to waste their time, to muddle their brains. They can afford for their sons to be Gaiety Johnnies. The labouring-classes cannot afford self-indulgence. Their battle is in front of them. It can only be won for their children by self-sacrifice.[687]

Another reader sought his advice on the question of divorce, a still-scandalous proceeding, as it would continue to be for several decades. Jerome himself had, of course, married a divorcée, and something of his own dislike of the inevitable publicity probably informs his response. Radically, he imagined a society that would replace the legal dissolution of marriage with an authoritative family council, designed both to avoid hasty divorce and to sanction irregular unions without the involvement of the courts. Reviving his never-quite-satisfied Edwin and Angelina, he declaimed with obvious feeling:

> Edwin is not as nice as Angelina thought he was going to be. Edwin yearns for something more sympathetic. Angelina discovers late her precious affinity. So the whole world of Edwin and Angelina is to be put into the melting-pot; an unsavoury mess of human folly is thrown out of window to poison the earth. ... Now the Family Council would make for sense and decency in these matters. The right and the wrong of the case could be discovered without the assistance of a low-comedy judge, a troupe of barristers paid according to their ability for confusing facts, and twelve indifferent gentlemen convinced of the notion that everything serves everybody right. Justice could be done without the grinning assistance of a garbage-

loving public. In many cases where the law is powerless the Family Council could act effectively. The lunatic husband or wife is a case in point. The law admits of no release; the Family Council could be left to decide the question. A union that might, strictly speaking, be illegal, would, practically speaking, be irreproachable, sanctioned by the Family Council on both sides. Public opinion is always of more importance than legal formula.[688]

This was an interesting article to write in the wake of the Jacobs affair, to say the least of it, and must have been painful for Ettie to read.

Something of Jerome's own domestic life during this period is known from interviews given by May Walker, the child of the Jeromes' housekeeper, and her account suggests that there was some kind of vacuum in the household at this time.[689] Mrs Walker was the daughter of Gertrude and Edward Hammond, both of whom worked for Jerome from 1906, when May was two, until about 1910, when Mrs Hammond left the family's service. Mrs Walker recalled in later life that Ettie Jerome decided her bedtime, bathed her, brushed her hair and gave her Harrods' frocks, treating her, in other words, as a child of her own. What Rowena thought of all this is unclear; Mrs Walker remembered finding both her and Jerome pleasant but remote. Another small and somehow surprising detail emerges from Douglas Sladen, who noted Jerome's scrupulous tidiness from the time he first knew him in the 1890s. As he put it, 'When you stay with him in the country, you cannot leave your stick and hat in the hall, handy for running out, as you might at Sandringham or Chatsworth. They are at once arrested, and are very lucky if they get off with a warning from the magistrate.'[690]

It was just before May joined the household that Elsie left home to marry Thomas Riggs-Miller, which might possibly explain Ettie's intense reaction to a child not her own. The marriage was evidently not a success, and May Walker remembered Elsie as being back at Gould's Grove, a semi-invalid, when she first joined the household. Given her own age at the time, this is not an entirely trustworthy claim, but it can safely be assumed that Elsie returned to her mother within a few years of her marriage.[691]

Despite these unsettling events, Jerome was able to produce another series of sketches, *Idle Ideas in 1905*. Continuing the format of a series of essays mixing humour and seriousness, Jerome offers a critique of Dickens, among other icons of Victorian literature. Describing himself as 'a person of gross appetites', Jerome praised the 'savage strength of the Brontë sisters'[692] while also expressing admiration for Olive Schreiner, 'Here, again, was a young girl with the voice of a strong man.'[693] In some moods, he told his readers, he turned to Walter Scott, in others to George Eliot or Thackeray, as well as eighteenth-century classics such as *Tom Jones, Peregrine Pickle* and *Tristram Shandy*. Importantly, he stressed the need for writing of both the realist and the 'fairy-land' school, 'May not both Dickens and Zola have their booths in Vanity Fair?'[694] But it is Dickens who benefits from a nine-page appreciation, albeit laced with some mature qualifications, 'Dickens suffered from too little of what some of us have too much of – criticism. His work met with too little resistance to call forth his powers. Too often his pathos sinks to bathos, and this not from want of skill, but from want of care.'[695] Nonetheless, Jerome was quick to point out that, 'We have to go back to Shakespeare to find a writer who, through fiction, has so enriched the thought of the people. Admit Dickens' faults twice over, we still have one of the greatest writers of modern times.'[696]

If his enthusiasm for Dickens remained largely unabated, he had clearly changed his mind on a number of political issues. Notably, he had renounced his former enthusiasm for empire-building, 'The happy Londoner on foggy days can warm himself with the reflection that the sun never sets on the British Empire. He does not often see the sun, but that is a mere detail.'[697] Specifically he criticised the annexation of China, commenting with a satirical nod to Kipling that, 'The present trouble in the East would never have occurred but for the white man's enthusiasm for bearing other people's burdens. What we call the yellow danger is the fear that the yellow man may before long request us, so far as he is concerned, to put his particular burden down. It may occur to him that, seeing it is his property, he would just as soon carry it himself.'[698]

'Creatures that shall one day be men' testifies to his continued interest in Russian politics. He begins by admitting that, 'I ought to like Russia better than I do, if only for the sake of the many good friends I am proud to possess among the Russians.'[699] But the tone quickly becomes apocalyptic, 'The workers – slaves it would be almost more correct to call them – allow themselves to be exploited with the uncomplaining patience of intelligent animals. Yet every educated Russian you talk to on the subject knows that revolution is coming.'[700] The parallels with late-eighteenth-century France are unavoidable, but Jerome comments that:

There will be no Maribeau, no Danton to be appalled at a people's ingratitude. The men who are to-day working for revolution in Russia number among their ranks statesmen, soldiers, delicately-nurtured women, rich landowners, prosperous tradesmen, students familiar with the lessons of history. They have no misconceptions concerning the blind Monster into which they are breathing life. He will crush them, they know it; but with them he will crush the injustice and stupidity they have grown to hate more than they love themselves.[701]

This article was percipient indeed, appearing in the year of the first Russian Revolution. The alterations to the typescript of an unpublished play, *The Russian Vagabond*, are also instructive. The original address given was Park Row, suggesting that it was probably written between 1895 and 1897. This was then amended to Gould's Grove and subsequently to Monk's Corner. Originally the play featured references to the Csar, but these were changed to Grand Duke, Governor of Moscow, underlining Jerome's point that both old and new regimes were equally oppressive. The plot concerns the idealistic rebellion of Paul Orloff, the son of a Countess who is disgraced after posting up a nihilist manifesto in a public building. He becomes involved in later scenes with a mysterious woman called Nona (in fact an aristocratic police spy), who infiltrates the nihilist group and exposes them as ruthless murderers. Her character is not the less interesting, incidentally, for its emphasis on resourcefulness and courage – at one point the conspirators attempt to break down her disguise as a deaf old woman by threatening to murder her on the spot, but she apparently does not hear them and carries on poking the fire.[702] Jerome took the play, along with five others, to Elisabeth Marbury, who was deeply unimpressed.

Despite the sensationalising, Jerome was also still defending his position as a humourist, and defending the position of the middle class in literature, 'A modern nursery rhymester to succeed would have to write of Lord Jack and Lady Jill ascending one of the many beautiful eminences belonging to the ancestral estates of their parents, bearing between them, on a silver rod, an exquisitely-painted Sèvres vase filled with attar of roses.' [703]

As if to reinforce the point, *Idle Ideas in 1905* was followed by a dramatic version of *Tommy & Co.* and another play, *Robina in Search of a Husband*, in 1906. In the latter, the second heroine Kate is separated from her husband at the church door and, before he can rejoin her, he is clubbed round the head and placed on a ship heading for a distant port. For reasons that are not entirely clear she agrees some years later to impersonate her friend, the wealthy and frivolous Robina (daughter of the Chewing Gum King), who has romantic memories of a Byronic young man, but is currently flirting with Lord Raffleton and wants to test his motives. Robina accordingly borrows Kate's clothes and becomes a hotel chamber maid for a week. Inevitably, Lord Raffleton turns out to be Kate's missing husband, who has newly come into a title, and is horrified to find that, in his honourable intention of acknowledging his wife, he is apparently going to end up with the wrong woman. The comedy reaches a climax when the lovers are all reunited, only for Robina to be accused of murdering her school teacher, who is believed to be on a cruise ship but turns up just in time to save her charge from an uncomfortable detention in the hotel. In true Jeromian fashion, the four lovers are all shown to be fallible – Robina has forgotten the Byronic lover (who has himself become engaged to another woman) sufficiently to flirt with Raffleton, who has paid her some attention before flirting with Kate in the belief that she is Robina. The first performance was on the Pier in Brighton, with a young Harold Chapin playing Lord Rathbone.[704]

Following in the footsteps of other successful Victorians of the previous generation, notably Dickens and Wilkie Collins, in 1905 Jerome made his first tour of America. He was invited to lecture under the management of the Pond Lecture Bureau, and was allocated a Mr Glass to supervise his tour.[705] On his last night in England, Pett Ridge and W. W. Jacobs arranged a farewell dinner and on 30 September he set off alone. On his arrival at his New York hotel he was cornered by a journalist, and initially denied that he was the famous novelist, who he claimed was 'sick'. Relenting under cross-examination he soon admitted that, yes, he was Jerome K. Jerome and confided, 'Young man, I have faced a Scotch audience on a damp night, and now I fear no foe. Anyhow, I will begin my tour at the Empire Theatre with readings on Oct. 17, after which I will keep on traveling and reading until the police or public stop me.' Shortly afterwards Mr Glass appeared and Jerome, as he was bustled away, completed the conspiracy by saying firmly, 'I will not be interviewed. I refuse to be interviewed. I will say Nothing of the Dog.'[706] A subsequent article in the *New York Times* remarks that, 'Jerome K. Jerome shares the misfortune of most men who write humorous matter. He is funnier to read than to hear.' Nonetheless, he had clearly made a good impression on his public, and the journalist assumes that by now everyone is familiar with the standard descriptions of his rosy face, twinkling eye and incipient bald spot.[707]

But within a fortnight Jerome had cabled to his wife to come to his aid, and she seems to have taken charge of him on arrival, teaming him up with the American humourist Charles Battell Loomis in order to reduce the pressure. Over the next six months Jerome made an extensive tour, with, as one journalist put it, 'no other signs of self-protection than a dress suit made in Bond Street and an accent picked up in Paddington'. In Texas and North Dakota they actually assumed he was speaking French. [708] In between lectures he was making arrangements for a production of *Robina in Search of a Husband*, writing to Eleanor Robson Belmont from Colorado Springs in January to establish whether she was interested in playing Kate or Robina. [709]

Throughout this gruelling six months tour Ettie seems to have been both game and supportive – where Jerome himself described the city street cars as 'chariots of execution', she claimed to have found the perpetual jolting 'exceedingly exciting'. While Jerome discoursed with the press she was there to make sure he was on an even keel, and, at the same time, to keep him organised. One amused journalist reported that, 'He was in his shirtsleeves, his evening trousers were in danger of Mrs Jerome's energetic instinct to pack them away, (and he needed them under a banquet table that night).' [710]

The same journalist was fascinated when this same Mrs Jerome insisted that she would be happy to sit down to tea with a 'negro'. Jerome himself qualified this statement by making the putative visitor 'educated', but his apparent hesitation should surely be seen in the context of early twentieth-century class bias, rather than racism. [711] Tellingly, the references to 'a low race' have disappeared altogether since his original discussions in the pages of *TO-DAY*. His comment that if black Americans are less civilised than their white counterparts, they should be given time to 'catch up', is tied to a point about civil and educational disadvantages, rather than any supposed deficiencies of race. He was, he told the journalist, outraged by the stories of lynching he had heard in Tennessee, and had spoken out in protest at the end of his reading in one city.

This well-known incident has rightly been cited as evidence of Jerome's courage in publicly denouncing cruelty, even where it was socially sanctioned and to protest was to court opprobrium. But it is complicated by the existence of at least three versions. In the interview given shortly afterwards Jerome told the *New York Times* that 'several men came up to me afterward and thanked me for my attack on lynch law, but while they were talking I could see they were looking furtively about for fear their own townpeople would overhear them'. The American people, he insisted, should 'Arouse public sentiment so thoroughly against lynching that any man or woman would be ashamed to support it.'[712] In *My Life and Times* in 1926 Jerome gives a dramatic account of the room falling silent and the audience walking out with hostile looks. However, recent research by Frank Rodgers suggests that Jerome may have been exaggerating when he claimed any opposition at all to his speech. While the evils he exposed were clearly real, the *Chattanooga Times* for 9 April reported that the denunciation of lynching had actually been greeted with applause.[713]

While in America, Jerome had also attended a bullfight near El Paso, and said with disgust that, 'It reminded me more of a slaughter house, a butcher's shop, where meat was being handled on business principles. ... The bull seemed quite the most intelligent thing in the ring.'[714] Again it was Ettie who ensured that the interview ended on the right note, covering her husband's slightly rude remark that he had seen so many beautiful American women that he was now rather sick of them, with the intriguing comment that 'the most fascinating thing about the American woman was her camaraderie with her own sex – her ready helpfulness toward another woman'.[715] In April 1906 the Jeromes returned to England, but they were briefly back in America in October 1907 on a promotional trip.

It was in 1907 that Jerome brought out *Sylvia of the Letters*, based on the earlier story of the same name. A version of this plot appears in *The Disagreeable Man*, probably written around this time but never produced.[716] While Ann Kavanagh shows a complete ineptitude for conciliating American journalists, the detail in which the photographer throws sticks onto the fire to create a blaze is instantly evocative of the behaviour of modern estate agents. Quizzed by the journalist, she shows more command of irony than common sense:

Journalist: 'Let me see, I did ask you your views on the Suffrage question? Ah, yes, I see I have got them. Oh, while I think of it, what would you say was the difference between English and American humour. One is so often asked that question?'

Ann: 'The difference between English and American humour? Oh, I should say, roughly, about fourteen days.'[717]

By now Jerome had exchanged his eye glass for a pair of glasses, and he was promoting himself very much as a dramatist rather than a novelist, an impression he would confirm a few years later when he said that 'Playwriting is to my mind the most interesting of literary work, as it is the most difficult'.[718] Asked about his most famous work of comedy, he told the *New York Times* that 'Three Men in a Boat was written because it had to be written. It was a mood, an opportunity of youth, a bit of work that had to be done. I don't suppose I shall ever be able to write anything like it again. You can't repeat that sort of temperamental effusiveness. Doubtless if I had delayed it for three years, and just kept my notes, I couldn't have written it at all. The mood was gone then.' The journalist wistfully noted that, 'He seems to regard the most vivid achievement of his career with the paternal tolerance of youthful indiscretion.'[719] But he still identified with his comic creations sufficiently to lament that no British humourists had been invited to meet Mark Twain on his recent visit to England.[720]

As this journalist noticed, Jerome was somewhat reserved and wary on this visit, expostulating with characteristic humour on a recent attempt to draw him out for a sensational paper:

> If you were all as industrious as a lady yellow journalist who inter-
> viewed me the other day, I should be afraid myself. After talking to
> me for over an hour, she finally began all over again by saying: "Now,
> Mr Jerome, can't we have a real heart-to-heart talk?" Fancy seeing
> one's self in a heart-to-heart talk in a yellow journal.[721]

Escaping hearts-to-heart with lady journalists, on 23 November he returned to England on the *Celtic*.[722]

It had been a successful year. Apart from his American trip, 1907 had also seen the publication of the collection of stories that would inspire one of his most successful plays of the same name, *The Passing of the Third Floor Back*. In her 1924 memoir, Elisabeth Marbury remembered that Jerome came to see her with six ideas for plays and, after her instantly rejecting the first five, '"What is the use of my going on?" said Jerome, "if you haven't cared for the others, you are certainly not going to like this one. Not a manager in the world would consider the story for a minute."'[723] The original plan was to bring the play out with David Warfield as the Stranger. According to Jerome his agent Belasco got cold feet, fortuitously enough, just as Forbes-Robertson had expressed an interest in taking the part himself after seeing some sketches for the characters done by the artist Percy Anderson.[724] In another version of the story it was Jerome who sabotaged the agreement, requesting payment in advance and ultimately failing to complete the script in time for the opening of Belasco's theatre in 1907.[725]

Again, according to Marbury, it was actually Golding Bright who managed to interest Johnston Forbes-Robertson in the play. It was first performed at the St James's, where it enjoyed 186 performances before transferring to Terry's for a run of three months. From here it went to Harrogate, where the audience took it for a farce and failed to see the joke. But in the long run, this story of a Christ-like figure who redeems the inmates of a third rate boarding house by the sheer force of his presence, became one of Jerome's most successful plays. Forbes-Robertson made a famously impressive 'stranger' with Gertrude Kingston playing Stasia the slavey. Enduringly popular, it was revived for Drury Lane in 1913, with Rowena playing Stasia, again in 1917, again in 1924 and twice between 1928 and 1930.[726] In 1922 Jerome was gratified to hear that it had been played to the prisoners in Gloucester Gaol.[727]

In 1908 came a series of essays, *The Angel and the Author – and Others*. Jerome's continuing interest in the position of women is evidenced in several of the articles he included. It is not known whether he attended a political meeting at the Albert Hall in December 1908, when violence broke out and a number of suffragettes were forcibly ejected by the stewards. According to one witness, the stewards acted for the protection of the audience and Lloyd George obtained a hearing from the platform through the exercise of 'tact, humour, and forbearance'.[728] Carl Hentschel was in the audience and a letter published in the same issue of *The Times* attacks Lloyd George for 'shilly-shallying', while expressing horror at the treatment of the women: 'to witness a few burly men hurl themselves on some slight and delicate woman, smother her mouth with their coarse hands, carry her bodily and with violence out of the hall, within a few feet of a Cabinet Minster, who views the scene with equanimity, was regrettable and scandalous.'[729]

The Angel and the Author was followed in 1909 by a new play, *Fanny and the Servant Problem* (the joke is that Fanny has herself been in service and marries well only to find that her new servants are all her relations); and the first novel for five years, *They and I*, a moving from the town to the country comedy in which the family is initially unable to cope with rustic life. In this spring Jerome was busy lecturing in Glasgow, travelling by night for a flying visit before returning to 'so much business' at Gould's Grove.[730] Little wonder that Jerome himself was grateful for the relative peace of life in the country, where, 'You have a blessed sense of being really alone; you look out on the unpeopled green fields; your nearest neighbour is not next door; you neither hear nor see anything of London, and have a soothing feeling that it and the critics are such a long way off that they don't matter.'[731]

Of course the critics were never far off and, unlike other writers of his generation, Jerome was still popular enough to be the object of mild satire. *Diminutive Dramas* (1910) features a spoof called 'The Member for Literature' in which Jerome (J-E K. J-E) vies for a newly-created seat in Parliament against Max Beerbohm (M-X B-B-M), Hall Caine (H-LL C-E) and Kipling (R-D-D K-P-G). Each candidate makes a speech:

> Mr J-E K.J-E (*rises*). Mr Chairman, ladies and gentlemen –
> A VOICE. Does your mother know you're out?
> Mr J-E K.J-E. Yes, but my mother-in-law doesn't. (*Terrific cheers*).
> Gentlemen, I don't think I need say any more. I'm the only man so far who has said to you a single word you've understood. (*Cheers*). So I think I'll let well alone. My politics are Home Rule at Home, and down with Mothers-in-Law. (*Renewed cheering*).[732]

But, just as this extraordinary output was appearing before the public, another disaster struck on the domestic front, in the shape of a house fire. Towards the end of her life, May Walker gave a vivid account of this fire, 'The Jeromes were away and she and her parents woke to the sound of crackling and the cries of animals. Through the window they saw that the farm adjoining the house was ablaze and beneath them, in the yard, the few poor creatures which had escaped were tearing around, alight.'[733] This account sounds fairly accurate, although in fact the Jeromes were not away when the fire broke out in the early hours of Monday 17 May. They had Pett Ridge staying with them for the weekend (Ridge had ironically said only a few months earlier that 'The quiet and calm of the country are, to me, rather disturbing'),[734] and were witness to the devastation left by the fire in a progress of just two hours. The motor house, containing their de Dion car, was totally destroyed, as was the billiard room, with the greater part of the farm buildings and the ricks belonging to the tenant farmer Sidney Roadnight. A cyclist had been despatched to Wallingford with the news, but the town is several miles away and valuable time was therefore lost. To make matters worse, there were only two water pumps, and the fire brigade, finding their steamer to be utterly useless, were reduced to manning a line of fifty buckets instead. Jerome is reported to have remained characteristically good-humoured, although he was heard to remark, 'You come down to the country for peace and quietness, and this is what you have to put up with.' He would have been deeply distressed by the devastation of his neighbour's livestock – while Pett Ridge helped in the rescue attempt, forty-eight pigs and three calves were lost; only six of Ettie's forty pigeons were found alive.[735] The disaster was reported as far away as New Zealand, where the *Evening Post* reported that Jerome and Ridge had taken the family to safety before returning to try and save the livestock.[736]

Cancelling a meeting with Herbert Thring of the Society of Authors, Jerome told him the next day that they were all at sixes and sevens.[737] On 23 September the family moved to Monk's Corner on Marlow Common. Here he would have been a near neighbour of Conrad Dressler of Medmenham Pottery.[738] He later recalled that Dressler and another acquaintance both 'courted bankruptcy, even if they did not achieve it, about which I am not sure, dreaming of the house beautiful. They designed and executed beautiful hand-painted tiles, but at a price. And the British house-builder shrugged his shoulders and preferred the machine-made article a half-a-crown a dozen.'[739] Of course, Jerome knew Marlow well from his boating expeditions, describing it in *Three Men in a Boat* as 'one of the pleasantest river centres I know of'.[740]

By November he was back on fighting form, putting his signature to a letter to *The Times* for the last time, on the question of censorship. He and the other undersigned wanted to know 'why we, alone among British subjects, are to be allowed to exercise our profession only on the impossible condition that we hurt nobody's feelings. We again demand as complete freedom of conscience and speech as our fellow subjects enjoy.'[741]

By her own account, it must have been shortly after this that May Walker was taken by her mother to a small cottage on Marlow Common. Mrs Hammond, by now expecting her second child, is supposed to have said that she intended bringing this one up herself. When Ettie Jerome enrolled May in a private school, Mrs Hammond responded by moving further off, to Bovingdon Green, and sending May to the village school. After the war, Ettie contacted May's mother again to ask if May would like to come back to them as a maid. Mrs Walker later said, 'I just couldn't get on at all. I think that after being made such a fuss of I couldn't knuckle down to being a maid.'[742] Jerome himself was, of course, a socialist by this point, but as an old lady Mrs Walker still remembered the unhappiness that ended this social experiment.

The death of Mark Twain in 1910 brought out the more introspective side of Jerome's own character. In his contribution to a series of 'reminiscences' in *The Bookman* he wrote of their one private meeting, 'In public he always carried – a little warily, so it seemed to me – the burden of the professional humourist, and at such times I thought wistfully of the man of deep feeling and broad sympathies – of the grave, earnest, shrewd, whimsical thinker – I should like to have met and talked with again.'[743]

In 1911 Jerome brought out his own latest play, *The Master of Mrs Chilvers*, with Rowena playing Mrs Peekin.[744] The theme of the play self-consciously captures much of Jerome's own ambivalence about women's emancipation, as the suffragist MP Geoffrey Chilvers assumes that change will come 'not in his time', and has a companionate, but evidently rather passionless marriage, to Annys, a type of the New Woman. Jerome's character note says that 'a generation ago she would have been the ideal woman: the ideal helpmeet. But new ideas are stirring in her blood, a new ideal of womanhood is forcing itself upon her.' That 'a new ideal' conflicts with what Jerome still posits as 'the ideal' reflects perfectly his own confusion about the changing role of women in his time. The action revolves around a fictitious court case in which an Irish lunatic has been accorded voting rights on a technicality, which in turns opens up the way for other 'mentally deficient' types such as women to run in by-elections.[745] Mrs Chilvers accordingly agrees to contest the seat in East Poplar, only to find that she will be standing against her own husband. Initially the couple believe that this political contest will prove their disinterested commitment to the same cause, but almost immediately tension starts to escalate, with Chilvers accusing his wife of failing in her natural duties and effectively abandoning her home. When she wins the seat her husband, who has fallen in love with her just in time to realise that he cannot after all face the prospect of his wife having a political career, threatens to put through a bill retarding women's rights, for purely personal reasons. The crisis is averted only when Mrs Chilvers learns that she is expecting their first child, and decides to stand down.

The closing lines of the play are dispiritingly conventional in every sense – 'I thought you were drifting away from me', Geoffrey explains, 'that strange voices were calling you away from life and motherhood. God has laughed at my fears. ... His chains are the children's hands.' His wife does not disagree. Nonetheless, the conflicting voices of the play have allowed this very question to be complicated, and in a significant debate on the perceived conflict between a woman's career and her maternal instinct, one character suggests that instinct is socially contrived and therefore mutable. While the controlling voice is Geoffrey's as the curtain falls, he can be seen to have fallen into the very trap of individualism over social duty of which the women's party is accused but that his wife has been able to avoid. While Annys ultimately renounces her own political ambition, she tells her husband that when she is 'strong again' she will clamour for the vote through his auspices. As he was to do throughout his twentieth-century writing on this subject, Jerome finally defers the question, evidently thinking that it would not come 'in his time'.

In January 1912 he was travelling in Switzerland, but he appears in *The Times* on 24 February as one of a list of well-known figures, including Pett Ridge and Ellen Terry, at a suffrage meeting in the Albert Hall.[746]

The year 1913 saw the production of *Esther Castways*, focusing on the issue of child labour in New York. Despite the play's popularity with audiences, it was withdrawn after forty-seven performances. Still, as Jerome philosophically put it,[747] 'disappointments of many kinds are the lot of the dramatist.'[748] Apart from his plays, Jerome was still enjoying the active lifestyle he had so often enjoined on readers of his journalism, if not of his fiction, enjoying skating and skiing and, especially, tennis.[749] This comment to a journalist in 1913 is one of the last moments in which he can be seen relaxing in the year before the war.

CHAPTER SEVEN

'all the little devils hold their sides with laughter' 1914 - 1921

'From this time onward, no man of letters who has the least sense of responsibility to his fellows should allow himself a single line that would foster the war-spirit.'

Jerome K. Jerome, 2 March 1918

The year 1914 saw two more plays, *Poor Little Thing* and *The Great Gamble*, the latter of which was abruptly taken off on the outbreak of war for its celebration of German drinking songs.[750] At the end of July, Jerome was writing to his old friend Douglas Sladen, 'Your letter has a good deal moved me. I should take it as a very great honour.'[751] Sladen superscribed the letter, 'This accepts the dedication of "Twenty Years of my Life"', a personal reminiscence containing episodes in Sladen's own life interspersed with anecdotes about his literary friends. Jerome had provided Sladen with an account of his own early writing career and his continued comic despair over the merciless propensities of critics:

> You write your book or play while talking to the morning stars. It seems to you beautiful – wonderful. You thank whatever gods there be for having made you a writer. The book or the play finished, the artist takes his departure, to dream of fresh triumphs. The shopkeeper – possibly a married shopkeeper with a family – comes into the study, finds the manuscript upon the desk. Then follows the selling, bargaining, advertising. It is a pretty hateful business, even with the help of agents. … It appears, and anything from a hundred

to two hundred and fifty experienced and capable journalists rush at it to tear it to pieces. It is marvellous – their unerring instinct. There was one sentence where the grammar was doubtful – you meant to reconsider it, but overlooked it; it appears quoted in every notice; nothing else in the book appears to have attracted the least attention.[752]

The self-deprecating humour, of course, conceals a certain assumption of status – only a very popular author could expect to receive so many reviews, negative or otherwise.

A few days after his letter to Sladen, Jerome – the bad timing seems remarkable for someone with his interest in international politics – was writing to Robert Donald of the *Daily Chronicle* with a proposal for a new twopenny paper.[753] Clearly he had compelling memories of editing *TO-DAY* in the '90s (*The Idler* seems never to have evoked anything like the same regret), and now wanted to recreate something comparable. Donald wrote back with his estimate of costs and suggested a penny paper along the lines of *London Opinion* instead, but Jerome was not to be moved by this allusion to the paper with which his own *TO-DAY* had merged nine years earlier, and for which he had himself written a column over a period of months. *TO-DAY* (itself a twopenny paper) had made its way, he felt sure, 'by its seriousness and its sincerity. It was a political and social organ with views that people wanted to hear. Its opinions on the Drama, on Art, on music, carried weight. The penny weekly public do not care for these things. It also made a strong appeal to the humanitarian public, avoiding fanaticism and exaggeration. This is a vast and growing public seeking a commonsense organ.' Ironically, he would soon be radically revising the opinions that he had so enthusiastically put forward in *TO-DAY*, and with them his idea of what a 'commonsense' journal constituted.

In the 1890s, of course, Jerome had been a staunch Conservative, but now he felt sure he could draw a reading public from among the Young Liberal party, 'undergraduates, the better class of artisan, the young professional man.' Here again he comes close to Dickens's imagined middle-class readership who are intelligent but rather afraid of being bored, explaining that:

My own idea would be not to compete with the penny weekly, where one has to cater chiefly for the office-boy, but to go for a public at present un-catered for: the man who takes life seriously but who does not want dullness. The man to whom the sixpenny weekly is either out of the question or extravagant. To whom a sixpenny magazine is three parts uninteresting and who, where he is interested, does not want to wait a month.[754]

Not surprisingly, this letter seems to have signalled the end of the correspondence. War was declared on 4 August, barely giving Donald time to read it before they would both have been preoccupied with other things entirely.

To anyone acquainted with his earlier journalism, Jerome's initial response was predictable. Within a few weeks he was writing to discuss the question of recruitment, and there is no ambivalence in his rush at the rhetorical guns. His language, consciously or otherwise, actually mimics the surge of a crowd, gaining a forward momentum through variations on repeated active verbs ('we are not fighting', 'we are fighting', 'we have fought', intensified through a series of imperative declarations 'we hate', 'we hate', 'we will leave', 'we will leave'):

I do not think we are at all an unimaginative or lethargic nation. We are a little slow moving at the beginning, but that goes with strength and determination. I do not think that England is in danger nor do I think that is quite the appeal to address to our manhood. No force is going to sweep England from the seas. Any force hurled against us would fall back from our shores as waves from a storm-girt rock. We are not fighting for our own safety – that God's sea and our own hearts has given us already. We are fighting for just an idea. We have fought for it against Pope. We have fought for it against King and Kaiser. We have fought for it amongst ourselves and won it. We have fought for it against Spain. We have fought for it against France. We are fighting for it now against Germany. We are not fighting for our own sake. I deprecate these appeals, "Save yourselves! You next!" They are appeals to fear and self-interest. We are fighting as Christian gentlemen should fight: for righteousness and justice to all people. I regard this not as a war to save ourselves but as a crusade in which we are risking much, making sacrifice in the service of mankind. We are fighting to win freedom for the people of Europe against the greatest enemy that has ever risen against them: the Minotaur of militarism devouring year by year their youth; turning the earth into a shambles.

That, I take it, underlying the homely expressions through which it finds vent, is the spirit that is moving us. We hate the Kaiser and his legions making of Europe a shell. We hate their boasting and their brutality. We hate burning villages, sacked towns, and murdered peasants. We hate the stench of human blood shed to glut the War-god's lust. We hate it that these harmless fisher folk should have their lives shattered out of them upon the seas. We hate it, these sobbing rivulets of women and children and old men pouring through the blackened fields. We will leave our homes – we will leave security behind us – we fill face wounds and death that with God's keep these things shall be put an end to.[755]

At the end of his life he would admit baldly that, at the news of war 'The animal in me rejoiced.'[756] This latent attraction to bloodshed was an aspect of his character that Jerome had already addressed, ironically in relation to the wounding of German students in the Mensur. He had repeatedly claimed that mankind in general contained elements of bestial cruelty that only an evolving civilisation could refine or contain. In his response to the outbreak of war it is the (admittedly misguided) enthusiast that comes to the fore. How far his rolling cadences were informed by a more sinister fascination with war for its own sake, Jerome himself might have found it hard to gauge. But at the time, newspapers were clamouring for just such rhetoric as he had unleashed in this early letter, and as he recalled sadly, 'The appalling nonsense we poured out, during those hysterical first weeks, must have made the angels weep, and all the little devils hold their sides with laughter.'[757] Jerome was hardly alone among his contemporaries in looking forward to war. In August 1914 Coulson Kernahan wrote to *The Times* on the subject of recruitment, suggesting that a recent sermon on the usefulness of office workers was likely to be used as 'an excuse for shirkers' and declaring, 'It is now for the people of this country instantly to make known their will and to call upon the Government, calmly and soberly, but promptly, to introduce some wise and fair system of compulsion.'[758] In a haunting evocation of the late-Victorian age, his letter is addressed from the Savage Club.

Later generations tend to imagine the horror of this World War I as lying precisely in its disruption of a peaceful tradition inherited from the Victorians. Jerome himself was well aware that it would not be a war to end war, 'I had heard that talk in my babyhood: since when I had lived through one of the bloodiest half centuries in history.'[759] By May 1915 he was warning his readers that 'The war is going to last quite a long time.'[760] In the first months of the war the renewal of military force was precisely what would have appealed to him, and he was sufficiently stirred by the excitement around him to want an active part in the war. He had spent the mid-1890s declaring in weekly editorials from the Strand that war was the only remedy for an effete nation. Now 'Men all around me were throwing up their jobs, sacrificing their careers. I felt ashamed of myself, sitting in safety at my desk, writing articles encouraging them, at so much a thousand words.'[761]

The Three Patriots makes some attempt to pre-empt hatred of the German people themselves. In the play Jerome splits a few hairs over the precise nationality of the second hero, who declares just before war starts that he is not a German. Nonetheless, he ends up being bayoneted by his English friend, who instantly recognises him and carries him to the field hospital, where he is nursed by the English woman who loves him. It seems to have had one matinee performance only in London, with Rowena taking the part of Lady Smith, but the *Stage Year Book* for 1916 lists Rowena among the cast at an unspecified number of performances in this year.[762]

Rowena kept up her dramatic career at least intermittently during the war, playing Pauline in Frederick Fenn's *A Scrap of Paper*, which had forty performances at the Criterion[763] and Dolly Tukes in Michael Orme's *Those Who Sit in Judgement*, at the St James's.[764]

At fifty-five Jerome was clearly too old to enlist but, as a journalist himself, he was a credible commentator on what happened in the ensuing months. In *My Life and Times*, he confirms that initially there was no hostility between the English and German people themselves, and 'Jokes and courtesies were exchanged between the front trenches. Our civilians, caught by the war in Germany, were well treated. The good feeling was acknowledged and returned.'[765] As for the relations between French and Germans, as late as 1916 he noted that:

During the two hours, every afternoon, when the little tramway was kept busy hauling up food, both French and German batteries fell silent. When the last barrel of flour, the last sack of potatoes, had been rolled in safety down the steps of the field kitchen the firing would break out again. When a German mine exploded, the Frenchmen who ought to have been killed were invariably a quarter of a mile away sawing wood. One takes it that the German peasant lads possessed like gifts of intuition, telling them when it would be good for their health's sake to take walking exercise.

A pity the common soldiers could not have been left to make the peace. There would have been no need for Leagues of Nations.[766]

But English propaganda did not work along these lines, and as 1914 went on, 'It became necessary to stimulate the common people to prolonged effort. What surer drug than Hate?' And so, as he uncompromisingly explains, 'The Atrocity stunt was let loose.'[767] From the start, Jerome protested against such sensationalising tactics:

> Half of these stories of atrocities I do not believe. I remember when I was living in Germany at the time of the Boer War the German papers were full of accounts of Tommy Atkins's brutality. He spent his leisure time in tossing babies on bayonets. There were photographs of him doing it. Detailed accounts certified by the most creditable witnesses. Such lies are the stock in trade of every tenth-rate journalist, who, careful not to expose himself to danger, slinks about the byways collecting hearsay.[768]

For a start, as he pointed out in a letter to *The Express*, it was inconceivable that a marching army would slow themselves down by using women and children as a human shield.[769]

To prove the point, he related the anecdote (perhaps as apocryphal as the stories of German atrocities in Belgium) of two Boy Scouts starting a panic after they had supposedly caught a spy trying to pour poison into a reservoir. It was the police sergeant's daughter who finally translated the French word 'poisson' (fish). Jerome himself came under fire 'for not believing that the entire German nation – among which I mixed for 4 years – is composed of Jack the Rippers' and he remained in touch with German friends who were likewise abused 'for being unable to hate England every morning'.[770] It was the hysterical attacks on the German nation that Jerome claimed first undermined his faith in the war (Hentschel was mistakenly said to be a German and his business suffered in consequence). He was sufficiently trusted to be sent as an ambassador to America assisting with English propaganda. But on the way out he met an American deputation from Belgium, who denied the stories of atrocity being circulated in the English media. The visit was not altogether a success. Jerome claimed afterwards that everywhere he went he met with accusations of English 'cowardice'. At a dinner at the New York

Canadian Club, 'I told them, when my turn to speak came, of the long queues I had seen waiting outside the recruiting offices, unable to get near the doors; of the hundreds of thousands I had left drilling in every open space in every city in Great Britain; of the closed factories; of the villages where no able-bodied man under forty is to be found.'[771] As far as he could see, 'While our chivalrous, kindly, cheery lads in khaki are pouring out their blood for England's honour, certain English journalists, behind their backs, are doing their dirty best to cover England's name with mud. Forgive my language: I feel hot about it.'[772] Nor had his interview with President Wilson gone well. As Jerome reported, 'His interest in English literature and the drama was quite uncanny. Again and again he persisted in returning to it.'[773]

Back in England, Jerome continued to call for British unity. It is in this context that he supported press censorship; arguing that bad news would only damage morale, he was infuriated by the aspersions cast on the courage of the young men in an effort to boost recruitment, and he had nothing but respect for the soldiers he met. He wrote after the retreat from the Marne in 1915, 'I have talked with men who have been through it. ... With nothing to help them but just that willingness to die that lifts a man out of himself, they fought it through. That is the soldier's job. The men who have put behind them their business and their pleasure to go into the trenches can do without encouragement and bucking up. Can, if need be, do without hope.'[774]

In the interests of national unity, he further insisted that party differences must be buried until the war was over. Completely reversing his position of twenty years earlier, he now opposed conscription, on the grounds that it 'would place the entire body of workers under the command of a small leisured class consisting of the landed aristocracy and the inheritors of wealth assisted by a guard of professional soldiers'.[775] However, he must have felt the irony of his position as he found himself calling for prohibition – hastily adding that at any other time he would be on the other side of this debate.

Inevitably this stance led to disagreements with some of his friends. As he wrote to Shaw, 'I dont [sic] agree with your views on this matter & I have said so in print. But I know you are labouring for humanity & justice according to the intuitions that our Commander has given to you & as Stevenson put it.[sic] there is no help but from every man's sincerity.'[776] Certainly there are passages in these early articles that one does not need to be an angel to weep over:

Just for love of a dear land, for hope of a far-off dream, they have come to offer their young lives. There is no hate in their young faces. There has come to them something that lifts them up above all thoughts that are mean and passing. They are the faces of the young men who love, of the young men who hope.[777]

Worse still, 'It was English voluntary adventures that won our colonies and established our Indian Empire.'[778] But while this type of rhetoric has not aged well, it is worth noting that Jerome also urged practical measures at home. He was horrified by stories of war-profiteering and nothing infuriated him more than the idea of 'old men' advising and criticising the soldiers from the safety of their own homes. In June 1916 he would comment grimly, 'One gathers that a not insignificant number of patriotic elderly gentlemen would like this war established as a permanent institution.'[779] Now a democrat himself, he argued that democracy needed to organise itself for the good of the country:

If it is to be an organisation that includes the whole country, that demands sacrifice from employers and dividend-seekers, from coal merchants and millers and beef trusts, as well as from the workers, then the workers will respond. We want ... two armies to finish this war: the army in the field and the army at home.[780]

But Jerome was, even at this stage, fair-minded enough to stick up for conscientious objectors, observing sarcastically that, 'More than one bishop has taken the trouble to explain to us the Sermon on the Mount; and we now know that any words that may have been let fall on that occasion, seeming to suggest that honest fighting might be incompatible with Christianity, must be taken in conjunction with other words and phrases, proving clearly that Christ, had he lived today, would have made a very excellent recruiting sergeant.'[781]

Like so many others at the time Jerome had to negotiate the tension between a personal sense of loss and the wider implications of mass warfare. In the early months of the war Marlow had sent four hundred out of a population of 4-5 thousand to the front.[782] When Harold Chapin died in 1915 it was initially Rowena who wrote to condole with his widow on behalf of herself, her parents and sister.[783] Later Jerome wrote himself, telling her that, 'Of all the younger men I knew I felt most in touch with him. This is the greatest loss the war as yet has brought me so I can understand your sorrow[.]

God be with you.'[784] Publicly, Jerome held up Chapin as an example of lost promise, taking him with Rupert Brooke as the type of a lost generation:

> I think of young Rupert Brooke, his sweet song ended with a splash of blood. Of young Harold Chapin, brimming over with life and hope, when I last saw him. He told me of his schemes, the new theatre he intended to found. Everyone connected with it was to be young, perhaps not in years, but always in enthusiasm. I believe he could have carried it through. His energy, his faith, was so abounding. Now he lies dead and useless.[785]

The images of an iconic poet and a young man whose aspirations will now be impossible to realise would, of course, resonate with readers whether or not they had sustained a personal loss – the point of this juxtaposition is that a generation of young men will never have the chance of singing the 'sweet song' that Brooke himself was unable to complete. But the emotional resonance is invoked, as the next lines make clear, as ballast for Jerome's fury against the older men whom he sees as so desirous of war. He goes on to detail the supposed use of inexperienced German soldiers as 'rifle bait' and demands:

> Wouldn't old gentlemen do just as well for this job? Boys grow into men. After the war, the world will have need of them. Is it not false economy to kill them all off while every country appears to be so well provided with its hosts of fierce greybeards demanding fights to an eternal finish; insisting upon the annihilation of England, the crushing of Germany?[786]

He was in a better position than many to comment on the possible impact of war on civilians, having seen for himself the devastation wreaked in France. In April 1915 he reported:

> There was something strange about this France. Only ten months since I saw it last, but I did not seem to recognise it. Until, at one of the weedy, wayside stations at which we stopped, it came to me.
>
> France has become a silent land....
>
> And nearer to the fighting line there was this added to it. A sense of people listening.[787]

Perhaps because of his access to the scene of action, and surely because of his own former residence in Germany, Jerome was reasonably temperate in his attitude to 'the enemy'. In response to stories about war crimes in Belgium, the shooting of Nurse Cavell and incidents involving civilian casualties, he wrote in 'God Punish Germany', 'We believe he will. ... May I suggest to some of my journalistic friends, to various elderly gentlemen writing from easy chairs, to a certain number of shrill women who have not yet found work more practically useful, that we would do well to leave it in his hands.'[788] This article is notable not least for its assumption that the war was drawing to a close. 'Hatred during war time may be necessary to a few poor creatures incapable of fighting for love of country. But now that the end of the contest is coming into sight, it will be well to get rid of it.'[789]

In April 1916, at the time of the Somme offensives, he was still claiming that, 'There is a feeling – I was going to say abroad: I should say both in this country and abroad – that the war has spent its energy: that it is moving to a close. In what precise way it will end – whether in a crushing victory for the Allies or the mere forcing of Germany back within her boundaries, which for her would mean a staggering and lasting defeat – one need not at this moment discuss.'[790]

In 1916 he published *Malvina of Brittany*, a whimsical treatment of an airman who falls in love with a suspiciously New-Womanish fairy. Ironically, it was also in 1916, the year conscription was introduced, that Jerome finally achieved his real ambition and got himself accepted for a stint at the front. At his age he would have been expected to join the Home Guard or simply remain at his desk churning out motivational articles. But, as he honestly expressed it a decade later, 'I wanted to see the real thing.'[791] The YMCA apparently approved him as an entertainer, only to be overruled by the War Office, who were sceptical about the motives of writers involving themselves in the life of the trenches.[792]

Finally, he managed to dodge the regulations by signing up as an ambulance driver for the French Red Cross at the beginning of August 1916,[793] work which took him right into the fighting line.[794] His continuing ambivalence about the war at this point is tellingly expressed in two articles published just two months earlier. 'After the Battle' confronts the fear that war is unstoppable, likening it to the relatively new experience of driving a motor car that could do up to 60mph:

For the owner who really wishes to avoid trouble it is the ideal car. The average driver of my acquaintance I would warn against it. I would not have one myself as a gift. For months I would drive that car to the admiration and envy of all the nervous old ladies and gentlemen in the neighbourhood. I would take the children out in it and they would come home with not a hair out of its place. And then one day the old original Adam would steal into my blood, and I should want to "let her out".[795]

In 'The Blessings of War' the familiar imagery of sacrifice as morally purifying the 'best' young men their country has to offer is temporarily suspended; instead Jerome reverts to the tone of much of his *fin-de-siècle* journalism, in which man's innate brutality is only thinly masked by civilisation. In the rather confused argument that follows, war is a disease that enervates the social body, which emerges 'enfeebled, fretful, degenerated'; but it is also a purifying agent, allowing virulent passions to be removed from the system:

War is a disease. The result of insanitary moral conditions: greed, passion, evil thinking, hatred, that collective selfishness that Lord Hugh Cecil denounces ... as "patriotism gone bad." Until these things are cleared out of our nature, until the tiger and the ape is worked out of our system, war is inevitable – may even be a necessary outlet for these poisons, lest, turning inward, they corrupt the whole body politic. From time to time we have to suffer war. We emerge enfeebled, fretful, degenerated.[796]

In this article Jerome is not simply trying to make sense of a national disaster, he is repeating arguments he had deployed years earlier (a point he would later forget). But even as he sets out a pessimistic view of man's moral nature, the anxiety about degeneration vies on the page with an insistence that suffering (rather than actual fighting) could strengthen character. By the end of the page, war itself has become a test of character in precisely the way he had initially denied:

The victory in this war is not going to be in territories and indemnities. It is going to be in Character. War will not purify us. The war, if we listen to the evil counsels round about us, to our own evil passions, will degrade us. But bearing our sores and tribulations with patience and courage we may purify ourselves – of our sloth, of our love of ease, of our vain boasting. Steadfast to the end, facing our tribulations with patience and courage, so shall we conquer not only our enemy, but a mightier still – Ourselves. War shall be our test.[797]

Shortly afterwards Jerome sailed from Southampton to Le Havre, from where he was ordered to the village of Bar-le-Duc. He promptly got lost and spent the night in the town of Revigny. In detailing this incident Jerome offers a balance of dark humour and understated horror, more convincing than anything he had yet attained in his fiction, 'Half of it was in ruins. It was crowded with troops, and trains kept coming in discharging thousands more.' In the only hotel 'The *salle à manger* was crammed to suffocation: so the landlady put me a chair in the kitchen. The cockroaches were having a bad time. They fell into the soups and stews, and no one took the trouble to rescue them.'[798]

As an officer Jerome remembers that he was supplied with a wholesome diet of meat and vegetables[799] but he offers a grimly humorous picture of the trenches, 'They say there is no smoke without fire. It is not true. You can have a dug-out so full of smoke that you have to light a match to find the fire.'[800] Like other commentators, he also remembered the prevalence of rats:

One takes off one's boots, and tunic, blows out the candle and turns in. A rat drops from somewhere on to the table, becomes immoveable. By the light of the smouldering logs, we look at one another. One tries to remember whether one really did put everything eatable back into the tin. Even then they work the covers off, somehow – clever little devils.[801]

As an ambulance driver he might still be summoned at any hour of the night, and *My Life and Times* describes at length the experience of driving in the dark along a '*mauvaise route*. ... The route becomes more and more mauvaise.'[802]

But it was not just the horror of these night journeys along bad roads that stayed with him. In almost his last novel, *All Roads Lead to Calvary*, he captures with disturbing brilliance the ambivalent position of a fictional woman who has gone out to nurse the wounded. A young French sergeant she is looking after asks her if she has ever seen a bull fight, and when she answers in the negative he rejoins, caustically:

...you would understand if you had. When one of the horses goes down gored, his entrails lying out upon the sand, you know what they do, don't you? They put a rope round him, and drag him, groaning, into the shambles behind. And once there, kind people like you and Monsieur the Médecin tend him and wash him, and put his entrails back, and sew him up again. He thinks it so kind of them – the first time. But the second! He understands. He will be sent back into the arena to be ripped up again, and again after that. This is the third time I have been wounded, and as soon as you've all patched me up and I've got my breath again, they'll send me back again. Mam'selle will forgive my not feeling grateful to her.[803]

Jerome always insisted that the Germans set an example to the English in their treatment of animals and he notes that one day he stumbled on an animal hospital where one donkey was wearing the Croix de Guerre.[804] He acknowledges that the Germans did indeed drop shells on the hospitals, as they were accused of doing, because the ammunition park and the hospital were either side of the railway head. He comments grimly, 'Those who talk about war being a game ought to be made to go out and play it. They'd find their little book of rules not much use.'[805] It was a freezing winter and, 'At the end of it, I was not much more good for the work. I came back cured of any sneaking regard I may ever have had for war',[806] compared with which, he said grimly in *My Life and Times*, 'a street scavenger's job is an exhilarating occupation, a rat-catcher's work more in keeping with the instincts of a gentleman.'[807] Towards the end of his life he said that '[always] it seemed the sky was ablaze, and death came suddenly and treacherously. There was no glory or romance about such killing. There was only filth and blood; men changed by tens of thousands into carrion.'[808] Shortly after his death Coulson Kernahan commented that, 'but for the strain he put upon a weakened heart in the Christlike task of bringing in the wounded during the War, he might have been alive today'.[809]

Back in England in 1917, Jerome, who would regard himself as an invalid from this time on,[810] joined a peace party including Ramsay MacDonald as well as his old friend Zangwill. Other friends, notably Kernahan and Douglas Sladen, remained committed to the idea of war as a holy cause. In addition to making speeches at Essex Hall, the peace party published *Common Sense*, edited by F. W. Hirst, and Jerome would write numerous articles for this journal over the next few years.

By 1918 he had spectacularly and publicly fallen out with H. G. Wells, Wells attacking Jerome's 'League of Reason' as Jerome protested against his 'God of the Sword', through the letters page of the *Daily News and Leader*. As Wells put it on 11 February, 'My objection to Mr Jerome is that he advocates non-resistance, cessation of warlike effort, and so forth, and calls all this quite unjustifiably Reason'.[811] Following up letters of 1, 3 and 7 February, Jerome insisted that Wells was misrepresenting his position, commenting on 14th that, 'I am sorry to have taken up so much of your space with the education of Mr Wells. His difficulty is that he seems unable to read.'[812] An appended note from the editor reads, 'This correspondence is now closed.'

It is somehow typical of Jerome that he contrived to suffer both ways, first by participating in the war and later by attacking it in the face of public opprobrium. Notably his 1917 play *Cook* is based on a much earlier story about class and shows no interest in the topical question of national difference.

But it would be simplistic to assume that he became a pacifist as the result of what he had seen or that he placed a higher value on human life than he had done before the killing began. While he repeatedly spoke on behalf of the working class, Jerome never fully accepted the doctrine of social equality, and his horror is based, at least in part, on the belief that the men who were prepared to give their lives were the very ones who could least be spared. In his fiction the characters who speak out against the war invariably possess the heroic qualities that fit them for it in the first place, and this moral authority is used to win over a potentially hostile reader.

Some time in 1918 the Jeromes moved from Monk's Corner to a smaller house, Wood End,[813] where they would remain almost until Elsie's death in 1921. By now Jerome, the one time campaigner for all healthy sport, was sufficiently shaken to tell Douglas Sladen that rugby made him nervous.[814] Despite his nerves, he retained enough of the fighting spirit to engage in yet another press battle, this time with Conan Doyle in the pages of *Common Sense* in 1919. Doyle's response to two articles attacking his spiritualist position was in turn sufficiently brusque, 'I note from his remarks that he is sceptical about the facts of the physical phenomena of Spiritualism. But from every word of his article it is evident that he has never examined these alleged facts...'[815]

In 1919 Jerome wrote what would be his last novel, revisiting the Woman Question that had so troubled him over the years, further complicated as it now was by the context of recent war. *All Roads Lead to Calvary* pitches its central protagonist Joan Allwood headfirst into the questions facing women in the work place immediately before and during World War I.

Joan, the beautiful daughter of a wealthy manufacturer, is Jerome's first female protagonist to receive a Cambridge education. His choice of a highly-educated woman for the heroine of the novel might seem to reflect a shift in his conservative view of the Woman Question in line with his adoption of more liberal political principles. In fact, Jerome's politics had always been more radical in focus than his affiliation with the Conservative party in the 1890s would suggest. His treatment of women's emancipation, on the other hand, shows a continued ambivalence that threatens in places to undermine the novel altogether. While Joan's education renders her the perfect match for a radical, but unfortunately married, Member of Parliament, her successful journalistic career leaves her unfulfilled and lonely. Indeed, she ruminates on the fate of single women in her position, living in dreary lodgings with limited opportunities for social enjoyment and forced to earn their own living. 'It was one of the drawbacks of civilisation that so many had to do it of necessity. It developed her on the wrong lines – against her nature.'[816] Joan's attachment to the suffrage movement is presented as a failed attempt to redirect her surplus energy, for which she finally finds an outlet through marriage to a committed social campaigner. In writing of 'middlebrow' novels of this period Rosa Bracco has argued that they:

> depict the period which represented for many the watershed between the reliable past and the confusing present, the tragic break between old and new. They attempt not to camouflage the horror of war but to soften the impact of the break it represented by reasserting links with the past; even when lamenting the disruptive consequences of the war they still imply the possibility of readjusting the various parts and making them whole and functional again.[817]

Jerome's account is actually more complex than this, insofar as the traumatic break of the war is intertwined with the social disruption associated, not least, with turn of the century feminism. Rather than attempt to recapture a vanished past, his narrator stresses the ways in which late-Victorian and Edwardian problems are part of the social disease that finds its fullest representation in war. Characters debate the tendency of workers to wreck their model cottages because they have only ever been used to slums, in an image that implicitly links the slum conditions of the workers with the mud of the trenches.

Jerome actively campaigned for the fulfilment of the government's promise that there would be 'homes for heroes'. By now he had little faith in the government and admitted, 'Of the hundreds and thousands of cottages that our loving Government is about to erect (the moment it has settled the affairs of Russia, Hungary, China, and the Balkans), I am doubtful. At present prices those cottages are going to work out at sixty pounds a year. To be of any use they will have to be let out at fifteen.'[818] He had by now come to see the use of women in public life. By the end of 1919 there were two hundred Working Women's Village Councils, fighting for cottages to be built, while the government apparently dithered over the relative practicality of brick versus slate tiles for the roofs. 'They appear to be unaware that all this has been settled for them by able editors and bright young members of Parliament. … It seems that young men and women are wanting to get married at some date *before* England becomes a land fit for heroes to dwell in. They want four rooms and a roof, *now*.'[819] *All Roads Lead to Calvary* ends with a vision of Joan and her husband metaphorically rebuilding workers' cottages after the war. In this context their crusade is imbued with metaphors of the front line as well as the abortive idealism of George Eliot's *Middlemarch*, as the narrative attempts to reconcile the repeated failures of history with a promised future.

But this ending leaves unresolved the subplot of Joan's mother, a talented actress psychologically destroyed by marriage to a man who forbids her to continue her career. This tragedy, sketched through the haunting motif of the 'drum' taken from her by her husband, persistently inflects Joan's own experience of listening to the drummer in her own head. Paradoxically, the narrator's confused discourse on women's choices stands as a far more suggestive commentary than any specific directive enjoined on the reader in the course of the novel.

But the most powerful passages in the novel are those concerned with the trauma of war. Jerome remained deeply conscious of the part he and other writers had played in creating an enthusiasm for war among their readers. Writing in the *Daily News* January 1918 he denounced the kind of propaganda he had initially been so ready to provide:

> I do not think I am giving to my own profession undue importance by
> expressing the conviction that, since the advent of the printing press,
> the world's lust of warfare has been chiefly fostered by the writers
> of fiction. If that is to continue, we can say good-bye to any dream

of lasting peace. ... I was brought up as a youngster on Erckmann-Chatrian and Alexander [sic] Dumas with tales of the Border feuds and the joyous days of the Round Table; and I can remember how my schoolboy blood leaped with delight when I heard that Prussia had declared war on France; and how I hoped that one day not far removed, my own dear country would call me to battle. On Sunday I did lip-service to peace, but in my heart of hearts I deemed it the prayer of a coward. You cannot play the Devil's music for ever and not expect the young men to dance to the tune.[820]

Equally to blame were the newspapers and visual artists, as he would remember bitterly in 1919, 'Was it not by advertisement that we prolonged the war? Would a million Englishmen have died to achieve Lloyd George's senseless knock-out blow if it had not been for those lurid posters? Germany sang her hymn of hate. We advertised ours on the hoardings. It was more effective.'[821] In *All Roads Lead to Calvary* the most contemptible figures are newspaper editors, and the reader is encouraged to feel threatened by unthinking mobs who respond in animal fashion to the articles they read.

Notably, the most tragic death in the novel is brought about not by German forces, but by an English crowd. Joan's friend and relation Arthur has initially worked as a mine sweeper, in order to avoid his conflicted feelings about killing. Later he explains to her why he can no longer subscribe to the doctrines of war and has become a conscientious objector, despite what he sees as his initial cowardice in conforming to social expectation. Arthur has been troubled by the idea that Christ's 'sword' is suffering rather than killing, and he tells Joan that one night a piece of driftwood in the shape of a cross led to a moment of epiphany, in which he realised that the best form of patriotism is to refuse to fight. It is possible that the character of Arthur was based on a real soldier whose story Jerome had read in the press:

he had gone to the front at the beginning of the war as a stretcher bearer, facing death a dozen times a day: death with honour. He had squared the matter with his conscience, could have continued till the end. Then came the new conscription law, which demands that not only the body of every citizen shall be handed over to the keeping of the State, but his soul also. What does the young fool do? He comes back to declare himself a Conscientious Objector.[822]

Joan's fears, mediated through the narrator, echo Jerome's earlier horrified denunications of American lynch mobs, 'Jeering mobs would follow him through the streets. More than once, of late, she had encountered such crowds made up of shrieking girls and foul-mouthed men, surging round some white-faced youngster while the well-dressed passersby looked on and grinned.'[823] Significantly, it is other soldiers who show sympathy when the mob catches up with Arthur. The narrator prepares the reader for a crowd 'yelping and snarling, curiously suggestive of a pack of hungry wolves' and the soldiers warn Joan not to go on, 'It's some poor devil of a Conchy, I expect. Must have a damned sight more pluck than I should.'[824] The final shock is that Arthur's death is finally caused by a young girl:

> The crowd gave way to them, and they had all but reached him. He was hatless and bespattered, but his tender eyes had neither fear nor anger in them. She reached out her arms and called to him. Another step and she would have been beside him, but at the moment, a slim, laughing girl darted in front of him and slipped her foot between his legs and he went down.[825]

The reader is surely expected to recall Joan's earlier contrast between 'the sleek, purring women who talked childish nonsense about killing every man, woman and child in Germany, but quite meant it' and 'the givers of their blood, the lads who suffered, who had made the sacrifice'. As Jerome had done in the early part of the war, Joan insists that 'war had taught them chivalry, manhood. She heard no revilings or hatred and revenge from those drawn lips. Patience, humour, forgiveness, they had learnt from war.'[826] Bracco notes that:

> Interestingly, Arthur's death links Joan more closely to the soldiers' experience by providing the motivation for her to go and work as a nurse in France; the hatred shown against her friend makes her want to fight for peace and freedom of conscience. The conclusion, to help a war that will end war, is not at all paradoxical in the context of the novel, where the only feelings of gentleness and tolerance of the enemy are to be found at the front...[827]

But this belief in the ennobling effect of war was something that Jerome had himself started to question long before the writing of the novel, and Joan's simplistic response is later undermined through her encounter with the cynical French officer who refuses to thank her for dressing his wounds.

Clearly it was an image of ardent, betrayed youth that remained important to Jerome, but it is surely no coincidence that this reflection is placed in 1916, just at the time when conscription was being introduced and just before the time when he himself had been forced to reassess the meaning of war. What the narrative does sustain is a sense of united feeling between the young men themselves. The narrator stresses that the men called upon to fight are the very ones who show compassion, even at the risk of drawing the anger of the crowd onto themselves. After the attack in the street, the two soldiers who have tried to intervene at Joan's request ask her if the dead Arthur would mind their taking him on a stretcher, if he could know of it. 'She had the feeling that he was being borne by comrades.'[828]

Despite his volte-face, Jerome's response to war remained deeply confused, as it did for many of his contemporaries. In a preface to his 1929 novel *The Middle Parts of Fortune*, Frederic Manning captures something of the uncertainty in his comment that he has presented the conversation of the soldiers on the front line as he remembers it, rather than trying to homogenise their position, 'Their judgements were necessarily partial and prejudiced; but prejudice and partialities provide most of the driving power of life. It is better to allow them to cancel each other, than attempt to strike an average between them. Averages are too colourless, indeed too abstract in every way, to represent concrete experience.'[829] The novel, subtitled 'Somme and Ancre, 1916', is set in the period when Jerome was serving as an ambulance driver and echoes his ambivalence about the qualities of nobility and savagery brought out by the experience of warfare. The narrator comments at one point that, 'It was useless to contrast the first challenging enthusiasm which had swept them into the army, with the long and bitter agony they endured afterwards.'[830] In the gap between enlisting and actually fighting, 'Men had reverted to a more primitive stage in their development, and had become nocturnal beasts of prey, hunting each other in packs: this was the uniformity, quite distinct from the effect of military discipline, which their own nature had imposed on them.'[831]

Following his own stint close to the front line, Jerome had reworked his experience in journalism, fiction and autobiography. But the inconsistencies in this thinking are never really resolved. Notably, *All Roads Lead to Calvary* presents a conscientious objector as a martyr, but only after he has engaged in sustained and dangerous war work, sweeping mines. When Joan's nursing work is attacked as supporting mere butchery, it is a wounded man who is allowed to comment. While he attacks the officials and members of the public who send young men to war, there is no suggestion that he condones those who refuse the order.

A year after the war ended Jerome wrote to Ramsay MacDonald, supporting Barbusse:

> I find that his hope for the future is mine. He says, "What do we seek? This – and it is everything: to multiply ourselves. On the day when we are innumerable – here, elsewhere, everywhere – ...[JKJ's ellipsis] we shall have triumphed." In my last book, "All Roads Lead to Calvary", I write, "The men and women in all lands......still nameless, scattered, unknown to one another,: still powerless as yet against the world's foul law of hate, they should continue to increase and multiply, until one day they should speak with God's voice and should be heard. And a new world shall be created."[832]

Nowhere is the tension in Jerome's philosophy more evident than in this invocation of a holy voice descending from God, but dependent on the Darwinian imperative (all the more urgent in the face of mass destruction) to multiply the race.

Despite this appeal (in the same letter he notes that 'if the internationalists are going to ridicule sentiment out of their propaganda, it can only be because they do not understand the primary laws governing human nature'), Jerome was by no means convinced that human nature was essentially benign, or 'regenerate', to use the term his parents would have employed. In the last line of his chapter on the war in *My Life and Times* he would write, 'The one thing certain is that mankind remains a race of low intelligence and evil instincts.'[833]

He resumed this theme in *Common Sense*, where he wrote in May 1919:

> Many other people beside the German Kaiser richly deserved hanging for their share in this devil's work that is not yet finished. And they do not all belong to one country. ... Europe's dead, done to death by this war, number, we are told, at least ten millions. And thousands are still dying daily. If the killing of one more human being would do anything to lift the curse of hatred that is threatening with dark menace the future of civilisation, one would welcome the doing of it. If any good can come of it, by all means hang the Kaiser. But I shall still hate the vicious faces with their cruel eyes and twitching mouths that I see gathering from every land to gloat upon the spectacle.[834]

This is a picture of the lynch mob as he had described it in late-nineteenth- and early-twentieth-century America. Jerome had lost his faith in war in 1916, and after it was over he decried the view that it 'brings out the best and the worst in a people'. Rather, he insisted, 'What little good it may bring forth is spent upon itself. The evil that it breeds comes home. Lost energy; selfishness and savagery and greed around the hearth, in the workshop, in the street; brutalised, degraded men and women; evil dreams and shattered ideals.'[835]

But if war had intensified his pessimism about the essential animalism of human nature, it had paradoxically raised his hopes for the future in refocusing his attention on the younger generation. While the laughing young girl who causes Arthur's death in *All Roads Lead to Calvary* is a source of horror, the young men in the novel symbolise the chance of regeneration. Writing to an American reader in 1920 Jerome told him:

I was especially glad that you – a young man – cared for "All Roads Lead to Calvary". It is you youngsters that have the future of the world in your hands. If sufficient of you could only get together and come out boldly for fellowship and chivalry all the world over – The Brotherhood of Man, Black, White, and Yellow, Europe, Asia and America – the old earth's sorrow would fade away.[836]

In December 1918 the German wireless had relayed a message from Jerome, Zangwill and Shaw, among others, to the German people. 'In the new era ahead, the modelling of which will be humanity's united task, it is our earnest hope to step forward in peace and friendship with other nations, and thus transform discord into harmony. So will old evils disappear and in time the unity of nations be realised. We send you a message of hope and friendship.'

Now an ally of Shaw, rather than Rider Haggard and Kipling, whom he denounced as 'teaching to the people the Sermon on the Mount – as rewritten and revised by Dora [Defence of the Realm Act]', Jerome himself had renounced all support for empire building and was horrified that still in 1920 the imperial adventure and war could take such hold of the childish imagination:

Our Empire Days have come and gone, the Union Jack has been duly waved, and the fact impressed upon [the schoolboy's] mind that the Englishman's God-appointed duty is to relieve every other country not strong enough to defend itself of the burden of its own possessions, that the sun has no right to set upon any part of the earth that does not belong to Great Britain. Every boy you speak to dreams of one day driving a tank or dropping bombs from an aeroplane. ... While every high-spirited girl dreams of being shot at sight as a Red Cross nurse and having a hideous memorial erected to her memory in Trafalgar Square.[837]

He had not changed his opinion of strikes since the 1890s, writing, 'It is to be regretted that hunger should threaten the land, that business should be brought to a standstill, and the interests and amenities of social life disorganised, because a section of the workers can see no other means of advocating their claims but by making war against the whole community. Who taught them that Force was the only remedy, Selfishness the only creed?'[838]
Nonetheless, the working class were as culpable as anyone:

Who shouted as loud as any for that Knock-Out Blow, that Fight to a Finish that has naturally resulted in the paralysing of industry, the squandering of the nation's wealth, disorganisation, and threatening bankruptcy? It was you, my working-class friends, you must remember, who threw the brickbats and drowned with your threats and yells every man to dared to raise his voice for Reason.[839]

Jerome made a similar point in 1921, giving three reasons why the working class had tended to support war. Firstly, because they suddenly became of value to the ruling class; secondly for the sake of adventure. 'Broken men, crouching under arches, dying in workhouse wards – wheezy old charwomen flitting pale and ghostlike through the dawn, might utter warnings: were they not dumb. Besides, who would heed them. Is not this war going to be different to all other wars.' But the third reason was that war could be played as a game, 'This game of killing – of sticking a bayonet into a fellow human creature's entrails and there twisting it round and round – the common man, together with his betters, likes playing it.'[840]
The last few years of Jerome's own life would involve further disruption, including two further house moves and the death of his stepdaughter Elsie in 1921.

CHAPTER EIGHT

'Behind your teeming streets and roaring factories' 1922-1927

'one of the very few pleasant fatalists I have ever encountered.'
Louis J. McQuilland on Jerome, 1926

A rare account of Jerome (and especially so of Ettie) in these years comes from G. B. Burgin:

He is growing bald, although a love-lock still overhangs his capacious forehead. Jerome has shaved off his moustache, given up taking snuff, and his shrewd eyes have the old kindly twinkle when anything amuses him. But he is rapidly getting a middleaged look, and has a slight tendency to what the old lady called "ong-bong-pong." He went up to a pretty girl who had a cup of coffee in one hand and a sandwich in the other. When she said she could not shake hands he entreated her to go on eating, as it brought her so much nearer to the level of a mere man. We are almost lifelong friends, and I always enjoy going down for a week-end to his charming house on Marlow Common. Marlow Common believes itself to be a Common, but it is in reality a magnificent beech forest, with bits of Common dotted in between the trees. A literary and artistic colony gradually grew up there. One well-known art critic, Alfred Lys Baldry, built himself a "Greek house" between the trees, and experienced great joy in discovering dormice curled up among their roots. His friends forgave him for erecting this somewhat austere residence by insisting on his also constructing a "hard" tennis court where they could play in winter. In order to be quiet, Jerome had a study built over his motor-house, and there, with his favourite books and pictures around him, continues to delight the world. Mrs. Jerome devotes herself to her poultry, and I take this opportunity of reminding her of a certain promise she once made me. I was confiding to her that I wanted to "retire" with a hundred a year certain, a nice little country cottage, and half-a-dozen hens.

"Well," said she, "If you get the cottage and the hundred a year, I'll give you the hens." As there are many predatory gipsies camping on and around the Common, Jerome bought the "biggest dog in England," a Great Dane, with a view to making them let the fowls alone. One day he was coming back from a long walk through the beech trees and discovered the Great Dane amicably sharing the gipsies' dinner.[841]

By now the Jeromes seem to have been living more quietly than they had done before the war. A letter from Phillpotts in 1921 implies that he has not seen them for some time. Inviting Jerome to come and bring Ettie and Rowena, he writes, 'It would be a real pleasure to have some yarns, although you'd probably vote me a d-d, old reactionary now-a-days!'[842]

Writing a letter of condolence on Jerome's death in 1927, J. M. Barrie said that 'my affection for him and my admiration for his work are as fresh and sincere as ever', but noted that he had seen little of him in recent years.[843] At some point he must at least have become reconciled with Wells – a note survives inviting Jerome and Ettie to tea in 1925.[844] Presumably Elsie was still living with her mother and stepfather at the time of her death from kidney disease in November 1921, but there are few surviving letters from Jerome at this time and no known account of his reaction. According to May Walker, who rejoined the family as a maid around this time, 'Mrs Riggs-Miller was very ill then and things were not at all happy.'[845] After her death they moved to Ridge End, Marlow.

In these last few years Jerome was still writing, albeit with the help of an amanuensis. The MS of his 1923 socialist novel *Anthony John* is carefully amended to his dictation. In 1924 Jerome and Ettie moved back to London, to Belsize Park. Jerome was still in demand as a speaker, although his health was now failing. In 1925 he felt well enough to address an audience in Glasgow on literary subjects, which suggests that he had not been shelved as 'Victorian' like some of his contemporaries. Even at this late stage of his career he was still forced to warn his correspondent that he would not be delivering an entirely comic address. Writing a provisional acceptance, he made it clear this was, 'Presuming that you and your friends, will be willing to let me talk, perhaps, on serious subjects, with say some readings from my later books. I am past my humorous days, though I will try not to be dull.'[846] Receiving a favourable response, Jerome duly promised a talk on 'The Author Abroad' for 15 December,[847] to comprise reflections and readings on 'France, Germany, America, Russia and Foreign devils generally'.[848]

Clearly, Jerome's interest in international politics had not declined and he in turn remained of interest to European writers. The poet Ivan Alekseevich Bunin met Jerome while on a visit to London in 1926, describing him in a memoir published three years later as 'a very strong and stocky old man'. Their brief encounter took place at an evening party, and Bunin remembered how:

> He slowly climbed the stairs, slowly went into the room amongst the worshipping public who parted before him, greeting acquaintances, interrogating the room with his eyes. It seemed that he had come only to meet me, as he was led up to me. He gave me his big, thick hand in an old-fashioned and somewhat simple fashion, and with his small, blue eyes, in which sparkled a lively flame, looked me intently in the face.
>
> "Very pleased to meet you, very pleased", he said. "These days I'm like a baby: in the evenings I don't want to go anywhere, and at ten-o'-clock it is already time for bed! But I decided to allow myself a small deviation from the rules and came for a few minutes to see you and to shake your hand..."
>
> ... After a few minutes, he actually left, leaving in me forever the impression of something very durable and very pleasant....[849]

Answering a question about which of his books he liked best, Jerome told a correspondent in 1924 that, 'Personally my affection is chiefly for "Paul Kelver". But for the life of me I could not tell you why. Does one ever know why one loves?'[850]

He spent part of the time in these last few summers near the sea in Dunwich, Suffolk. To the end he retained his acerbic sense of humour, writing to one correspondent:

Just got your telegram, for which by the bye I have had to pay 3/3 which, if you are feeling generous you might refund me.

I am really not old enough to decide questions of immortality. Perhaps you & I & Kipling may meet on some other planet after this world has been wound up. Then, it seems to be, will be the time to decide.[851]

It was here that he wrote the memoir that would become *My Life and Times*, in which '…half clown, half preacher, he comments on his sixty-odd years of experiences'.[852] That Jerome should choose to write his autobiography is, on the face of it, surprising. He was, after all, known for his reticence in all things pertaining to his private life. He and Philip Marston had agreed as young men that no one would dare to write a truthful account of their own life, a conversation that he teasingly includes in his text. Nor did he believe in the kind of authorised biography that Victorian readers had expected when he was a young man. As he had once said, 'Of what value is a man's life to the world if the truth is never to be spoken?'[853]

How far Jerome meant to tell 'the truth' in *My Life and Times* is a difficult question. The chapter headings, 'I become a poor scholar', 'Record of a discontented youth' are overtly literary in their invocation of such fictional autobiographies as *David Copperfield* and his own *Paul Kelver*; certainly there are places where he tells what, in a biography, would be termed outright lies, such as his claim to be descended from Clapa the Dane.[854] There are several points where he attributes his current opinions to his younger self, as when he comments somewhat wearily that, 'Henley, and even dear Stevenson, used to warble about how fine a thing a blood-bath would be for freshening up civilisation.'[855] There is no acknowledgement at all that this was also his own view in the 1890s.

Even the supposedly unimpeachable evidence of his mother's diary is occasionally embellished when it serves his purpose. The narrative voice controls this source in various ways, most obviously through direct comment:

On 13 November, my mother tells Eliza that she can no longer afford to keep her. 'She wept and was sorry to leave' [the original entry reads 'Said couldn't keep Eliza']

'2 December. Jerome had his watch stolen. An elegant gold lever with his crest engraved that I gave him on our wedding day. Oh, how mysterious are God's dealings with us!' [original entry reads 'Jerome's watch stolen'.]

On 4 December the sun seems to have peeped out. ... but early the following year it is dark again.

'12 January. A very severe frost this week. Skating by torchlight in Victoria Park. Coals have risen to eight shillings a ton. It is a fearful prospect. I have asked the Lord to remove it.

18 January. Today *suddenly*, to the surprise of all, a thaw began. The skating by torchlight all knocked on the head. Coals have gone down again just as we were at the last. "How much better are ye than many sparrows."'[856]

Jerome's attitude to his mother's very sparse diary accounts is notably cavalier, as he edits, or at times rewrites them completely for greater effect (the entry where Marguerite asks the Lord to remove the trouble of cold and increased coal prices actually reads more prosaically 'No gas' and the miracle of the thaw a few days later was originally, 'The snow thawed and brought the walls dripping all over our bed').[857] While such rewritings suggest a kindly laugh at his mother's expense, the conflation of several disasters: the departure of the servant Eliza, the theft of Jerome's watch and the subsequent rise in coal prices as the snow and frost set in, make a serious enough point about his parents' poverty at this time. While he seems to have invented his mother's textual obsession with diet, 'I see from my mother's diary that one of her crosses was that for a growing boy I was not getting proper nourishing food',[858] this is probably a sense he retained from remembered conversations and claimed to have learned through reading her diary. Ironically, such a strategy in ostensibly sharing his mother's journal with the world would at least allow him to keep their conversations private. Notably, *My Life and Times* itself does give detailed accounts of what the young Jerome ate at different times, and how much it cost.

At one level this substitution of more textured language for Marguerite's brief notes suggests a very modern preoccupation with 'giving a voice' to the disempowered or 'voiceless' of Victorian London.[859] At a purely personal level, Jerome fleetingly admits to the shock he received on reading of his parents' deprivations and anxieties years after their death, 'It was a revelation to me, reading her diary. It did not come into my hands until some twenty years later. I had always thought of her as rather a happy lady.'[860] Elsewhere in the autobiography there is an emotional honesty to which only the confessions of alienation and loneliness in *Paul Kelver* come anywhere close. Certainly the themes of invisibility and the impossibility of quite knowing the inner life of another person, resonate through *My Life and Times* as through the autobiographical novel.

It is here that Jerome famously admits to his 'brooding, melancholy disposition' and his first attempts at approaching girls. In evidence also is his distrust of the written word and his reluctant determination to confront particular episodes from his past. At one point Jerome interrupts his own presentation of the founding of the Playgoers' Club with the remark that 'All this, however, belongs in another chapter.'[861] While there are two passing references in later chapters, the subject is never properly resumed. By contrast, in detailing the disruption of his friendship with Bernard Partridge, Jerome relays the events not once but twice. Clearly, the subject is a painful one and the initial appeal to Partridge in the consciously digressive, 'this again belongs elsewhere, and I content myself, here, with saying that he was right and I was wrong'[862] paradoxically operates at two levels and to opposite effect: firstly, it allows Jerome to apologise unreservedly and without revisiting the controversy; secondly it encourages Partridge himself to revisit the subject of their falling out in the later pages, where it needs to be set out for the comprehension of the reader. Of course, in making this public apology, Jerome both offers the best recompense in his power and avoids the possible rejection attending a more private confession of his own fault.

The urgency of such attempts at reconciliation is underscored by one of the oddest passages in the book, in which Jerome described Marie Corelli as someone with whom it was difficult to remain friends. Having commented on her opinionated behaviour, he adds, apparently almost as an afterthought, 'I always admired her pluck and sincerity. She died while I was writing this chapter.'[863] Ironically, the death of a much closer friend went unrecorded, presumably because the book had already been, or was about to be, published. On 1 August 1926 Israel Zangwill died of pneumonia brought on by overwork.[864]

In an interview with Louis McQuilland in September of this year, Jerome's appearance reminded him of 'a good kind of eighteenth century bishop'. He confided that he hated jazz and enjoyed life better when it was not lived 'at whirlwind speed'[865] (a complaint that surfaces it seems in every generation). His views on humanity had not substantially changed, and he told McQuilland that he was 'a pessimist about the world … but an optimist about the individual. It is the individual who counts always. An oak tree drops its acorns. Most of them become food for pigs; one of them becomes an oak.'[866]

In January 1927 the Old Playgoers' Club hosted a dinner to honour Jerome. The menu cards carried a picture of him with George Wingrave and Carl Hentschel, and *The Times* reported happily '"Three Men in a Boat." Originals Present at Dinner to Mr Jerome.' Ensuring that the evening did not get too stuck on this famous theme, Johnston Forbes-Robertson proposed a toast in which he praised *The Passing of the Third Floor Back*, and Jerome himself responded with an account of his early life, including his venture onto the stage at seventeen (if his audience noticed the poetic licence they were doubtless too good humoured to pick him up on it). Gracefully sliding a moral into the humour which had first made him famous, Jerome commented that, 'His successes as a dramatist he had never had any difficulty in explaining himself (laughter), but his failures always puzzled him till one day there came to him the explanation, which was "Life is a gamble." Successes and disappointments were all part of the game.'[867]

But by now he knew he was seriously unwell, writing in response to an evening invitation a fortnight later, 'Thanks for your kind invitation for Wednesday evening. I shall try to come, though I am really somewhat of an invalid in spite of my not looking it, & I may have to economise my strength for Thursday.'[868] The event for which he needed to conserve his strength was nothing less than his first official visit to Walsall since his move to London with his mother and sisters in 1862. On 17 February 1927 he was awarded the Freedom of the Borough of Walsall at a ceremony presided over by large numbers of townspeople. For this important public event Jerome was escorted by none other than W. W. Jacobs, whose wife had been, by her own admission, in love with him.

Jerome himself responded with an unusual display of emotion, reading a carefully prepared speech on his own attachment to the place of his birth and his hopes for its future. He began by remarking that most of his literary friends had been given titles, but he alone had received his title from the people. Anticipating by nearly fifty years the famous 'Queen of Hearts' speech by Princess Diana, he said that 'This Freedom of the City … it is the People's knighthood. I take it you have conferred upon me the knighthood of Walsall, and I shall always be proud of my spurs.' In more humorous vein he went on to tell his audience that, 'I came to Walsall in 1859. Three years later I left it. This seems to call for explanation. The truth is that, soon after my arrival, there was trouble in the coalfields. I do hope all that has now been settled. But for that, the probability is I should have stayed longer.'[869]

In a letter of public thanks, he wrote:

> You gave me the feeling that, behind your formal greetings, there was genuine affection for me - that all these years you had remembered me, & had been looking forward to my coming back. ... I felt I was the guest of all of you: there were no class distinctions: your quiet, undemonstrative men, your placid, smiling women, your grave faced little children, who clamoured to be lifted up so that they might wave their hands to me – you were all of you so evidently pleased to have me among you: you gave me the freedom of your hearts.
>
> There were many things I forgot to say when I was with you. As a child in London, I heard no music, that I can remember. If I had remained with you, I should have come to love it earlier.[870]

It was presumably on this occasion that Jerome got talking to a local admirer, Alfred Moss, and the subject turned to religion. In his biography written soon afterwards, Moss remarked that Jerome had told him 'he had not the stomach of an ostrich, and was unable to digest nails'.[871]

At around this period Jerome answered a letter from another reader, asking for a list of his own favourite authors and books. The response shows an undiminished love of Schreiner's *Story of an African Farm*, as well as of *David Copperfield* and – doubts notwithstanding – the Bible (although the agnostic Ernest Renan's *Life of Jesus* also appears on the list). His list of authors runs: 'Carlyle, Geo Eliot, Dickens, Tennyson, Scott, Chs Kingsley, Stevenson and Daudet'.

In 1927 Jerome brought out his last play, based on one of his many explorations of the double, *The Soul of Nicholas Snyders*. Revolving round the theme of emotional miserliness, it is ultimately an expression of human potential for good as much as for evil. In his speech to the citizens of Walsall Jerome had said that, 'if you ask me what I did during the War, I answer you that I saw it with my own eyes, and hope I shall have passed away before the next begins. But most of the boys and girls I talk to – and a good many of their Fathers and Mothers – seem eager for another, and maybe I will have to hurry up.'[872] In 1940 his old rival Bernard Shaw wrote to Rowena, 'I am glad J.K.J. did not live to see it. Aren't you?'[873] Just months after being granted the freedom of Walsall Jerome died, in the summer of 1927, on the way back from a motoring holiday in Devon with Ettie and Rowena. Coming back via Northampton he had suffered a stroke on the last day of May and was treated unsuccessfully in the local hospital. As the news spread across the world, the international press gave a blow-by-blow account of his apparent progress, but on 14 June they told their readers that it was all over. A day later *The Times* asserted bluffly that he had not 'kept pace with the changes of public taste and remained to the end both in the naïveté of his laughter and his tears a typical humourist of the eighties.'[874] The last word of the London press, in other words, was a veiled assault on *Three Men in a Boat*.

A few months later three men came to stand beside Jerome's grave. They were George Wingrave, Frank Shorland and Alfred Moss.[875]

EPILOGUE

For most of his adult life Jerome was haunted by the figure of Dickens and by his own inability to equal him. There seems to have been a sort of fatality in this as, sure enough, the year of Dickens's bicentenary has seen a flurry of academic conferences, books, press articles and festivals. Three years earlier, Jerome's 150th birthday was barely acknowledged in Walsall, let alone the rest of the country. As Jeremy Nicholas points out, there is no statue to Jerome in the town of his birth, nor has there been a museum since the withdrawal of funding in 2007. In the words of the *Daily Telegraph*, 'the ghost of Jerome K Jerome must still walk its pedestrianised precincts in search of recognition.'[876]

If Jerome never matched the achievements of Dickens (and, let us be honest, few writers have), he achieved more than simply writing one of the most popular comic novels in English fiction. His correspondence with Arrowsmith testifies to the seriousness with which the virtually unknown *Weeds* set out to challenge late-Victorian sexual ideology, and *Paul Kelver* is a superb rendering of the London of Jerome's early years.

Jerome's writing career spanned more than four decades, in the course of which he told many stories about himself, only to admit at last that 'No man will ever write the true story of himself.'[877] One reason for this was his own sense that the truth is quite simply impossible to express. But a wonderful paradox of literary talent is that it so often finds its best expression in registering precisely this failure, 'You judge me, of course, by the stories of mine that you have read – by this sort of thing, perhaps; but that is not just to me. The stories I have *not* told you, that I am going to tell you one day, I would that you judge me by those.'[878]

Attacked for vulgarity in his lifetime, Jerome has been largely ignored by recent critics, who are more drawn to working class anger than the ebullient behaviour of respectable bank clerks out of hours. One recent book on the literary suburban landscape foregrounds his cultural significance as a social iconoclast, usefully comparing him to William Morris and noting perceptively that, 'The critical reception of *Three Men in a Boat* is an interesting case study in cultural snobbery. The class and culture war sparked by its publication is a measure of its radicalism.'[879]

One purpose of this biography is to reassess Jerome's position in the literary culture of the *fin de siècle*, by going beyond *Three Men in a Boat* and uncovering the work that remains out of print, with its satire, its religious questioning and, yes, inevitably, its irrepressible humour. If Jerome is famous for his rendering of his own disasters in comic terms, to judge him by this alone is surely, as he says, unjust to him.

REFERENCES

Preface

1. Ruth Faurot, *Jerome K. Jerome* (New York: Twayne 1974), pp.42-3.

2. Jerome K. Jerome, 'TO-DAY', TO-DAY, 27 October 1893, p.371.

3. Based on notes made by Hall Caine for a speech to the Vagabonds Club, cited in G. B. Burgin, *More Memoirs (and some travels)* (London: Hutchinson 1922), p.97.

4. Faurot, unpaginated preface.

5. Faurot, p.45.

6. Martin Green, ed, *The Other Jerome* (Stroud: the History Press, 2009).

7. *The Other Jerome*, p.7.

8. Jerome K. Jerome, 'On the exceptional merit attaching to the things we meant to do', *The Second Idle Thoughts of an Idle Fellow* (London: Hurst & Blackett, 1898), pp.53-90, p.73.

9. Barry Pain, 'Idlers' Club, Are Interviewers a Blessing or a Curse? by the interviewed', *The Idler* (February – July 1895) pp. 491-494, pp. 493-4.

10. Jerome K. Jerome, 'The Playing of Marches at the Funerals of Marionettes', *The Second Idle Thoughts of an Idle Fellow* (London: Hurst & Blackett, 1898), pp.335-60, p.358.

11. A. Zverev, 'Ulybka Dzheroma' (Jerome's Smile), excerpt from 'Dzherom K. Dzherom. Troe v lodke, ne schitaia sobaki. Troe na chetyrekh kolesakh', (Moscow: 1995). www.jeromekjerome.ru/ulybka_dzheroma.shtml (accessed 25/07/2011).

12. Jerome K. Jerome, cutting from *Westminster Gazette*, 9 Dec 1914, Jerome K. Jerome, Special Collections, Bodleian. Box 8.

13. 'TO-DAY', *TO-DAY*, 7 March 1896, p.147.

Prologue

14. Jerome K. Jerome, 'Charles Dickens. The Fellowship of Love.', *Youth's Companion*, 86:01, 4 January 1912, p.3.

15. 'Charles Dickens. The Fellowship of Love.' The article suggests that Dickens died some time after Jerome saw his portrait in a gallery. By inference the encounter was recent enough for a young boy to recognise the portrait of a man he had met only once, which helps to date the encounter in the early part of 1870 or more probably (the weather was clement enough and the evenings sufficiently drawn out for the two to sit on a bench talking for an extended period) the summer or autumn of 1869.

16. 'Charles Dickens. The Fellowship of Love.'

17. *Paul Kelver* (London: Hutchinson and Co., 1902), p.152.

18. *Paul Kelver*, p.152.

19. *Paul Kelver*, p.155.

20. 'Charles Dickens. The Fellowship of Love.', p.3. The article does not suggest that Dickens had died at this point, which helps to date the encounter in the early part of 1870 or more probably the summer or autumn of 1869.

Chapter 1

21. The census for 1841 gives an estimated birth year of 1808, 1851 and 1861 give 1810. The census for 1851 gives place of birth as Queen's Square, Bath, and the Devon birthplace given in the census of 1841 is most likely due to a confusion with current place of residence.

22. With thanks to Frank Rodgers for generously sharing his years of research on the family.

23. There is a Yorkshire school of the same name, but there are no extant records before 1850. The most likely possibility is that Clapp was educated in Bath, but again there are no records that would confirm this supposition.

24. *My Life and Times* (London: Folio Society, 1992), p.14.

25. No records exist of Clapp's time at Rothwell, possibly because only students who became chapel members are included.

26. The records show that the chapel was founded under Rev Robert Tozer on 4 May 1823, when at least the first sixteen members were admitted. Clapp is listed as the 27th member to be admitted, presumably at this time. See 2194/1, Wiltshire & Swindon History Centre. The salver is mentioned in Jerome K. Jerome's *My Life and Times*, but its current whereabouts is unknown.

27. For further details see the 1841 census. As Mrs Morgan's age is given as 70 this was presumably a wholly platonic relationship.

28. Alan Argent, 'The Tale of an Idle Fellow: Jerome K. Jerome', Congregational History Circle 3:4, 1996, p. 21.

29. Argent, p.21.

30. For this and further details of Clapp's time in Appledore see Peter Christie, 'The Reverend Jerome Clapp in Appledore 1840-1855' in *Idle Thoughts on Jerome K. Jerome: A 150th Anniversary Celebration* (Jerome K. Jerome Society 2009) pp. 11-32.

31. An 1860 entry in his wife's diary notes that this is the first Christmas they have spent apart in twenty years.

32. 'The Conference of Ministers', *Sheffield and Rotherham Independent*, 21 August 1841, p. 5.

33. 'The Arbitration Movement', 'News', *Daily News*, 27 March 1849.

34. For Clapp's organisation of abstinence meetings during his ministry in Walsall, see Christie.

35. Jerome K. Jerome, *My Life and Times* (London: the Folio Society 1992), p.7.

36. In the notice of her marriage in the Births, Deaths, Marriages and Obituaries section of *The Bristol Mercury*, 18 June 1842, Marguerite is described as 'the youngest daughter of the late Mr Thos Jones, Swansea'.

37. Christie, p.14.

38. Mary Jones, death certificate, 24 September 1843, Bideford Union.

39. In 'Advertisements and Notices' on 5 November 1857, *The Era* (taken from Trewman's *Flying Post or Plymouth and Cornish* Advertiser) record Jerome K. Jerome Esq. as the yearly tenant of Windmill Field and East Hill on the Knapp estate.

40. Christie, pp.12-13.

41. 10 September 1853, *Bristol Mercury*.

42. For an account of this incident see Christie, pp.22-23.

43. Christie places the family's departure between July and October 1855; Marguerite Jerome noted in her diary on 23 September 1867 that they had left Appledore twelve years earlier.

44. Argent, p.23.

45. 'Dudley', 'News', *Birmingham Daily Post*, 12 November 1858. Interestingly Clapp was not a total abstainer in later life at least, and his son makes several references to his parents having alcohol in the house.

46. *My Life and Times*, p.8.

47. 'Opening of a new coal field', 'News', *Daily News,*, 8 September 1853.

48. 'Ironmasters' Quarterly Meeting', 'News', *Daily News*, 18 July 1853.

49. 'Staffordshire', 'News', *The Derby Mercury*, 26 December 1855.

50. Louis J. McQuilland, 'Jerome Klapka Jerome', *The Bookman* 70:420 (September 1926), pp.282-4, p.282.

51. Peter Barker, Maurice Davies et al, *The Cannock Chase Coalfield and Its Coal Mines* (Cannock Chase Mining Historical Society, 2006), p. 189.

52. *The Cannock Chase Coalfield and Its Coal Mines*, p.89.

53. In a diary entry of 26 January 1862 Marguerite Jerome alludes to her husband's going to Walsall from Milton's deathbed, presumably to arrange the funeral. By implication the family is no longer living in the town by this point.

54. Marguerite Jerome, MS diary, 15 [December 1861].

55. Marguerite Jerome, MS diary, 27 January 1862.

56. Marguerite Jerome, MS diary, 29 January 1862.

57. Alfred Moss, *Jerome K. Jerome: His Life and Work: From Poverty to the Knighthood of the People*, (London, Selwyn and Blount 1928), p.52

58. Marguerite Jerome, MS diary, 28 February 1862.

59. Marguerite Jerome, MS diary, 24 February 1862.

60. Marguerite Jerome, MS diary, 25 June 1862.

61. Marguerite Jerome, MS diary, 28 September 1862.

62. Jerome K. Jerome, speech on being awarded the Freedom of the Borough of Walsall, 17 February 1927, Jerome K. Jerome collection, Box 9, Bodleian Library, Oxford.

63. *Paul Kelver*, p.24.

64. *Paul Kelver*, p.23.

65. Jerry White, *London in the Nineteenth Century* (London: Vintage, 2008), p.51.

66. 'The Smoke Nuisance Act', *The Lancaster Gazette, and General Advertiser for Lancashire, Westmorland, Yorkshire etc*, 31 August 1861, p.8.

67. 'The London Poor', *The Morning Post*, 12 March 1863, p.5.

68. Jerome K. Jerome, introduction to Dickens, *Our Mutual Friend* (London:1966), p.17.

69. *My Life and Times*, p.11.

70. Marguerite Jerome, MS diary, 16 March 1863.

71. Marguerite Jerome, MS diary, 31 July 1863. In *My Life and Times* JKJ wrongly gives the date as 13 November.

72. Marguerite Jerome, MS diary, 3 November 1863.

73. Marguerite Jerome, MS diary, 15 March 1864.

74. *My Life and Times*, p. 12. It is possible that JKJ is confused here, in that Wood later proposed to Paulina.

75. *My Life and Times*, p. 11.

76. 'Great Eastern Railway', *Daily News*, 8 June 1864.

77. Jerry White, *London in the Nineteenth Century*, p.45.

78. Marguerite Jerome, MS diary, 17 March 1864.

79. Marguerite Jerome, MS diary, 1 January 1866.

80. Jerome K. Jerome, 'Gossip's Corner', *Home Chimes*, 2:9 (October 1886), pp.235-40, p.236.

81. Marguerite Jerome, MS diary, 31 January 1866.

82. Marguerite Jerome, MS diary, 21 July 1866.

83. Jerry White, *London in the Nineteenth Century*, p.54.

84. Michelle Allan, *Cleansing the City: Sanitary Geographies in Victorian London*, pp.8-9.

85. 'Cholera', *The Essex Standard, and General Advertiser for the Eastern Counties*, 17 August 1866.

86. Marguerite Jerome, MS diary, 12 August 1866.

87. 'TO-DAY', *TO-DAY*, 14 December 1895, pp.177-179, p.178.

88. 'Starvation amongst working men in London', *Dundee Courier and Argus*, 24 December 1866.

89. 'The distress in the East of London' *Lloyd's Weekly Newspaper*, 31 March 1867.

90. 'Births and Deaths in London', Daily News, 21 February 1868.

91. Marguerite Jerome, MS diary, 1 January 1868.

92. 'The sick poor of Poplar', *Daily News*, 27 January 1868.

93. Marguerite Jerome, MS diary, 18 July 1868.

94. *My Life and Times*, p.17.

95. *My Life and Times*, p.18.

96. Marguerite Jerome, MS diary, August 1868.

97. *My Life and Times*, p.18.

98. Jerome K. Jerome, speech on being awarded the Freedom of the Borough of Walsall, 17 February 1927, Jerome K. Jerome collection, Box 9, Bodleian Library, Oxford.

99. J.H. Stratton, cited in Moss, p.58.

100. Marguerite Jerome, MS diary, 16 November 1868. JKJ's embellished account appears in *My Life and Times*, p. 19.

101. Louis J. McQuilland, 'Jerome Klapka Jerome', *The Bookman* 70:420 (September 1926), pp.282-3, p.282.

102. Records of Marylebone Philological School, Acc1172, City of Westminster Archives Centre.

103. The records show that he was ranked number 6 in the 2nd form by this date. See Examination papers, City of Westminster Archives Centre, Acc1172/a/(e)2.

104. Paul Kelver, p.75.

105. 'TO-DAY', *TO-DAY*, 11 July 1896, p.306.

106. *My Life and Times*, p.22.

107. Jerome K. Jerome, 'How to be Happy Though Little', in *Idle Ideas in 1905* (London: Hurst and Blackett, 1905), pp.158-172, p.170.

108. Examination papers, City of Westminster Archives Centre, Acc1172/a/(e)2.

109. 'TO-DAY', *TO-DAY*, 10 March 1894, p.146; 'TO-DAY', *TO-DAY*, 19 September 1896, p.210.

110. *My Life and Times*, p.23.

111. *My Life and Times*, p.22.

112. *My Life and Times*, p.21.

113. March 1870. Exact date not given.

114. Marguerite Jerome, MS diary, 10 November 1870.

115. *Paul Kelver*, pp.157-8.

116. Jerome K. Jerome, *My Life and Times*, p.31.

117. Jerome K. Jerome, *My Life and Times*, p.206.

118. *My Life and Times*, pp.206-7.

119. 'Correspondence', *TO-DAY*, 16 October 1898, p.330.

Chapter 2

120. 'TO-DAY', *TO-DAY*, 17 November 1894, p.50.

121. Jerome K. Jerome, 'Thrice I wished my life would stand still', *Idle Thoughts* pp.177 – 179, p.178. First published in *Cassell's Weekly*, 5 February 1927.

122. *My Life and Times*, p.30.

123. David Fink, 'On the Rails and Off', *Idle Thoughts on Jerome K. Jerome*, pp.35-38. For further details of Neele's career Fink cites C. J. L. Elwell, 'A Nobleman's Agent and his Family', *Blackcountryman* 22: 1, Winter 1989. [pages not given].

124. Marguerite Jerome, MS diary, 2 May 1874.

125. Marguerite Jerome, MS diary, 3 June 1874.

126. Marguerite Jerome, MS diary, 21 May 1874. Her death certificate gives the address as 12 Moray Road, West Islington.

127. Marguerite Jerome, MS diary, undated January 1872.

128. *My Life and Times*, p.209.

129. *Paul Kelver*, p.137.

130. *My Life and Times*, p.33.

131. *My Life and Times*, p.33.

132. *Paul Kelver*, p.196.

133. *Paul Kelver*, p.196.

134. *My Life and Times*, p.33. I have not been able to trace any account of this incident in the London papers and it is possible that the incident is fictitious.

135. Jerome K. Jerome to the British Library, 8 November 18:80: MS 48341 F2525, British Library. The MS letter is given as 253 in the bound volume itself. For details of the apocryphal story that Jerome was named after General

Klapka, see Frank Rodgers, 'Answers to Conundrums – and Some New Conundrums' in *Idle Thoughts on Jerome K. Jerome*, pp.98-103, p.102.

136. The reader's slip survives and is held by the British Museum. It is not recorded what the book was.

137. *On the Stage – and Off* (Stroud: Sutton, 1991), p.1.

138. Jerome K. Jerome, speech on being awarded the Freedom of the Borough of Walsall, 17 February 1927, Jerome K. Jerome collection, Box 9, Bodleian Library, Oxford.

139. This first season can be traced with some accuracy through advertisements in *The Era* between 20 April and 5 October. The plays advertised tally exactly with Jerome's account in *My Life and Times*.

140. *My Life and Times*, p.38.

141. 'Police Intelligence', *Morning Post*, 4 April 1850.

142. Advertisements and Notices, *The Era*, 10 November 1878.

143. Beth Palmer, 'Working through the *Era* and the *Stage*', RSVP 43rd Annual Conference, Canterbury Christ Church University, July 2011.

144. *My Life and Times*, p.39. In a speech given at a dinner in his honour in 1927, Jerome remembered one of his sisters as having 'believed he had gone the way of destruction.' See '"Three Men in a Boat." Originals Present at Dinner to Mr Jerome.', *The Times*, 31 January, p.9.

145. Louis J. McQuilland, 'Jerome Klapka Jerome', p.284.

146. In *My Life and Times* Jerome records that his new company opened at Torquay on Boxing Day with a pantomime, a two-act drama and a farce. He had already identified the pantomime as *Whittington and his Cat* in *On the Stage – and Off* (see p.85).Our Girls were advertising for a cat to play in Dick Whittington at the Lyceum Theatre, Torquay with rehearsals starting on 14 December. See 'Advertisements and Notices', *The Era*, 1 December 1878.

147. *My Life and Times*, p.39.

148. 'Advertisements and Notices', *The Era*, 9 February 1879 details both Harold Crichton's appearance with Auguste Creamer's company and Haldane Crichton's availability. Understandably newspapers did misprint Harold for Haldane on at least one occasion. However Jerome states in *My Life and* Times that he was appearing in the eastern counties around this time. Given that Creamer's company remained in King's Lynn until 12 April and then toured

the surrounding towns until at least June, it is also highly unlikely that Haldane would be appearing in King's Lynn and inviting offers to his London address as early as February. There is no evidence for Jerome's further claim that Crichton had adopted Jerome as a stage name (*On the Stage – and Off* p.23).

149. With thanks to the Stockport / Yarmouth archives.

150. Josephine Harrop, *Victorian Portable Theatres* (London: Society for Theatre Research, 1989), p.23.

151. *On the Stage and Off*, p.135.

152. See *On the Stage and Off*, p.138 for the claim that 'I left London exactly twelve months from the day on which I had started to fulfil my first provincial engagement.'

153. *On the Stage and Off*, p.142. In *My Life and Times* p.39 Jerome claims to have been on the stage for a period of 3 years. In fact the internal evidence of *My Life and Times* and *On the Stage and Off* alone shows that it was closer to 2.

154. *My Life and Times*, p. 40.

155. *My Life and Times*, p.63.

156. *Penny Illustrated Paper and Illustrated Times*, 12 May 1883, p.298.

157. Alfred Moss, *Jerome K. Jerome: His Life and Work: From Poverty to the Knighthood of the People*, (London, Selwyn and Blount 1928), p.74.

158. *Journal of Sacred Literature and Biblical Record*, vol V. (new series), 1864, no. X, p.356.

159. Jerome K. Jerome, 'Gossip's Corner', Home Chimes, 1:4 (May 1886), pp.315-20, p.320.

160. Coulson Kernahan, *Celebrities: Little Stories About Famous Folk* (London, Hutchinson 1923), p.245.

161. Jerome K. Jerome, 'Correspondence', *TO-DAY*, 31 July 1897, p.439.

162. *My Life and Times*, p.41.

163. Emma Liggins, '"Having a Good Time Single?": The Bachelor Girl in 1890s New Woman Fiction' in Adrienne E. Gavin and Carolyn W de la L. Oulton, eds, *Writing Women of the Fin de Siècle: Authors of Change* (Basingstoke: Palgrave Macmillan, 2011), pp.98-110, p.99.

164. Trevor Fisher, *Scandal: The Sexual Politics of Late Victorian Britain* (Stroud: Alan Sutton, 1995), p.14.

165. Deborah Epstein Nord, *Walking the Victorian Streets: Women, Representation, and the City* (Ithaca: Cornell University Press, 1995), p.182.

166. *My Life and Times*, p.35.

167. *My Life and Times*, p.36.

168. Jerome K. Jerome to Eleanor Robson Belmont, 1 January 1906, Spec Ms Coll. Belmont, Columbia University Libraries.

169. 'Curtain-Raisers', News, *The Era*, 14 November 1885.

170. 'A Reader of Plays', News, *The Era*, 5 December 1885.

171. *My Life and Times*, p.47. The story was 'Jack's Wife', *Lamp* 3rd series, 21 (July 1881), pp.6-8. Reprinted in *Idle Thoughts* no. 23, Spring 2000, pp.16-19.

172. *My Life and Times*, pp.47-48.

173. *My Life and Times*, p.48.

174. Introduction to *On the Stage – and Off*, p. ix.

175. G. B. Burgin, *Memoirs of a Clubman* (London: Hutchinson, 1922), p.221. Jerome apparently told Burgin that as a young man he had written 'gushing letters to all sorts of people' but that he liked to keep this reply.

176. Jerome K. Jerome to Clement Scott, 27 June 1882, Harry Ransom Center, University of Texas, uncatalogued.

177. Jerome K. Jerome, speech on being awarded the Freedom of the Borough of Walsall, 17 February 1927, Jerome K. Jerome collection, Box 9, Bodleian Library, Oxford.

178. Jerome K. Jerome to Clement Scott, 29 June 1882, Harry Ransom Center, University of Texas., uncatalogued.

179. Louis J. McQuilland, 'Jerome Klapka Jerome', *The Bookman* 70:420 (September 1926), pp.282-4, p.283.

180. 'Interview with Eden Phillpotts', *TO-DAY*, 17 March 1894, p.184.

181. A letter from 16 February 1886 gives this address. See Jerome K. Jerome to the manager of the Drury Lane Theatre, MS Coll Ray, Rare Book and Manuscript Library, Columbia University.

182. *My Life and Times*, p.56.

183. Obituary, Mr Carl Hentschel, *The Times*, 10 January 1930, p.14b, reprinted in *Idle Thoughts on Jerome K. Jerome*, pp.185-7.

184. Obituary, Mr Carl Hentschel.

185. G. B. Burgin, *More Memoirs (and some travels)* (London: Hutchinson 1922), p.199. Kernahan's preface to Moss's biography states that he was in fact introduced to Jerome by George Wingrave's brother Tom.

186. *My Life and Times*, p.96.

187. Kevin Telfer, *Peter Pan's First XI: The Extraordinary Story of J. M. Barrie's Cricket Team* (London: Sceptre, 2010), pp.34-5.

188. *More Memoirs (and some travels)*, p.200.

189. Playgoers' Club Archive. Playgoers' Club Records (MS 351), Special Collections and University Archives, University of Massachusetts Amherst Libraries.

190. 'Society and the Stage', News, *Manchester Times*, 26 October 1889. For Jerome's succession by J. T. Grein see 'Theatrical and Muscial Intelligence', Arts and Entertainment, Morning Post, 19 October 1891, p.2. Jerome claims in a letter of 1888, the year before he became President, that he had insisted on *The Playgoer* having nothing to do with the club. See Jerome K. Jerome to Clement Scott, 10 November 1888, Harry Ransom Center, University of Texas, uncatalogued.

191. 'Gleanings', News, *Birmingham Daily Post*, 13 January 1890.

192. Faurot, p.104.

193. G. B. Shaw to H. G. Wells, 29 September 1904, *Bernard Shaw Collected Letters 1898-1910*, ed Dan H. Lawrence (London: Max Reinhardt, 1972), p.454.

194. Jerome K. Jerome to Clement Scott, 18 February 1891, Harry Ransom Center, University of Texas, uncatalogued.

195. 'Chats with Celebrities. Miss Rose Norreys', *Hearth and Home*, 11 June 1891, p.109.

196. Meri-Jane Rochelson, *A Jew in the Public Arena: The Career of Israel Zangwill* (Detroit: Wayne State University Press, 2008), p.1.

197. Jerome K. Jerome to Clement Scott, 4 November 1888, Harry Ransom Center, University of Texas, uncatalogued.

198. For an account of this disagreement see 'Club Chatter', *TO-DAY*, 7 December 1895, p.147. Further context is provided by a defence of the club offered by Percy Hunt. See 'The Playgoers' Club', News, *The Era*, 9 November 1895.

199. B. W. Findon, *The Playgoers' Club 1884-1905: Its History and Memories* (1905), p.4.

200. *More Memoirs (and some travels)*, p.199.

201. 'The End of the Playgoers', *The Era*, 20 October 1900.

202. 'The End of the Playgoers', *The Era*, 20 October 1900.

203. Findon, pp.44-45.

204. 'Views and Reviews', *Judy*, 14 November 1900, p.543.

205. Findon, p.46.

206. 'The Man About Town', *Judy*, p.494.

207. 'Multiple News Items', *Penny Illustrated Paper and Illustrated Times*, 28 November 1903, p.341.

208. Douglas Sladen, *Twenty Years of My Life* (London: Constable and Company, 1915), p.60.

209. Untitled, Atalanta Constitution, 26 (10 June 1894), p.3.

210. 'Gossips' Corner', *Home Chimes* 2:12 (January 1887), pp.471-76, p.476. 'Idlers Club', *The Idler* vol 7 (February - July 1895), p.419. Her verdict on the Laureateship was that Swinburne was the greatest poet but that a Republican could not 'with grace, wear a crown queen-given.' Her choice therefore fell on Kipling.

211. Jerome K. Jerome, 'Gossip's Corner', *Home Chimes*, 1:4 (May 1886), pp.315-20, p.319.

212. Moss, p.82.

213. *Memoirs of a Clubman*, p.71.

214. *My Life and Times*, p54.

215. See 'Answers to Enquiries', *TO-DAY*, 7 April 1894, p.275.

216. *My Life and Times*, p55.

217. *My Life and Times*, p.55.

218. 'To the Editor of *The Times*', *The Times*, 23 May 1885, p.10. Jerome's response was one of several printed in the same issue. The original letter, entitled 'A Woman's Plea', appeared on 20 May on p.13.

219. 'TO-DAY', *TO-DAY*, 10 May 1897, p.57. Jerome claims that he must have been about 19 when this happened. In fact he was 26.

220. *My Life and Times*, p.211.

221. *My Life and Times*, p.212.

222. 'TO-DAY', *TO-DAY*, 12 October 1895, p.305.

223. 'TO-DAY', *TO-DAY*, 5 September 1896, p.146.

224. *My Life and Times*, p.211.

225. 'Answers to Enquirers', *TO-DAY*, 12 October 1895. Jerome *Sartor Resartus* as one of his favourite books shortly before his death.

226. 'Mat Traps', 'To the Editor of *The Times*', *The Times*, 21 April 1885, p.9.

227. 'Cruelty to Horses', 'Letters to the Editor', *The Times*, 31 December 1885, p.4.

228. 'The Condition of the Strand', 'Letters to the Editor', *The Times*, 22 September 1883.

229. 'Insecurity of London', 'Letters to the Editor', *The Times*, 8 August, 1884, p.5.

230. 'Mat Traps'. 'Tip-cats' is presumably a misspelling of 'carts'.

231. Jerome K. Jerome, 'Gossip's Corner', Home Chimes 5:26 (March 1888) pp.155-60, p.155.

232. *My Life and Times*, p.49.

233. 'Mat Traps'.

234. Review of *On the Stage – and Off*, The Sporting Times, 26 September 1885, p.3.

235. *My Life and Times*, p. 47. Originally serialised as *Reminiscences of a Brief Stage Career. A Chronicle of the London Stage. By a Would-be Actor*, Play 2, no. 67 (25 January 1883), pp. 114-15 to no. 83 (17 May 1883), pp. 242-43.

236. Jerome K. Jerome to Stanley Weiser, quoted in Alfred Moss, *Jerome K. Jerome: His Life and Work: From Poverty to the Knighthood of the People*, (London, Selwyn and Blount 1928), p.182. Moss notes that the accents are in answer to Weiser's query as to pronunciation.

237. 'Our Booking-office', *Punch*, 3 January 1891, p.4.

238. *My Life and Times*, p.48.

239. *My Life and Times*, p.92.

240. *My Life and Times*, p.74.

241. 'Sad Story of a Popular Actress', *North-Eastern Daily Gazette*, 9 September 1895.

242. 'Miss Rose Norreys', *The Era*, 16 December 1899.

243. *My Life and Times*, p.74.

244. 'The London Theatres', *The Era*, 26 June 1886.

245. 'Theatrical Gossip', *The Era*, 3 July 1886.

246. 'The Amateur Nuisance', Letters to the Editor, *The Era*, 4 September 1886.

247. Jerome K. Jerome, Preface, *Idle Thoughts of an Idle Fellow*, (Bristol: Arrowsmith, 1946), p.7.

248. 'On being hard up' in *Idle Thoughts of an Idle Fellow*, pp. 11-19, p. 12.

249. 'On being hard up', p.14.

250. Paulina Shorland, death certificate, 28 September 1886, Edmonton.

251. Especial thanks are due to Frank Rodgers for this information.

252. National Archives, J77/386/1711 C397617

253. Judith Flanders, *The Invention of Murder: how the Victorians revelled in death and detection and created modern crime* (London: Harper, 2011), pp.32-3.

254. Jerome K. Jerome, 'The hero', *Stage-Land: Curious Manners & Customs of its Inhabitants* (London: Chatto & Windus, 1890), p.6.

255. Jerome K. Jerome, 'The comic man', *Stage-Land: Curious Manners & Customs of its Inhabitants* (London: Chatto & Windus, 1890), p.21.

256. Jerome K. Jerome, 'The hero', *Stage-Land: Curious Manners & Customs of its Inhabitants*, p.3.

257. Jerome K. Jerome, 'The Troubles and Joys of Jerome K. Jerome', *Penny Illustrated Paper*, 22 March 1913, p.11.

258. Jerome K. Jerome, 'Are we as interesting as we think we are?', in *Idle Ideas in 1905* (London: Hurst and Blackett, 1905), pp.1-15, p.11.

259. Jerome K. Jerome to Clement Scott, [circa 1891.letterhead is 104 Chelsea Gardens], Harry Ransom Center, University of Texas., uncatalogued.

260. Jerome K. Jerome, 'Gossip's Corner', Home Chimes 4:24 (January 1888), pp.471-6, p.471.

261. 'Gossip's Corner', Home Chimes 4:24 (January 1888), pp.471-6,472.

262. 'Gossip's Corner', Home Chimes 4:24 (January 1888), pp.471-6, p.474.

263. Jerome K. Jerome, 'Should Soldiers be Polite?', in *Idle Ideas in 1905* (London Hurst and Blackett, 1905), pp.105-121, p.112.

264. Jerome K. Jerome to Clement Scott, 17 February 1888, Harry Ransom Center, University of Texas, uncatalogued.

265. Jerome K. Jerome to Clement Scott, 28 May 1888, Harry Ransom Center, University of Texas, uncatalogued.

266. Untitled, *Penny Illustrated Paper and Illustrated Times*, 31 January 1891, p.67.

267. London Metropolitan Archives, Saint Luke, Chelsea, Register of marriages, P74/LUK, Item 236.

268. 'Ought Stories to be true?' in *Idle Ideas in 1905* (London: Hurst and Blackett, 1905), pp.122-140, p.132.

269. Elsie Jerome to unnamed correspondent, undated, private archive.

270. Elsie Jerome, 'How I bring up my parents', *The Idler*, 7 (February - July 1895), pp.293-4.

271. In the correspondence column he wrote on 25 September 1895 that *The Fruits of Philosophy*, a book banned for its advocacy of birth control, dealt with a difficult subject in an accessible and dignified way.

272. Jerome K. Jerome, *Idle Thoughts of an Idle Fellow*, (Bristol: Arrowsmith, 1946), p.121.

273. *My Life and Times*, p.83.

274. Marie Corelli, *The Sorrows of Satan* (Kansas: Valancourt, 2008), p.1.

275. With thanks to Jane Jordan for confirming the Ouida connection.

276. *My Life and Times*, pp.44-5.

277. 'Politics and Society', News, *The Leeds Mercury*, 22 September 1890.

Chapter 3

278. *My Life and Times*, p.75.

279. Jerome K. Jerome, *Three Men in a Boat* (London: Penguin, 1999), preface.

280. Excerpted in Douglas Sladen, *Twenty Years of My Life* (London: Constable and Company, 1915).

281. *My Life and Times*, pp.74-75.

282. See *Publishers' Circular*, 53 (15 February 1890), p.171.

283. *My Life and Times*, p.75.

284. Excerpted in *Twenty Years of My Life*, p.89.

285. *My Life and Times*, p.75.

286. The entire correspondence is reproduced in Joseph Connolly, *Jerome K. Jerome: A Critical Biography*, pp.70-74.

287. Jerome K. Jerome to J. W. Arrowsmith, 24 February 1889: reprinted in Connolly, p.70.

288. With thanks to Peter Merchant, the most recent editor of *Vice Versâ*.

289. Jerome K. Jerome to J. W. Arrowsmith, 19 March 1889: reprinted in Connolly, p.73.

290. R. R. Bolland, *In the Wake of Three Men in a Boat*, (Tunbridge Wells: Oast Books, 1995), p.58.

291. *Three Men in a Boat*, p.131.

292. In the author's youth it appeared unattributed on posters of yawning animals and was a popular decoration in dormitories and cubicles.

293. *Three Men in a Boat*, p.16.

294. *Three Men in a Boat*, p.41.

295. Moss, p.143.

296. *Three Men in a Boat*, p.12.

297. *Three Men in a Boat*, p.145.

298. *Paul Kelver*, pp.97-8.

299. *Paul Kelver*, p.53.

300. *Idle Thoughts*, pp. 72-76. Bollard infers from this that Jerome attended the inquest and that it was from this he first learned of the suicide itself. However it is equally likely that he gained his knowledge from newspaper accounts, having already seen the body as he describes.

301. Mary Cholmondeley to George Bentley, 3 February 1894, L41, Mic.B.53/177, Bentley Archive, British Library.

302. Jerome K. Jerome, *Tea-Table Talk* (London: Hutchinson & Co., 1903), p.37.

303. *The Diary of a Nobody* (London, Penguin 1975), p.199.

304. Jeremy Lewis, Introduction to *Three Men in a Boat*, p.xiii.

305. *Three Men in a Boat*, p.41.

306. Editorial, *TO-DAY*, 15 September 1894, p.178.

307. Olof E. Bosson, *Slang and Cant in Jerome K. Jerome's Works* (Cambridge: Heffer and Sons, 1911) p.5.

308. Bosson, p.41.

309. Faurot, p.179.

310. Faurot, p.178.

311. 'An evening with Jerome K. Jerome', *The Star* (Saint Peter Port), 16 February 1893.

312. 'The Boycotting of Dulness', Oberammergau, 2 April 1892.

313. *My Life and Times*, p.52.

314. 'Mr Sloggington Blowford, Author of Three Monkeys in the Dusthole', *Punch*, 10 (16 October 1897), p.169.

315. Philip Waller, *Writers, Readers, and Reputations: Literary Life in Britain 1870-1918* (Oxford: Oxford University Press, 2008), p.78.

316. Jerome K. Jerome to Clement Scott, 24 January 1890, Harry Ransom Center, University of Texas, uncatalogued.

317. *My Life and Times*, p.59.

318. *My Life and Times*, p.59.

319. Introduction, Programme for the Oberammergau passion play 2010, p.7.

320. Jerome K. Jerome, 'The Oberammergau Passion Play', *Theatre* 16:1, 1890, pp.1-5, p.3.

321. Introduction, Programme for the Oberammergau passion play 2010, p.7.

322. *My Life and Times*, p.80.

323. Jerome K. Jerome, *Diary of a Pilgrimage* (Gloucester: Alan Sutton, 1990), p.49.

324. *Diary of a Pilgrimage*, p.43.

325. Jerome K. Jerome to Thomas Helmore, Spec MS Coll Samuels, JH, Columbia University Libraries.

326. Jerome K. Jerome, 'The Oberammergau Passion Play', *Theatre* 16:1, 1890, pp.1-5, p.4.

327. Jerome K. Jerome, 'The Oberammergau Passion Play', p.4.

328. 'TO-DAY', *TO-DAY*, 11 August 1894, p.18.

329. Jerome K. Jerome, 'The Oberammergau Passion Play', p.5.

330. Jerome K. Jerome, *The Diary of a Pilgrimage* (Gloucester: Alan Sutton, 1990), p.106.

331. *My Life and Times*, pp.80-81.

332. *My Life and Times*, p.81. In fact the duration of the Jeromes' residence in Germany was probably closer to 2 ½ years, from the autumn of 1898 to the spring of 1901.

333. Untitled, The Times, 15 December 1890, p.9.

334. 'Mr Jerome K. Jerome and the Cabman', *Birmingham Daily Post*, 27 June 1891, p8.

335. Intriguingly this was published in *Pot pourri of gifts literary and artistic: Contributed as a Souvenir of the Grand Masonic Bazaar in aid of the annuity fund of Scottish Masonic Benevolence. Edinburgh 1890.*

336. Jerome K. Jerome to unknown correspondent, 15 September [year unknown], sent from Gould's Grove: uncatalogued, Harry Ransom Center, University of Texas.

337. G. B. Burgin, *Memoirs of a Clubman*, p. 220. This is the kind of story at which Jerome likewise excelled – it ought to be true, but sadly *The Diary of a Pilgrimage* contains two references to flies and only one to fleas.

338. *Diary of a Pilgrimage*, p.68.

339. *Diary of a Pilgrimage*, p.69.

340. *Diary of a Pilgrimage*, p.71.

341. *My Life and Times*, p.54.

342. "'Arry Abroad", *Punch*, 16 May 1891, p.239.

343. Elisabeth Marbury, *My Crystal Ball* (London: Hurst and Blackett, 1924), p.134.

344. 'Theatrical Gossip', Arts and Entertainment, *The Era*.

345. 'Terry's Theatre', *The Times*, 10 February 1890, p.7.

346. A. B. Walkley, *Playhouse Impressions* (London: Fisher Unwin, 1892), p.166.

347. *Playhouse Impressions*, p.172.

348. Untitled review, *Penny Illustrated Paper and Illustrated Times*, 31 January 1891, p.67.

349. *Ruth*, Act 1, Add. 53447 F, British Library.

350. *Ruth*, Act 1, Add. 53447 F, British Library.

351. Jerome K. Jerome to Clement Scott, undated, Harry Ransom Center, University of Texas., uncatalogued.

352. Jerome K. Jerome to J. W. Arrowsmith, undated: uncatalogued, Harry Ransom Center, University of Texas.

353. 'Answers to Correspondents', *London Opinion and TO-DAY*, 29 July 1905, p.137.

354. *My Life and Times*, p.114.

355. 'Jerome Klapka Jerome', Louis J. McQuilland, *The Bookman* 70:420 (September 1926), p.282.

356. *My Life and Times*, pp.114-15.

357. G. B. Burgin, *Memoirs of a Clubman*, pp.96-97. Unlike the 'flies' story this is perfectly plausible. As early as 1896 Burgin was saying that 'I can date most of my literary friendships from the time when, with heart in mouth, and

shorthand book up my sleeve, I timidly knocked at the gorgeous doors of my "subjects."' See Idlers' Club, 'Are Interviewers a Blessing or a Curse? by the interviewers', *The Idler*, 8 (August 1895-January 1896), pp.592-4, p.592.

358. G. B. Burgin, *Memoirs of a Clubman*, p.97.

359. Raymond Blathwayt, 'A Talk with Mr Jerome K. Jerome', *Idle Thoughts* 31, The Souvenir Sesqicentenary Edition, pp.31-37, p.31. An advertisement for the forthcoming edition of *Cassell's Family Magazine* dated 1 December 1893 cites this interview as being in the magazine.

360. *Review of Reviews*, February 1892, p.188.

361. *Review of Reviews*, April 1892, p.395.

362. G. B. Burgin, *Memoirs of a Clubman*, p.98.

363. *My Life and Times*, pp.114-15.

364. *Twenty Years of My Life*, p.334.

365. Jerome K. Jerome to Arthur Conan Doyle, 18 June 1892. Private archive.

366. Coulson Kernahan, *Celebrities: Little Stories About Famous Folk* (London, Hutchinson 1923), p.243.

367. Pett Ridge, 'On giving presents', Idlers' Club, *The Idler*, October 1896, vol 10, pp.420-6, p.423.

368. Jerome K. Jerome to J. W. Arrowsmith, 14 April 1893, with Arrowsmith's response: uncatalogued, Harry Ransom Center, University of Texas. It is possible that this break with Chatto predated Jerome's letters in connection with *TO-DAY*.

369. W. W. Jacobs, 'On giving presents', Idlers Club, *The Idler*, October 1896, vol 10, pp.420-6, p.424.

370. See Douglas Sladen, *Twenty Years of My Life* (London: Constable and Company, 1915) p.61.

371. Wearing, 1890-99, p.515.

372. Wearing, 1890-99, p.478.

373. *My Life and Times*, p.103.

374. *The Prude's Progress*, Act 1, p6. ts Special Collections, Templeman Library, University of Kent.

375. *The Prude's Progress*, Act 1, p.13.

376. *The Prude's Progress*, Act 1, p.21.

377. *The Prude's Progress*, Act 1, p.15.

378. 'Mr Stanley', *The Times*, 9 June 1890, p.6.

379. 'The Press Club', *The Times*, 20 April 1891, p.9 D.

380. 'The Retail News Agents and Booksellers', *The Times*, 15 May 1894, p3.

381. 'The Article Club', *The Times*, 6 January 1898, p4 E.

382. 'Mr Hall Caine on Fiction', *The Times*, 20 December 1904, p5 F.

383. Anthony Hope, *Memories and Notes* (London: Hutchinson 1927)

384. Anne Humpherys, 'Putting Women in the Boat in *The Idler* (1892-1898) and *TO-DAY* (1893-1897), *19: Interdisciplinary Studies in the Long Nineteenth Century*, 1 (2005), pp.1-22, p.8, www.19.bbk.ac.uk, accessed 4 January 2011.

385. G. B. Burgin, *Memoirs of a Clubman*, p.251.

386. Anthony Hope, *Memories and Notes*, p.186.

387. Jerome K. Jerome, 'Some Spring Books. Critics v Public', *Common Sense*, 27 May 1920, p.187.

388. G. B. Burgin, *Memoirs of a Clubman*, p.189.

389. In contrast to today's habits, friends and family members would often exchange valentine cards during this period.

390. Jerome K. Jerome, 'Idlers' Club', *The Idler*, 1: 1 (February 1892), pp.113-18.

391. I. Zangwill, 'Idlers' Club', *The Idler*, 1:4 (May 1892) p.481.

392. G. B. Burgin, *Memoirs of a Clubman*, pp.100-101.

393. While it is unclear when they met, Weyman is one of the relatively few friends named in Hope's memoir *Memories and Notes*, and at Stevenson's death he left a letter for Hope, whom he had never met, expressing admiration of *The Prisoner of Zenda*. See *Memories and Notes* p.34.

394. Jerome K. Jerome to J. W. Arrowsmith, undated: uncatalogued, Harry Ransom Center, University of Texas.

395. Jerome K. Jerome to J. W. Arrowsmith, 30 September 1892: uncatalogued, Harry Ransom Center, University of Texas.

396. Jerome K. Jerome to J. W. Arrowsmith, 30 September 1892

397. Jerome K. Jerome to J. W. Arrowsmith, 30 September 1892

398. Jerome K. Jerome to J. W. Arrowsmith, 30 September 1892

399. Jerome K. Jerome to J. W. Arrowsmith, undated: uncatalogued, Harry Ransom Center, University of Texas.

400. See 'Jerome's Rarest Book – *Weeds*' in *Idle Thoughts on Jerome K. Jerome*, pp.51-55, p.52.

401. Jerome K. Jerome, *Weeds* (Bristol, Arrowsmith, 1892), p.39.

402. *Weeds*, p.86.

403. *Weeds*, p.33.

404. *Weeds*, p.76.

405. Jerome K. Jerome to J. W. Arrowsmith, undated: uncatalogued, Harry Ransom Center, University of Texas.

406. Jerome K. Jerome to J. W. Arrowsmith, undated: uncatalogued, Harry Ransom Center, University of Texas.

407. Jerome K. Jerome to J. W. Arrowsmith, undated: uncatalogued, Harry Ransom Center, University of Texas.

408. Jerome K. Jerome, *Novel Notes* (Stroud: Sutton, 1991), p.vi.

409. Anthony Hope, *Memories and Notes*, p.135.

410. Aaron Watson with a chapter by Mark Twain, *The Savage Club: a Medley of History,*

Anecdote, and Reminiscences (London: Unwin, 1907), p.14.

411. *Novel Notes*, p.86.

412. *Novel Notes*, p.87.

413. *Novel Notes*, pp.42-44.

414. Jerome K. Jerome, 'The Woman of the Saeter', *The Idler* 3 (February - July 1893) pp. 579-593, p.592.

415. Jerome K. Jerome, 'Two Extracts from a Diary', *The Idler* 5 (February – July 1894), pp. 558-60, p.559.

416. 'Arise and fly / The reeling Faun, the sensual feast; / Move upward, working out the beast, / And let the ape and tiger die.' CXVIII

417. *Novel Notes*, p.128.

418. Jerome K. Jerome to Clement Scott, [undated but refers to the last of the series being at proof stage], Harry Ransom Center, University of Texas., uncatalogued.

419. *Novel Notes*, p.96.

420. 'TO-DAY', *TO-DAY*, 29 December 1894, p.243.

421. Jerome K. Jerome to Arthur Conan Doyle, quoted in Moss, p. 90.

422. Jerome K. Jerome to Theodore Watts-Dunton, 8 October 1892, Berg Collection, New York Public Library.

423. Jerome K. Jerome to Hall Caine, 3 January 1893, Berg Collection, New York Public Library.

424. G. B. Burgin, 'Some Literary Critics', *The Idler*, 5 (February-July 1894), pp.498-517.

425. Philip Marston, 'Poet and Cobbler', 'Idlers' Club', *The Idler* 4 (August 1893 - January 1894), pp. 416-17, p.416.

426. 'Jeromania', *Glasgow Herald*, 9 April 1892.

427. The care with which this attack is formulated can be demonstrated by a simple test – it is not at all easy, as the reviewer suggests, to come up with alternative examples of this type of double entendre.

428. 'The Academy of New Humour', *Fun*, 31 October 1893, p.184.

429. 'The Idlers' Club', *The Idler*, 4 (August 1893 - January 1894), p.108.

430. Jerome K. Jerome to J. W. Arrowsmith, undated: uncatalogued, Harry Ransom Center, University of Texas.

Jerome does not specify that the new journal is *TO-DAY*, but he writes on *Idler* letter paper, and it is therefore unlikely that he was talking about the original journal as if it had not yet started publication. The letter cited below can be dated with greater accuracy and appears to be part of the same correspondence.

431. Jerome K. Jerome to J. W. Arrowsmith, undated: uncatalogued, Harry Ransom Center, University of Texas. The reference to the publishing business suggests that this letter was probably written in early 1893.

432. Jerome K. Jerome to J. W. Arrowsmith, 31 October 1893, 40145/P/12b, Bristol Record Office.

433. Jerome K. Jerome to Arthur Conan Doyle, undated. Private archive.

434. Raymond Blathwayt, 'A Talk with Mr Jerome K. Jerome', p.31.

435. Douglas Sladen, *Twenty Years of My Life* (London: Constable and Company, 1915), p.58.

436. Douglas Sladen, *My Long Life* (London: Hutchinson, 1939).

437. *Twenty Years of My Life*, pp.82-3.

438. G. B. Burgin, *More Memoirs*, p. 29.

439. 'Mr Zangwill on the New Humour', *TO-DAY*, 10 March 1894, p.152.

440. 'TO-DAY', *TO-DAY*, 3 March 1894, p.113.

441. *Twenty Years of My Life*, p.84.

442. *Twenty Years of My Life*, p.84.

443. Editorial, *TO-DAY*, 23 June 1894, p.209.

444. A letter survives from Jerome to the manager of the Avenue Theatre, 2 November 1893, detailing the plan. Private archive.

445. 'Arts and Entertainment', *Pall Mall Gazette*, 28 October 1893.

446. 'Literary Notes', *Pall Mall Gazette*, 11 November 1893. In fact the journalist was right about the paper – in the bound edition of *TO-DAY* the issues before 16 December onwards are notably discoloured and brittle as compared to the later issues.

447. 'TO-DAY', *TO-DAY*, 18 November 1893, p.18.

448. Jerome K. Jerome to Coulson Kernahan, undated, reprinted in Moss, p.97.

449. *Twenty Years of My Life*, p.83.

450. Jerome K. Jerome, 'Who is the biggest fool in the world?', *The Idler*, April 1896, volume 9, pp.478-82, p.479.

451. Interestingly the original text reads 'honest gentleman'.

452. 'Suggestions re Editorial 'pars', *Idler* letterhead, Harry Ransom Center, Jerome K. Jerome papers, uncatalogued.

453. 'TO-DAY', *TO-DAY*, 30 December 1893, p.17.

454. 'TO-DAY', *TO-DAY*, 2 December 1893, p.18.

455. Spencer Jerome, 'The New Woman, *The Idler*, 7 (February – July 1895), p.291.

456. *The Idler*, 7 (February – July 1895), pp. 198-200, p.199.

457. Miss F. L. Fuller, 'Girton Collge. By an ex-Girtonian', *The Idler*, 5 (February – July 1894), pp. 532-9.

458. 'TO-DAY', *TO-DAY*, 23 December 1893, p.17.

459. 'TO-DAY', *TO-DAY*, 17 November 1894, p.82.

460. Untitled article, New Readerships, *Hearth and Home*, 18 October 1894, p.807. The idea of 'new readerships' promoted in this column reinforces the sense in which the new humour actually created its own readership, to the horror of some critics.

461. Untitled, *Hearth and Home*, 18 October 1894, p.807.

462. 'Bristol Volunteer Diary', *Bristol Mercury and Daily Post*, 13 March 1895.

463. Barry Pain, 'If he had lived TO-DAY. A specimen of the New Criticism', *TO-DAY*, 23 February 1894, p.10.

464. Jerome K. Jerome to Robert McClure, 26 October 1893, MS Collection no. 174, Series 1, Correspondence, F3, Special Collections, University of Delaware Library.

465. Jerome K. Jerome to Robert Donald, [August] 1914, Berg Collection, NYPL.

466. *My Life and Times*, pp.122-3.

467. Wilson, p.38.

468. *My Long Life*, p.131.

469. Again, the advice is typically temperate. A reply of 5 May 1894 advises a 24-year- old bank clerk that all work is interesting if one can put one's heart into it but not otherwise, and that he should try to 'take the thing that is to his hand, and see what can be done with it.' See Correspondence column, p.403.

470. 'TO-DAY', *TO-DAY*, 20 January 1894, p.19.

471. 'TO-DAY', *TO-DAY*, 31 October 1896, p.403.

472. 'TO-DAY', *TO-DAY*, 7 March 1896, p.147. One would like to know the gender of the correspondent.

473. This query is answered in 'TO-DAY' on 17 October 1896, p.339. Jerome's advice is that the man would only be compounding his original fault if he married the woman knowing he would not make her a good husband.

474. Jerome K. Jerome, 'TO-DAY', *TO-DAY*, 5 January 1895, p.275.

475. *My Life and Times*, p.130.

476. 'TO-DAY', *TO-DAY*, 13 June 1895, p.306.

477. 'Authors at Work. The disadvantages of working in London and out of it.', *The Bookman*, November 1908, pp.83-88. Jerome's contribution is on pp.83-84.

478. 'TO-DAY', *TO-DAY*, 9 January 1897, p.328.

479. 'TO-DAY', *TO-DAY*, 20 January 1894, p.18.

480. G. B. Burgin, *Memoirs of a Clubman*, p.73.

481. As Frank Rodgers points out (in an e-mail to the author, 25 July 2008), Jerome somewhat disingenuously failed to mention that he was Shorland's uncle.

482. 'The N.C.U. and its Record', *TO-DAY*, 16 December 1893, p.23. The article is unattributed but almost certainly by Jerome.

483. Ezra, 'Extract from "Electro-Cycling" of July 7th 2075', *Cycling: An Illustrated Weekly*, 3 March 1894, p.108.

484. Jerome K. Jerome, 'Are we as interesting as we think we are?', in *Idle Ideas in 1905* (London: Hurst and Blackett, 1905), pp.1-15, p.9.

485. 'Twenty-Four Hours on the Cycling Track', New Readerships, *Chums*, 14 February 1894, p.399.

486. 'Cycling Notes', 'Sports', *Leeds Mercury*, 6 July 1894.

487. 'Cycling', *The Morning Post*, 28 July 1894, p.3.

488. 'Twenty-Four Hours Cycling Race', *Reynolds's Newspaper*, 29 July 1894.

489. 'TO-DAY', *TO-DAY*, 4 August 1894, p.401.

Chapter 4

490. 'Cyclers of the Day', *Cycling: An Illustrated Weekly*, 23 January 1892, p.7

491. 'A Chat with "TO-DAY"', *Cycling: An Illustrated Weekly*, 20 October 1894, p.215.

492. 'G. W. Moore v Jerome K. Jerome and Another', *The Times*, 7 February 1895, p14 A.

493. 'TO-DAY', *TO-DAY*, 16 February 1895, p.49.

494. 'In the City', *TO-DAY*, 12 May 1894, p.14.

495. 'Birds of a Feather', *TO-DAY*, 19 May 1894, p.46.

496. 'In the City', TO-DAY, 23 June 1894, p.206.

497. 'In the City', 'The Water-Gas Bubble', *TO-DAY*, 7 July 1894, p. 270.

498. 'TO-DAY', *TO-DAY*, 7 July 1894, p.273.

499. 'In the City', *TO-DAY*, 14 July 1894, p.302.

500. 'TO-DAY', *TO-DAY*, 16 December 1893, p.17.

501. Thomas Hardy to Jerome K. Jerome, 26 August 1894, Rare Books and Manuscripts, Yale University Library.

502. Jerome K. Jerome to Hall Caine, 2 May 1895, MS09542, Manx Museum.

503. The first of these protests appeared in the 'TO-DAY' for 6 January 1894, p.18. While he repeatedly spoke out against voyeuristic reporting of 'horrors' in other contexts, Jerome is unflinching in his presentation of torture where there is a point to be made.

504. 'TO-DAY', *TO-DAY*, 30 June 1894, p.242.

505. 'TO-DAY', *TO-DAY*, 16 March 1895, p.210.

506. 'TO-DAY', *TO-DAY*, 21 December 1895, p.211.

507. 'TO-DAY', *TO-DAY*, 27 January 1894, p.18.

508. Jerome K. Jerome to unknown corresopondent, 15 September [year unknown], sent from Gould's Grove: uncatalogued, Harry Ransom Center, University of Texas.

509. 'The Pioneer Club and its President. A chat with Mrs Massingberd', *Hearth and Home*, 2 February 1893, p.339.

510. *My Life and Times*, p.68.

511. Jerome K. Jerome, 'Gossip's Corner', *Home Chimes*, 6:33, October 1888, pp.235-40, p.235.

512. 'TO-DAY', *TO-DAY*, 17 February 1894, p.50.

513. Jerome K. Jerome, *Biarritz*, Act 2, p.71.

514. Answers to Enquirers, *TO-DAY*, 19 September 1996, p.211

515. 'Correspondence', *TO-DAY*, 1 May 1897, p.403.

516. *Twenty Years of My Life*, p.84.

517. 'Interview with Eden Phillpotts', *TO-DAY*, 17 March 1894, p.184.

518. Barry Pain, 'Men I have murdered. William Gorlsford', *TO-DAY*, 10 March 1894, p.152. This is reprinted from the *Granta*.

519. 'Today', *TO-DAY*, 5 October 1895, p.274.

520. Jerome K. Jerome, 'To the Readers of "The Idler"', *The Idler*, 7 (February – July 1895), pp.97-100, p.98.

521. Jerome K. Jerome, 'To the Readers of "The Idler"', *The Idler*, 7 (February – July 1895), pp.97-100, pp.99-100.

522. Anthony Hope, *The Prisoner of Zenda* (Oxford: Oxford World's Classics 2009), p.37.

523. 'TO-DAY', *TO-DAY*, 18 May 1895, p.50.

524. *The Idler*, 7 (February – July 1895), pp. 198-200, p.198.

525. 'Today', *TO-DAY*, 25 November 1893, p.19.

526. 'Today', *TO-DAY*, 16 June 1894, p.178.

527. 'Today', *TO-DAY*, 22 September 1894, p.210.

528. Christine Bayles Kortsch, *Dress Culture in Late Victorian Women's Fiction: Literacy, Textiles, and Activism* (Farnham, Ashgate 2009), p.77.

529. Kortsch, p.79.

530. 'Today', *TO-DAY*, 29 September 1894, p.243.

531. 'TO-DAY', *TO-DAY*, 15 December 1894, p.178.

Chapter 5

532. 'TO-DAY', *TO-DAY*, 9 February 1895, p.19.

533. 'TO-DAY', *TO-DAY*, 18 April, p.369.

534. 'TO-DAY', *TO-DAY*, 12 October 1895, p.306.

535. 'TO-DAY', *TO-DAY*, 4 July 1896, p.275.

536. 'TO-DAY', TO-DAY, 5 October 1896, p.274.

537. 'TO-DAY', TO-DAY , 12 December 1896, p.182.

538. 'TO-DAY', *TO-DAY*, 27 March 1897, p.243.

539. Correspondence, *TO-DAY* 19 June 1897, p.237.

540. 'TO-DAY', *TO-DAY*, 9 March 1895, p.147.

541. 'TO-DAY', *TO-DAY*, 13 June 1895, p.306. The allusion is to Wilde's *Pen, Pencil and Poison* published in 1889.

542. 'TO-DAY', *TO-DAY*, 29 December 1894, p.241.

543. 'TO-DAY', *TO-DAY,* 5 January 1895, p.273

544. 'The new master of art. Mr Aubrey Beardsley', *TO-DAY,* 12 May 1894, pp.28-29.

545. 'TO-DAY', *TO-DAY,* 13 April 1895, p.305.

546. 'TO-DAY', *TO-DAY,* 13 April 1895, p.305.

547. Fisher, *Scandal: The Sexual Politics of Late Victorian Britain*, p.149.

548. See Oulton, Carolyn W. de la L., *Romantic Friendship in Victorian Literature* (Aldershot: Ashgate, 2007).

549. Jerome K. Jerome, 'The Rise of Dick Halward', letter to the editor, *The Times*, 21 October 1895, p.8; 'TO-DAY', *TO-DAY,* p.147.

550. *Novel Notes*, p.229. The speaker is Jephson.

551. 'Music and the Drama', Arts and Entertainment, *Glasgow Herald*, 14 December 1891.

552. 'TO-DAY', *TO-DAY,* 22 My 1897, p.92.

553. Wearing 1890-99, p.637.

554. Jerome K. Jerome, My Life and Times, p.100.

555. 'TO-DAY', *TO-DAY*, 13 April 1895, p.305.

556. Stanley Weyman, *The Red Cockade* (London: T. Nelson & Sons, undated), p.335.

557. 'TO-DAY', *TO-DAY*, 13 April 1895, p.305.

558. 'TO-DAY', *TO-DAY*, 21 April 1894, p.338.

559. 'TO-DAY', *TO-DAY*, 13 April 1895, p.305.

560. 'TO-DAY', *TO-DAY*, 20 April 1895, p.337.

561. 'Correspondence', *TO-DAY*, 7 November 1896, p.19.

562. 'Correspondence', *TO-DAY*, 27 February 1897, p.115.

563. 'TO-DAY', *TO-DAY*, 11 April 1896, p.307.

564. George Bernard Shaw, *Our Theatres in the Nineties* (London: Constable & Co., 3 vols, vol 2, 1948), p.102.

565. *Our Theatres in the Nineties*, p.104.

566. TO-DAY', *TO-DAY*, 27 June 1896, p.242.

567. Jerome K. Jerome to Hall Caine, 2 May 1895, MS09542, Manx Museum.

568. *My Life and Times*, p.89.

569. 'TO-DAY', *TO-DAY*, 3 August 1895, p.402.

570. 'The New Line to London', *Sheffield and Rotherham Independent*, 26 July 1895, p.7.

571. 'Jerome K. Jerome wins a Suit', reproduced in *New York Times*, 9 August 1895, p.9.

572. 'TO-DAY', *TO-DAY*, 12 October 1895, p.305. Jerome notes in this 'TO-DAY' that in a compensation case brought by a dentist and tried by the same judge, a similar verdict was returned under questionable circumstances. He points out that out of a possible forty jurymen, each side has the chance to reject a quota until the final number of twelve is reached, and that the jury in each case is therefore essentially handpicked.

573. 'TO-DAY', *TO-DAY*, 3 August 1895, p.402.

574. 'Mark Twain. Some Personal Recollections and Opinions', *The Bookman* 38:225 (June 1910), pp.116-119, p. 116.

575. *My Life and Times*, p.90.

576. 'TO-DAY', *TO-DAY*, 28 December 1895, p.243.

577. SL8/20/D/01, Oxford History Centre.

578. *My Life and Times*, p.124.

579. 'TO-DAY', *TO-DAY*, 6 June 1896, p.146.

580. For Jerome's account of this incident see 'TO-DAY', *TO-DAY*, 3 October 1896, p.306.

581. Jerome K. Jerome to Clement Shorter, 1 February 1897: Ms9862, Correspondence files of Clement K. Shorter and John Malcolm Bulloch, NLS.

582. 'TO-DAY', *TO-DAY*, 7 March 1896, p.146.

583. Jerome K. Jerome to J. W. Arrowsmith, [1897], 40145/P/15, Bristol Record Office.

584. Jerome K. Jerome to J. W. Arrowsmith, 7 March 1897: uncatalogued, Harry Ransom Center, University of Texas.

585. Jerome K. Jerome to J. W. Arrowsmith, undated (from Albert Gate): uncatalogued, Harry Ransom Center, University of Texas.

586. Jerome K. Jerome to J. W. Arrowsmith, undated (sent from Park Gate, Albert Mansions): uncatalogued, Harry Ransom Center, University of Texas.

587. Jerome K. Jerome to J. W. Arrowsmith, undated (sent from Park Gate, Albert Mansions): uncatalogued, Harry Ransom Center, University of Texas.

588. 'TO-DAY', *TO-DAY*, 15 May 1897, p.56. Jerome offers the suppositious case of a burglar claiming that he thought he was robbing his own house and therefore getting off, as a comparable scenario.

589. Cited in 'TO-DAY', *TO-DAY*, 15 May 1897, p.56.

590. 'TO-DAY', *TO-DAY*, 15 May 1897, p.56.

591. 'In the City', *TO-DAY*, 8 May 1897, p53.

592. Correspondence, *TO-DAY*, 19 June 1897, p.237. In a letter to another correspondent calling himself 'Juryman' (possibly one of the actual jury in the case), Jerome gave a still higher estimate, based on 16 days in court at £300 per day, plus the associated costs of preparing the case and travelling to gather evidence. See Correspondence, *TO-DAY*, 22 May 1897, p.93.

593. Correspondence, *TO-DAY*, 19 June 1897, p.237.

594. 'Theatrical Gossip', *The Era*, 19 June 1897.

595. 'TO-DAY', *TO-DAY*, 4 January 1896, p.275.

596. 'Literature', Arts and Entertainments, *Leeds Mercury*, 5 February 1896.

597. 'TO-DAY', *TO-DAY*, 22 August 1896, p.82.

598. 'TO-DAY', *TO-DAY*, 10 May 1897, pp.56-7.

599. Jerome saw the death of Cuthbert Evans as a sign of the brutality allowed by the public school system, but he was particularly outraged by the headmaster's assumption that 'a school of boys is like a box of oranges or eggs, at ten a

shilling – all much of the same quality, size and flavour' and his resulting failure to allow for individual opinions among the boys. See 'TO-DAY', *TO-DAY*, 12 June 1897, p.199.

600. 'TO-DAY', *TO-DAY*, 5 June 1897, p. 163.

601. 'Three Men in a Boat', *Oxford Chronicle and Berks and Bucks Gazette*, 25 September 1897, p.5

602. 'In the City', *TO-DAY*, 13 November, p.51.

603. Jerome K. Jerome to Arthur Conan Doyle, undated. Private archive.

604. Jerome K. Jerome to J. W. Arrowsmith, 1 December 1897: uncatalogued, Harry Ransom Center, University of Texas.

605. Jerome K. Jerome to A. P. Watt, 26 September 1914, Berg Collection, NYPL. Jerome gives details of the paper's circulation and costs from memory but as 'an honourable man'.

606. Jerome K. Jerome, speech on being awarded the Freedom of the Borough of Walsall, 17 February 1927, Jerome K. Jerome collection, Box 9, Bodleian Library, Oxford.

607. 'J. K. Jerome on the Stump'. Playwright Addresses Workmen in Favor of Liberal Party', *New York Times*, 20 December 1909, p.1.

608. Jerome K. Jerome to unknown corresopondent,[1897]: uncatalogued, Harry Ransom Center, University of Texas.

609. 'Words of Consolation and of Caution to Mr Jerome', *Saturday Review*, 12 June 1897, pp.653-4, p.653.

610. Jerome K. Jerome to Douglas Sladen, undated, V7.4.4, Douglas Sladen Papers, Richmond Central Reference Library.

611. Jerome K. Jerome to Douglas Sladen, undated, V7.4.18/1, Douglas Sladen Papers, Richmond Central Reference Library.

612. Jerome gives one possible spelling of her name transliterated from the Russian. The friend in question was probably Nadezhda Alekseevna Iarintseva, a translator and critic of Russian poetry. In 1917 she spent some time in London and Oxford where she could have met the Jeromes.. With thanks to Vicky Davis.

613. Jerome K. Jerome to Douglas Sladen, 6 January 1898, V7.4.64, Douglas Sladen Papers, Richmond Central Reference Library.

614. 'Notes and News', *The Academy*, 8 January 1898, p.31. This may well be a

reference to the *Anglo-Russian*, begun in 1897. Jerome was sent a copy of the first issue and expressed his approval in a letter published in the second issue.

615. For an account of this incident see A. Zverev, 'Ulybka Dzheroma' (Jerome's Smile), excerpt from 'Dzherom K. Dzherom. Troe v lodke, ne schitaia sobaki. Troe na chetyrekh kolesakh. Rasskazy', (Moscow: Russiko, 1995). (Vicky Davis). http://www.jeromekjerome.ru/ulybka_dzheroma.shtml (accessed 23/01/2012) Trans Vicky Davis.

616. Jerome K. Jerome to Douglas Sladen, [January? 1898], V7.4.85, Douglas Sladen Papers, Richmond Central Reference Library.

617. Jerome K. Jerome to Bram Stoker, [March 1898], Stoker Correspondence, Brotherton Library, University of Leeds.

618. Jerome K. Jerome to Coulson Kernahan, undated, cited in Moss, p.103.

619. 'People, Places and Things', *Hearth and Home: An Illustrated Weekly Journal for Gentlewomen*, 16 March 1899, p.737.

620. SL8/20/D/01, Oxford History Centre.

621. See Jerome K. Jerome to Clement Shorter, 17 December 1899, Shorter Correspondence, Brotherton Library, University of Leeds.

622. *My Life and Times*, p.140.

623. Jerome K. Jerome, *Three Men on the Bummel* (London: Penguin, 1985), pp.99-100.

624. *Diary of a* Pilgrimage, pp.140-1.

625. 24 April 1899, Shorter Correspondence, Brotherton Library, University of Leeds.

626. Jerome K. Jerome to Clement Shorter, [1900], Shorter Correspondence, Brotherton Library, University of Leeds.

627. Jerome K. Jerome to Clement Shorter, [1900], Shorter Correspondence, Brotherton Library, University of Leeds.

628. Wearing 1900-1909, p.848.

629. The H. G. Wells Collection at the University of Illinois contains a letter from Jerome to Wells of 12 August 1899 mentioning that he is about to set off on a bicycling tour of the Black Forest. With thanks to Frank Rodgers.

630. *My Life and Times*, p.62.

631. *Three Men on the Bummel*, p.146.

632. Jerome K. Jerome to Coulson Kernahan, 1900?, cited in Moss, p.155.

633. *Three Men on the Bummel,* pp.78-9.

634. *Three Men on the Bummel,* p.99.

635. *Three Men on the Bummel,* p.107.

636. *Three Men on the Bummel,* pp.8-9.

637. *Three Men on the Bummel,* p.186.

638. 'The Fighting Instinct', *Common Sense,* 20 March 1920, p.170.

639. *My Life and Times,* p.143.

640. Jerome K. Jerome to Clement Scott, 3 November 1899, Harry Ransom Center, University of Texas., uncatalogued.

641. As this incident took place in the spring, it must have been early in the year of either 1899 or 1900.

642. *My Life and Times,* pp. 144-5.

643. Jerome K. Jerome to Clement Scott, Christmas [1899 Addressed from Ludwig Strasse], Harry Ransom Center, University of Texas., uncatalogued.

Chapter 6

644. Jerome K. Jerome to A. P. Watt, 9 January 1901, MS Coll Watt, Columbia University Rare Book and Manuscript Library.

645. Writing from Brussels to turn down an invitation to lecture at the Edinburgh Philosophical Institute, Jerome explains that he has been abroad for the last few winters and expects to winter abroad for several more years. See Jerome K. Jerome to unknown correspondent, 15 March 1902, QYAS 122P, Edinburgh Room, Central Library, Edinburgh. A letter held in the Harry Ransom Center dated 9 December 1903 is written from 3 Rue de Naples, Bruxelles.

646. This is a supposition, based on the registration of Blandina's death in Wallingford in 1904, the first year that the Jeromes did not leave England for the winter. Jerome does state in *My Life and Times* that he spent this winter also abroad, but his letters of the period are addressed from England, making it unlikely.

647. Jerome K. Jerome to Clement Shorter, 30 May 1901, Shorter Correspondence, Brotherton Library, University of Leeds.

648. Wilson's excerpt, citing Appendix in Chistopher Jacobs's *Nobody in Particular*, an MS biography of his father W. W. Jacobs.

649. Jerome K. Jerome, *Tea-Table Talk* (London: Hutchinson & Co., 1903), p.112.

650. *Tea-Table Talk*, p.78.

651. Faurot, p.89.

652. Jerome K. Jerome to Coulson Kernahan, undated: cited in Moss, p.167. The most obvious reference would be to Kernahan's *Celebrities: Little Stories About Famous Folk* (London, Hutchinson 1923). However it is unlikely that Jerome would be talking about his work 'for some time to come' given the state of his health by this point, or that he would have 'the fight all over again' after the overtly serious nature of his most recent work. The language points rather to a first effort at serious fiction i.e. *Paul Kelver*. Equally the letter may have been written much earlier. Following the success of *Three Men in a Boat* Jerome had told other correspondents that he would be writing more serious work for some time to come, although he did not write another novel until *Three Men on the Bummel* in 1900.

653. Jerome K. Jerome, 'The Troubles and Joys of Jerome K. Jerome', *Penny Illustrated Paper*, 22 March 1913, p.11.

654. Jerome K. Jerome to Francis Gribble, undated. Private archive.

655. 'The New Jerome', The Bookman, 23:137 (February 1903), p.213.

656. *Paul Kelver*, p.1.

657. Faurot, p.145.

658. *Paul Kelver*, p.47.

659. *Paul Kelver*, pp.35-6.

660. *Paul Kelver*, p.50.

661. While the Victoria Embankment was completed by 1870, untreated sewage caused problems downriver until the 1880s. See White p.55.

662. *Paul Kelver*, p.50.

663. *Paul Kelver*, pp.129-30.

664. *Paul Kelver*, pp.147-8.

665. *Paul Kelver*, p.156.

666. *Paul Kelver*, p.176.

667. *Paul Kelver*, p.185.

668. *Paul Kelver*, p.186.

669. 'Are Clever Women or Stupid the More Attractive to Men?', Idlers Club, *The Idler*, 7 (February - July 1895), p.87.

670. *Paul Kelver*, p.4

671. *Paul Kelver*, p.171.

672. *Paul Kelver*, p.299.

673. *Paul Kelver*, p.303.

674. *Paul Kelver*, p.303.

675. *Paul Kelver*, p.335.

676. 'Interview with Jerome K. Jerome. A talk on the young man's journal', *TO-DAY and London Opinion*, 25 January 1905, pp. 369-70, p.370.

677. 'TO-DAY', *TO-DAY*, 21 March 1896, p.210.

678. *Paul Kelver*, p.319.

679. *Paul Kelver*, p.134.

680. Jerome K. Jerome, 'On the exceptional merit attaching to the things we meant to do', *The Second Idle Thoughts of an Idle Fellow* (London: Hurst & Blackett, 1898), pp.53-90, p.81.

681. Jerome K. Jerome, 'On the exceptional merit attaching to the things we meant to do', p.90.

682. ' Interview with Jerome K. Jerome. A talk on the young man's journal', *TO-DAY / London Opinion*, 25 January 1905, pp.369-70, p.369

683. 'Interview with Jerome K. Jerome. A talk on the young man's journal', p.369.

684. 'Interview with Jerome K. Jerome. A talk on the young man's journal', p.369.

685. Jerome K. Jerome, 'On dress and deportment', *Idle Thoughts*, p.152.

686. 'Interview with Jerome K. Jerome. A talk on the young man's journal', p.370.

687. Jerome K. Jerome, 'Answers to Correspondents', *TO-DAY and London Opinion*, 30 September 1905, p.430.

688. 'The Family Council', Answers to Correspondents, *TO-DAY and London Opinion*, 12 August 1905, p.205.

689. The interview of which a transcript exists was given in 1989, judging by internal evidence. However there is also an extant recorded interview, held by the Marlow Society, giving far less detail than appears in the transcript. The probability therefore is that more than one interview was conducted at around the same time, the first of which provided material for a more specific programme of questions at a later date.

690. *Twenty Years of My Life*, p.85.

691. In the new year of 1912 she wrote to one of Jerome's correspondents to say that she was forwarding a letter to him in Switzerland.

692. 'Ought Stories to be True?', in *Idle Ideas in 1905* (London: Hurst and Blackett, 1905), pp.122-140, p.122.

693. 'Ought Stories to be True?', p.124.

694. 'Ought Stories to be True?', p. 128.

695. 'Ought Stories to be True?', p.137.

696. 'Ought Stories to be True?', p.138.

697. 'How to be Happy Though Little', in in *Idle Ideas in 1905*, pp.158-172, p.159.

698. Jerome K. Jerome, 'The White Man's Burden! Need it be so Heavy?', in *Idle Ideas in 1905*, 225-250, p.235.

699. Jerome K. Jerome, 'Creatures that one day shall be men', in *Idle Ideas in 1905*, pp.141-158, p.141.

700. 'Creatures that one day shall be men', p.146.

701. 'Creatures that one day shall be men', pp.147-8.

702. Jerome K. Jerome, *A Russian Vagabond*, Jerome K. Jerome Collection, Box 5, Bodleian Library, Oxford.

703. Jerome K. Jerome, 'Difficulties of a Modern Author', *TO-DAY and London Opinion*, 9 December 1905, pp.323-4, p. 323.

704. Wearing, 1910-19, p.408.

705. The manager is named in 'Jerome K. Jerome here and has a lively day. Dodges the cameras only to get lost in a hotel. His name tangled too.', *New York Times*, 8 October 1905, p.9. The bureau itself is identified by 'Pendennis' in 'Jerome K. Jerome Returns to England Indignant', *New York Times*, 29 April 1906, p.4.

706. 'Jerome K. Jerome here and has a lively day.'

707. 'Jerome K. Jerome Talks on Women', *New York Times*, 18 October 1905, p.11.

708. 'Jerome K. Jerome Returns to England Indignant'.

709. Jerome K. Jerome to Eleanor Robson Belmont, 1 January 1906, Spec MS Coll. Belmont, Columbia University Libraries.

710. 'Jerome K. Jerome Returns to England Indignant'.

711. Specifically it is reminiscent of his relation of comic dismay when he was supposedly invited to tea by a number of shop keepers on his arrival in Germany a few years earlier, and was unsure whether to pay or to reciprocate the invitation.

712. 'Jerome K. Jerome Returns to England Indignant'.

713. For this and a detailed account of Jerome's three American tours, see Frank Rodgers, 'Jerome in America: Problems of a Biographer', *Idle Thoughts*, pp.141-44.

714. 'Jerome K. Jerome Returns to England Indignant'.

715. 'Jerome K. Jerome Returns to England Indignant'.

716. The MS in the Bodleian gives Jerome's forwarding address as c/o Pond at the Lyceum Bureau in New York. See Jerome 8, Special Collections, Bodleian.

717. *The Disagreeable Man*, Act 2.

718. Jerome K. Jerome, 'The Troubles and Joys of Jerome K. Jerome', *Penny Illustrated Paper*, 22 March 1913, p.11.

719. 'Jerome K. Jerome's Explanation of Himself', *New York Times*, 20 October 1907, p.7.

720. This comment throws question on the report that Jerome had refused to meet Twain at a dinner in March 1906, saying that he must be the guest of honour and would not play second fiddle to his fellow author. See Rodgers, 'Jerome in America', p.143. The source is William Dana Orcutt. *Celebrities off Parade*. (Chicago, Willett, Clark & Company, 1935, pp. 175-9).

721. 'Jerome K. Jerome's Explanation of Himself'.

722. www.ancestry.co.uk, BT26: Piece:297: Item:12. UK Passenger Lists.

723. Marbury, p.34.

724. *My Life and Times*, p.111.

725. For details of this affair see William Winter, *The Life of David Belasco*, vol 2 (New York: Moffat, Yard & Co.,1918), pp.257-61.

726. For full details see the relevant volumes of J. P. Wearing, *The London Stage: A Calendar of Plays and Players*.

727. Jerome K. Jerome to Mr Hannam-Clark, 14 February 1922, cited in Moss, p.131.

728. Larua McClaren to the Editor of *The Times*, 7 December 1908, p.6.

729. Carl Hentschel, to the Editor of *The Times*, 7 December 1908, p.6.

730. Jerorme K. Jerome to unnamed correspondent, 14 April 1908. Private archive.

731. 'Authors at Work. The disadvantages of working in London and out of it.', *The Bookman*, November 1908, p.84.

732. Maurice Baring, 'The Member for Literature' in *Diminutive Dramas* (London: William Henemann, 1938) pp.70-77, p.76.

733. 'May Walker – Life With Jerome', *Idle Thoughts on Jerome K. Jerome*, pp.154-8, p.156. Original transcript held by the Marlow Society.

734. 'Authors at Work. The disadvantages of working in London and out of it.', *The Bookman*, November 1908, p.86.

735. 'Serious fire at Gould's Grove. 50 pigs and calves burned', *Jackson's Oxford Journal and Wantage Herald*, 22 May 1909, p.5.

736. 'Fictionists and a Fire', [New Zealand] *Evening Post*, 10 July 1909, p.10.

737. Jerome K. Jerome to Herbert Thring, 18 May 1909, 75, Society of Authors Archive, BL.

738. A letter described on the Jerome K. Jerome Society forum shows that Dressler lived in a property called White Cottage, which is clearly not Monk's Corner as sometimes assumed.

739. Jerome K. Jerome, 'Idle Thoughts on Youth', *Common Sense*, 5 June 1920, p.311.

740. *Three Men in a Boat*, p.108.

741. Dramatic Committee of Society of Authors to *The Times*, 29 November 1909.

742. 'May Walker – Life With Jerome', p.158.

743. 'Mark Twain. Some Personal Recollections and Opinions by Jerome K. Jerome' et al, *The Bookman* 38:225 (June 1910), pp.116-119, p. 116.

744. See Wearing, 1910-19, p.127.

745. As Victorian feminists complained, women, children and the insane were treated alike in this context.

746. 'The Woman Suffrage Movement. Mr Lloyd George at the Albert Hall', *The Times*, 24 February 1912, p.8.

747. Wearing, 1910-19, p.307.

748. Jerome K. Jerome, 'The Troubles and Joys of Jerome K. Jerome', *Penny Illustrated Paper*, 22 March 1913, p.11.

749. 'The Troubles and Joys of Jerome K. Jerome'.

Chapter 7

750. It had eighteen performances. See Wearing, 1910-19, p.451.

751. Jerome K. Jerome to Douglas Sladen, 24 July 1914, V66.10J8, Sladen Correspondence, Richmond Central Reference Library.

752. Sladen, *Twenty Years of My Life*, p.88.

753. This letter has not been found but see Robert Donald to Jerome K. Jerome, 30 July 1914, Berg Collection, NYPL.

754. Jerome K. Jerome to Robert Donald, [August] 1914, Berg Collection, NYPL.

755. Jerome K. Jerome to Perriton Maxwell, 7 September 1914, Berg Collection, NYPL.

756. *My Life and Times*, p.190

757. *My Life and Times*, p.191.

758. Coulson Kernahan to the editor of *The Times*, 25 August 1914, p.81

759. *My Life and Times*, p.191. It is worth noting that in the 1890s Jerome was perturbed by the supposed lack of opportunity for military engagement, rather than by the violence overseas on which he was reporting week by week.

760. Jerome K. Jerome, 'Wanted: a Man with a Torch. The Coalition Government must Put an End to National Dawdling.', *Illustrated Sunday Herald*, 23 May 1915, p.10. However in an article written for *New Days* in December he assumed that 'the end of the contest is coming into sight'

761. *My Life and Times*, p.190.

762. *Stage Year Book* (Carson & Comerford Ltd: 1916), p.136.

763. Wearing, 1910-19, vol 1., p.451.

764. Wearing, 1910-19, vol 1., p.490.

765. *My Life and Times*, p.191.

766. *My Life and Times*, pp.198-99.

767. *My Life and Times*, p.192.

768. Jerome K. Jerome, 'Hard Blows, not Hard Words' *New York Times* 1:1 (12 Dec 1914), pp.103-6, pp.103-4. Originally published as 'How Not to be Useful in War Time. Talking and Doing', *Daily News and Leader*, 4 September 1914.

769. Jerome K. Jerome, letter to *The Express*, 10 September 1914, page unknown, Jerome 8, Special Collections, Bodleian Library, Oxford.

770. Jerome K. Jerome to G. B. Shaw, 29 October 1915, 50517 f 299, BL.

771. Jerome K. Jerome, cutting from *Westminster Gazette*, 9 Dec 1914, page unknown, Jerome 8, Special Collections, Bodleian Library, Oxford.

772. Jerome K. Jerome, cutting from *Westminster Gazette*, 9 Dec 1914, page unknown, Jerome 8, Special Collections, Bodleian Library, Oxford.

773. Unreferenced press cutting, *Daily News* [1914], Jerome 8, Special Collections, Bodleian Library, Oxford.

774. Cutting from *Illustrated Sunday Herald*, 9 May 1915, page unknown, Jerome 8, Special Collections, Bodleian Library, Oxford.

775. Jerome K. Jerome letter to the editor, *Westminster Gazette*, 29.1.1915, Jerome 8, Special Collections, Bodleian Library, Oxford.

776. Jerome K. Jerome to G. B. Shaw, 29 October 1915, 50517 f 299, BL.

777. Jerome K. Jerome, 'The Voice of the Young Men. What Youth can Do in the Securing of a Lasting Peace.' *Illustrated Sunday Herald*, 6 June 1915, p.14.

778. '"No German Methods Wanted Here." Jerome K. Jerome on the Armies England Wants to Finish the War.', *Illustrated Sunday Herald*, 13 June 1915, p.11.

779. Jerome K. Jerome, 'After the Battle', *Lloyd's Weekly News*, 18 June 1916, page unknown.

780. '"No German Methods Wanted Here." Jerome K. Jerome on the Armies England Wants to Finish the War.', p.11.

781. Jerome K. Jerome, 'The New Christianity', unreferenced but probably from May or June 1916, Jerome 8, Special Collections, Bodleian Library, Oxford.

782. Jerome K. Jerome, cutting from *Westminster Gazette*, 9 Dec 1914, page unknown, Jerome 8, Special Collections, Bodleian Library, Oxford.

783. Rowena Jerome to Mrs Harold Chapin, 12 November 1915, Rare Books & MSS., Penn State Univ. Library.

784. Jerome K. Jerome to Mrs Harold Chapin, [1915], Rare Books & Mss., Penn State Univ. Library.

785. Jerome K. Jerome, 'Business Not as Usual', *Lloyd's Weekly News*, 4 June 1916, page unknown.

786. 'Business Not as Usual'.

787. Jerome K. Jerome, 'Land of Silence. Famous Writer on the New France. On the Borders of War. Enemy Cocksure he is not to be Beaten.' *Illustrated Sunday Herald*, 4 April 1915, p.6.

788. Jerome K. Jerome, 'God Punish Germany!', *New Days*, 4 December 1915, pp.299-300, p.299.

789. 'God Punish Germany!', pp.299-300, p.300.

790. Jerome K. Jerome, 'The Stomach of the People', *Lloyd's Weekly News*, 9 April 1916, page unknown.

791. *My Life and Times*, p.193.

792. *My Life and Times*, p.193.

793. See Certificate issued by L'Ambassadeur de France, London 4 August 1916, Letters and papers concerning Jerome K. Jerome, Walsall, compiled for a centenary of birth exhibition in 1959, Walsall Local History Centre.

794. In an interview with the *Bookman* in 1926 Jerome noted that in the English service this proximity to the fighting was the province of stretcher bearers not ambulance drivers.

795. Jerome K. Jerome, 'After the Battle', *Lloyd's Weekly News*, 18 June 1916, page unknown.

796. Jerome K. Jerome, 'The Blessings of War', *Lloyd's Weekly News*, 11 June 1916, page unknown.

797. Jerome K. Jerome, 'The Blessings of War', *Lloyd's Weekly News*, 11 June 1916, page unknown.

798. *My Life and Times*, p.196.

799. *My Life and Times*, p.197.

800. *My Life and Times*, p.198.

801. *My Life and Times*, p.199.

802. A bad road. *My Life and Times*, p.200.

803. Jerome K. Jerome, *All Roads Lead to Calvary* (New York: Dodd, Mead and Company), 1919, pp.312-13.

804. *My Life and Times*, p.203.

805. *My Life and Times*, p.203.

806. *My Life and Times*, p.205.

807. *My Life and Times*, p.205.

808. Louis J. McQuilland, 'Jerome Klapka Jerome', *The Bookman* 70:420 (September 1926), pp.282-4, p.283.

809. Coulson Kernahan, introduction to Moss, *Jerome K. Jerome: His Life and Work: From Poverty to the Knighthood of the People*, p.15.

810. Louis J. McQuilland, 'Jerome Klapka Jerome', p.284.

811. H. G. Wells, *Daily News and Leader*, 11 Feb 1918, page unkown, Jerome 8, Special Collections, Bodleian Library, Oxford.

812. Jerome K. Jerome, *Daily News and Leader*, 14 Feb 1918, page unkown, Jerome 8, Special Collections, Bodleian Library, Oxford.

813. With thanks to Hazel Malpass, Marlow Society.

814. Jerome K. Jerome to Douglas Sladen.

815. Arthur Conan Doyle, *Common Sense*, 16 August 1919, p101.

816. Jerome K. Jerome, *All Roads Lead to Calvary* (New York: Dodd, Mead & Co., 1919) p. 261.

817. Rosa Maria Bracco, *Merchants of Hope: British Middlebrow Writers of the First World War, 1919-1939* (Oxford: Bert, 1993), pp.12-13.

818. 'Idle Thoughts - Houses and Miracles', *Common Sense*, 23 August 1919, p.115.

819. Jerome K. Jerome, 'Idle Thoughts on Village Life & Village Concerts', *Common Sense*, 20 December 1919, p.382.

820. Jerome K. Jerome, 'A League of Reason', *Daily News*, 18 January 1918, page unknown.

821. Jerome K. Jerome, 'Idle Thoughts on Government by Advertisement', *Common Sense*, 11 October 1919, pp.18-19, p.19.

822. Jerome K. Jerome, 'The New Christianity', unreferenced but probably from May or June 1916, Jerome 8, Special Collections, Bodleian Library, Oxford.

823. *All Roads Lead to Calvary*, p.304.

824. *All Roads Lead to Calvary*, p.305.

825. *All Roads Lead to Calvary*, p.306.

826. *All Roads Lead to Calvary*, p.297.

827. Bracco, *Merchants of Hope*, p.109.

828. *All Roads Lead to Calvary*, p.307.

829. Frederic Manning, *The Middle Parts of Fortune* (London: Penguin, 2000), Author's Prefatory Note.

830. *The Middle Parts of Fortune*, p.201.

831. *The Middle Parts of Fortune*, p.40.

832. Jerome K. Jerome to Ramsay MacDonald, 20 November 1919, PRO30/69/1163, PRO.

833. *My Life and Times*, p.205.

834. Jerome K. Jerome, 'Idle Thoughts. By Jerome K. Jerome', *Common Sense*, 17 May 1919, pp. 301-2, p.302.

835. Jerome K. Jerome, 'Idle Thoughts After Dinner', *Common Sense*, 8 November 1919, pp.281-2, p.282.

836. Jerome K. Jerome to Stanley Weiser, 24 October 1920, cited in Moss, p.182.

837. Jerome K. Jerome, 'Burn Your School-Books', *Common Sense*, 15 May 1920, p.271.

838. Jerome K. Jerome, 'Idle Thoughts', 'The Gospel of the Jungle', *Common Sense*, 4 October 1919, pp.205-6, p.205.

839. Jerome K. Jerome, 'After Dinner', 'Idle Thoughts', *Common Sense*, 8 November 1919, pp.281-2, p. 282.

840. Jerome K. Jerome, 'War, and the Common People', *Foreign Affairs*, 11:8, February 1921, pp.117-118, p.118.

Chapter 8

841. Burgin, *Memoirs of a Clubman*, pp.28-29.

842. Eden Phllpotts to Jerome K. Jerome, 26 October 1921, Jerome 9, Special Collections, Bodleian Library, Oxford.

843. J.M. Barrie to Ettie Jerome, 3 July 1927, Jerome 9, Special Collections, Bodleian Library, Oxford.

844. H. G. Wells to Jerome K. Jerome, 3 November 1925, Jerome 9, Special Collections, Bodleian Library, Oxford.

845. Transcript of interview with May Walker, archives of the Marlow Society. This transcript is republished in *Idle Thoughts on Jerome K. Jerome.*

846. Jerome K. Jerome to Henry McClelland, 9 September 1925, MS.152/53/3, Mitchell Library, Glasgow.

847. Jerome K. Jerome to Henry McClelland, 24 October 1925, MS.152/53/3, Mitchell Library, Glasgow.

848. Jerome K. Jerome to Henry McClelland, 24 September 1925, MS.152/53/2, Mitchell Library, Glasgow.

849. 'Jerome Jerome', by Ivan Alekseevich Bunin, 1929. (Vicky Davis) The article is an excerpt from Bunin's memoir and appears in *Polnoe sobranie sochinenii v XIII tomakh*, vol. 9, ed. G. V. Priakhin (Moscow: Voskresen'e, 2006), pp.45-6.

850. Jerome K. Jerome to unknown corresopondent, 12 January 1924: uncatalogued, Harry Ransom Center, University of Texas.

851. Jerome K. Jerome to unnamed correspondent, 9 July 1926. Private archive.

852. Faurot, p.29.

853. 'TO-DAY', *TO-DAY*, 7 March 1896, p.147.

854. *My Life and Times*, p.14.

855. *My Life and Times*, p.142.

856. *My Life and Times*, pp.12-13.

857. Jerome gives the dates as 12 January and 18 January, placing them a few weeks after incidents recorded on 13 November and 2 December in the preceding year when first Eliza leaves and then Jerome's watch is stolen. These earlier entries are inaccurately transcribed, but seem to be based on real entries of 9 November 1863 and 12 September 1863 respectively. However the entries concerning the gas and the snow are from 5 and 6 January 1867, suggesting that Jerome has condensed a series of disasters for literary reasons.

858. *My Life and Times*, pp.19-20.

859. Neo-Victorian fiction most obviously exemplifies this trend; equally the increased critical focus on women's diaries from this era testifies to a concern with representing women and decoding the ways in which they attempted to represent their own experience through domestic imagery.

860. *My Life and Times*, p.30.

861. *My Life and Times*, p.58.

862. *My Life and Times*, p.58.

863. *My Life and Times*, p.83. Corelli had died in April 1924.

864. See Rochelson, p.221.

865. Louis J. McQuilland, 'Jerome Klapka Jerome', p.283.

866. Louis J. McQuilland, 'Jerome Klapka Jerome', p.283.

867. '"Three Men in a Boat." Originals Present at Dinner to Mr Jerome.', *The Times*, 31 January, p.9.

868. Jerome K. Jerome to Mrs Leckie, 15 February 1927, 417, 137/10, Letters and papers concerning Jerome K Jerome, Walsall, compiled for a centenary of

birth exhibition in 1959. Walsall Local History Centre.

869. Jerome K. Jerome, speech on being awarded the Freedom of the Borough of Walsall, 17 February 1927, Jerome K. Jerome collection, Box 9, Bodleian Library, Oxford.

870. Jerome K. Jerome to unnamed correspondent, undated, 137/11, Letters and papers concerning Jerome K Jerome, Walsall, compiled for a centenary of birth exhibition in 1959. Walsall Local History Centre.

871. Moss, p.217.

872. Jerome K. Jerome, speech on being awarded the Freedom of the Borough of Walsall, 17 February 1927, Jerome K. Jerome collection, Box 9, Bodleian Library, Oxford.

873. G. B. Shaw to Rowena Jerome, 27 November 1940, Jerome K. Jerome Collection, Bodleian, Box 9.

874. 'Obituaries. Mr Jerome K. Jerome', *The Times*, 15 June 1927, p.18.

875. Moss, p.242.

Epilogue

876. 14 May 2009 http://www.telegraph.co.uk/news/uknews/5319957/Why-wont-Walsall-honour-Jerome-K-Jerome.html. Accessed 8 February 2012.

877. *My Life and Times*, p.4.

878. Jerome K. Jerome, 'On the exceptional merit attaching to the things we meant to do', *The Second Idle Thoughts of an Idle Fellow* (London: Hurst & Blackett, 1898), pp.53-90, p.81.

879. Lynn Hapgood, *Margins of Desire: The Suburbs in Fiction and Culture 1880-1925* (Manchester: Manchester University Press, 2005) p.20.

BIBLIOGRAPHY

TO-DAY. The corrected proof of the first issue is held at the Harry Ransom Research Center, University of Texas.

Archival sources

Marguerite Jerome, MS diary, private archive.
Divorce papers J77/386/1711 C397617
The Church Book of the Independent Church, Marlborough. 2194/1, Wiltshire & Swindon History Centre.

Jerome, Jerome K.

All Roads Lead to Calvary (New York: Dodd, Mead and Company, 1919)
'Charles Dickens. The Fellowship of Love.', *Youth's Companion*, 86:01, 4 January 1912, p.3.
Diary of a Pilgrimage (Gloucester: Alan Sutton, 1990).
Idle Thoughts of an Idle Fellow (Bristol: Arrowsmith, 1946).
Idle Ideas in 1905 (London: Hurst and Blackett, 1905).
My Life and Times (London: Folio Society, 1992)
Novel Notes (Stroud: Sutton, 1991).
On the Stage – and Off: the brief career of a would-be actor (Stroud: Sutton, 1991).
Paul Kelver (London: Hutchinson and Co., 1902).
The Second Thoughts of an Idle Fellow (London: Hurst & Blackett, 1898).
Stage-Land: Curious Manners & Customs of its Inhabitants (London: Chatto & Windus, 1890).
'The Night Call', *Reveille* 1 (August 1918) pp.98-102.
'The Oberammergau Passion Play', *The Theatre* 16:1, 1890, pp.1-5.

Tea-Table Talk (London: Hutchinson & Co., 1903).
Three Men in Boat (London: Penguin, 1999).
Three Men on the Bummel (London: Penguin, 1985).

Plays

Barbara Add. 53361 F "Barbara", British Library.
Biarritz Add. 53599 B, British Library.
Birth and Breeding (typescript), Add. 53458 E, British Library.
The Disagreeable Man Jerome K. Jerome, Special Collections, Bodleian. Box 2
Fennel, Add. 53399 H, British Library.
The MacHaggis Add. 53625 E "The MacHaggis", British Library.
New Lamps for Old (MS), Add. 53458 E, British Library.
The Prude's Progress ts Special Collections, Templeman Library, University of
    Kent
Robina in Search of a Husband Lacy's Acting Edition of Plays, 2304.i.8, British
    Library
The Russian Vagabond (Jerome K. Jerome, Special Collections, Bodleian. Box 5
Ruth (typescript), Add. 53447 F, British Library.
Sunset, Add. 53395 G, British Library.
The Three Patriots Jerome K. Jerome, Special Collections, Bodleian. Box 6
Wood Barrow Farm, Add. 53405 K, British Library.

Primary Sources

Abbot, Angus Evan et al, 'How to court the "Advanced Woman"' Idlers'
    Club. *The Idler* 6 (August 1894-January 1895): 192-211.
'Advertisements & Notices', *The Era,* (fully referenced in chapter footnotes).
'Authors at Work. The disadvantages of working in London and out of it.',
    The Bookman, 35:206 (November 1908), pp.83-88.
Baring, Maurice, *Diminutive Dramas* (London: William Heinemann, 1938).
Bernard Shaw Collected Letters 1898-1910, ed Dan H. Lawrence (London: Max
    Reinhardt, 1972).
Blathwyt, Raymond, 'A Talk with Mr Jerome K. Jerome', *Idle Thoughts* 31, The
    Souvenir Sesquicentenary Edition, pp.31-37.
Burgin, G. B., *Memoirs of a Clubman* (London: Hutchinson, 1922).
-- *More Memoirs (and some travels)* (London: Hutchinson, 1922).
Corelli, Marie, *The Sorrows of Satan* (Kansas: Valancourt, 2008).

Douglas, F.A., 'Woman and her Clubs', *Hearth and Home*, 8 November 1894, p.926.

Grossmith, George and Weedon, *The Diary of a Nobody* (London, Penguin, 1975).

Hope, Anthony, *The Prisoner of Zenda* (Oxford: Oxford World's Classics, 2009).

-- *Memories and Notes* (London: Hutchinson 1927), p.186.

-- *Journal of Sacred Literature and Biblical Record*, vol V. (new series), 1864, no. X.

Lovesey, Peter, *Swing, Swing Together* (London: Penguin, 1980).

McQuilland, Louis J., 'Jerome Klapka Jerome', *The Bookman* 70:420 (September 1926), pp.282-4.

Manning, Frederic, *The Middle Parts of Fortune* (London: Peguin, 2000)

Marbury, Elisabeth, *My Crystal Ball* (London: Hurst and Blackett, 1924).

'Mark Twain. Some Personal Recollections and Opinions', *The Bookman* 38:225 (June 1910), pp.116-119, p. 116.

Nelson, Carolyn Christensen, ed, *A New Woman Reader* (Hertfordshire: Broadview, 2001).

Programme for the Oberammergau passion play 2010.

The Queen's Gift Book (London: Hodder & Stoughton, 1915).

Shaw, G. B., *What I Really Wrote About the War* (London: Constable and Company, 1930).

-- *Our Theatres in the Nineties* (London: Constable & Co., 3 vols, vol 2, 1948).

Sladen, Douglas, *Twenty Years of My Life* (London: Constable and Company, 1915).

--*My Long Life* (London: Hutchinson, 1939).

'"Three Men in a Boat." Originals Present at Dinner to Mr Jerome.', *The Times*, 31 January, p.9.

Watson, Aaaron, with a chapter by Mark Twain, *The Savage Club: a Medley of History, Anecdote, and Reminiscences* (London: Unwin, 1907).

Weyman, Stanley, *The Red Cockade* (London: T. Nelson & Sons, undated).

Secondary Sources

Agathocleous, Tanya, *Urban Realism and the Cosmopolitan Imagination in the Nineteenth Century: Visible City, Invisible World* (Cambridge, Cambridge University Press, 2011).

Argent, Alan, 'The Tale of an Idle Fellow: Jerome K. Jerome', *Congregational History Circle* 3:4, 1996, pp.18-30.

Batts, John S., "American Humor: The Mark of Twain on Jerome K. Jerome.",

The Victorian Comic Spirit. New Perspectives, Jennifer A. Wagner-Lawlor (ed.) (Aldershot, Ashgate, 2000).

Bracco, Rosa Maria, *Merchants of Hope: British Middlebrow Writers of the First World War, 1919-1939* (Oxford: Berg, 1993).

R. R. Bolland, *In the Wake of Three Men in a Boat,* (Tunbridge Wells: Oast Books, 1995)

Bosson, Olef E., *Slang and Cant in Jerome K. Jerome's Works* (Cambridge: Heffer and Sons, 1911).

Chapman, Raymond, *Forms of Speech in Victorian Fiction* (Harlow: Longman, 1994).

Christie, Peter, 'The Reverend Jerome Clapp in Appledore 1840-1855' in *Idle Thoughts on Jerome K. Jerome: A 150th Anniversary Celebration* (Jerome K. Jerome Society, 2009) pp. 11-32.

Faurot, Ruth, *Jerome K. Jerome* (New York: Twayne, 1974).

Findon, B. W., *The Playgoers' Club 1884-1905: Its History and Memories* (1905).

Fisher, Trevor, *Scandal: The Sexual Politics of Late Victorian Britain* (Stroud: Alan Sutton, 1995).

Gilmour, Robin, *The Victorian Period: the Intellectual and Cultural Context of English Literature 1830-1890* (London: Longman, 1993).

Harrop, Josephine, *Victorian Portable Theatres* (London: Society for Theatre Research, 1989).

Herlihy, David V., *Bicycle: the History* (Yale: Yale University Press, 2006).

Humphreys, Anne, 'Putting Women in the Boat in *The Idler* (1892-1898) and *TO-DAY* (1893-1897), *19: Interdisciplinary Studies in the Long Nineteenth Century*, 1 (2005), pp.1-22, www.19.bbk.ac.uk, accessed 4 January 2011.

Kernahan, Coulson, *Celebrities: Little Stories About Famous Folk* (London: Hutchinson 1923).

Kortsch, Christine Bayles, *Dress Culture in Late Victorian Women's Fiction: Literacy, Textiles, and Activism* (Farnham: Ashgate, 2009).

Liggins, Emma, '"The Life of a Bachelor Girl in the Big City": Selling the Single Lifestyle to Readers of *Woman* and the *Young Woman* in the 1890s', *Victorian Periodicals Review* 40:3, Fall 2007, pp.216-238.

--'"Having a Good Time Single?": The Bachelor Girl in 1890s New Woman Fiction' in Adrienne E. Gavin and Carolyn W. de la L. Oulton, eds, *Writing Women of the Fin de Siècle: Authors of Change* (Basingstoke: Palgrave Macmillan, 2011), pp.98-110, p.99.

Lutz, Deoborah, 'The Dead Still Among Us: Victorian Secular Relics, Hair

Jewelry, and Death Culture', *Victorian Literature and Culture* 39 (2011), pp.127-142.

Miller, Russell, *The Adventures of Arthur Conan Doyle* (London, Harvill Secker, 2008).

Michie, Ranald C., *Guilty Money: the City of London in Victorian and Edwardian Culture, 1815-1914* (London: Pickering & Chatto, 2009).

Moss, Alfred , *Jerome K. Jerome: His Life and Work: From Poverty to the Knighthood of the People* (London: Selwyn and Blount, 1928).

Nicholas, Jeremy (ed.), *Idle Thoughts on Jerome K. Jerome* (Essex: Jerome K. Jerome Society / Toynbee Editorial Services, 2009).

Nord, Deborah Epstein, *Walking the Victorian Streets: Women, Representation, and the City* (Ithaca: Cornell University Press, 1995), p.182.

Telfer, Kevin, *Peter Pan's First XI: The Extraordinary Story of J. M. Barrie's Cricket Team* (London: Sceptre, 2010).

Walkley, A. B., *Playhouse Impressions* (London: Fisher Unwin, 1892).

Waller, Philip, *Writers, Readers, and Reputations: Literary Life in Britain 1870-1918* (Oxford: Oxford University Press, 2008).

White, Jerry, *London in the Nineteenth Century* (London: Vintage, 2008).

Wilson, Aubrey, *The Search for Ernest Bramah* (London: Creighton & Read, 2007).

--unpublished biography of W. W. Jacobs.

Winks, Robin W. and Joan Neuberger, *Europe and the Making of Modernity* (Oxford: Oxford University Press, 2005).

Winter, William, *The Life of David Belasco*, vol 2 (New York: Moffat, Yard & Co., 1918).

Jerome K. Jerome Bibliography

First English editions of books written by Jerome K. Jerome

On the Stage — and Off: the Brief Career of a Would-be Actor. London, Field & Tuer, 1885.

Barbara. Play in One Act. London, Samuel French, [1886].

The Idle Thoughts of an Idle Fellow. A Book for an Idle Holiday. London, Field & Tuer, The Leadenhall Press, [1886].

Sunset. Play, in One Act. London, Samuel French. [1888]

Fennel. A New Romantic Play. From the French of François Coppée. London, Samuel French, [1888].

Stage-land: Curious Habits and Customs of its Inhabitants. London, Chatto & Windus, 1889.

Three Men in a Boat (to Say Nothing of the Dog). Bristol, J. W. Arrowsmith, 1889.

Told After Supper. London, The Leadenhall Press, 1891.

Diary of a Pilgrimage (and Six Essays). Bristol, J. W. Arrowsmith, 1891.

Novel Notes. London, The Leadenhall Press, Ltd., 1893.

John Ingerfield, and Other Stories. London, McClure & Co., [1893].

The Prude's Progress. A Comedy in Three Acts. By Jerome K. Jerome and Eden Phillpotts. London, Chatto & Windus, 1895.

Sketches in Lavender Blue and Green. London, Longmans, Green and Co., 1897.

The Second Thoughts of an Idle Fellow. London, Hurst and Blackett, 1898.

Three Men on the Bummel. Bristol, J. W. Arrowsmith, [1900].

    Published in the USA as *Three Men on Wheels.*

The Observations of Henry. Bristol , J. W. Arrowsmith, 1901.

Miss Hobbs. London, Samuel French, [1902].

Paul Kelver. London, Hutchinson & Co., 1902.

Tea-Table Talk. London, Hutchinson & Co., 1903.

Woodbarrow Farm. London, Samuel French, 1904.

Tommy and Co. London, Hutchinson and Co., 1904.

Idle Ideas in 1905. London, Hurst and Blackett, [1905].
Most of the essays in this collection were originally published in 1904 in the USA, with different titles, in a volume entitled *American Wives and Others.*

The Passing of the Third Floor Back and Other Stories. London, Hurst & Blackett, 1907.

The Angel and the Author – and Others. London, Hurst & Blackett, 1908.
Includes five essays originally published in 1904 in the USA in *American Wives and Others.*

Fanny and the Servant Problem. A Quite Possible Play in Four Acts. London, Samuel French, 1909.

They and I. London, Hutchinson & Co., 1909.

The Passing of the Third Floor Back. An Idle Fancy in a Prologue, a Play and an Epilogue. London, Hurst & Blackett, Ltd., Paternoster House, 1910.

The Master of Mrs. Chilvers. An Improbable Comedy, London, T. Fisher Unwin, [1911].

Robina in Search of a Husband. A Farce in Four Acts. London, Samuel French, 1914.

Malvina of Brittany. London, Cassell and Company, Limited, [1916].
Published in the USA as *The Street of the Blank Wall and Other Stories.*

All Roads Lead to Calvary. London, Hutchinson & Co., [1919].

Anthony John, a Biography. London, Cassell and Company, Ltd., 1923.

A Miscellany of Sense and Nonsense. From the Writings of Jerome K. Jerome. Selected by the Author, with Many Apologies. London, J. W. Arrowsmith, 1923.

The Celebrity. A Play in Three Acts. London, Hodder and Stoughton Limited, [1926].

My Life and Times. London, Hodder and Stoughton Limited, [1926].

The Soul of Nicholas Snyders. A Mystery Play in Three Acts. London, Hodder and Stoughton, [1927].

Books written by Jerome but published anonymously

Playwriting: a Handbook for Would-be Dramatic Authors. By a Dramatist. London, The Stage Office, Clement's Inn Passage, Strand, W. C., 1888.

Weeds. A Story in Seven Chapters. By K. McK. Bristol , J. W. Arrowsmith, [1892]. (Arrowsmith's Note-Book Series).
Copies were sent to the copyright deposit libraries, but the book was probably not released for general sale.

Books edited by Jerome

My First Book... London, Chatto & Windus, 1894.
Essays by twenty-two authors, originally published in *The Idler*.

Periodicals edited by Jerome

The Idler. Vol.1, February-July 1892 to Vol. 12, August 1897-January, 1898.
To-Day. A Weekly Magazine-Journal. Vol. 1, 11 November, 1893 - 3 February, 1894 to Vol. 16, 7 August-30 October, 1897.

A comprehensive bibliography, listing all editions of Jerome's books to the year 2000, and all of his contributions to periodicals and newspapers, compiled by Frank Rodgers and Andrew P. Read, is available on the website of the Jerome K. Jerome Society, www.jeromekjerome.com.

INDEX

Victorian Secrets

Victorian Secrets is an independent publisher dedicated to producing high-quality books from and about the nineteenth century, including critical editions of neglected novels.

The Angel of the Revolution by George Chetwynd Griffith
The Autobiography of Christopher Kirkland by Eliza Lynn Linton
The Blood of the Vampire by Florence Marryat
The Dead Man's Message by Florence Marryat
Demos by George Gissing
Dorothea's Daughter and Other Nineteenth-Century Postscripts by Barbara Hardy
East of Suez by Alice Perrin
Grania: The Story of an Island by Emily Lawless
Henry Dunbar by Mary Elizabeth Braddon
Her Father's Name by Florence Marryat
The Light that Failed by Rudyard Kipling
A Mummer's Wife by George Moore
Notable Women Authors of the Day by Helen C. Black
Robert Elsmere by Mrs Humphry Ward
Thyrza by George Gissing
Twilight Stories by Rhoda Broughton
Vice Versâ by F. Anstey
Weeds by Jerome K. Jerome
Weird Stories by Charlotte Riddell
Workers in the Dawn by George Gissing

Our critical editions are edited by scholars and include introductions, explanatory footnotes, author biographies, and extensive contextual material.

For more information on any of our titles, please visit:

www.victoriansecrets.co.uk

Victorian Secrets

Weeds: A Story in Seven Chapters
by Jerome K. Jerome

edited with an introduction and notes by Carolyn W. de la L. Oulton

First published anonymously in 1892, *Weeds* marked a significant departure from the humour that made Jerome K. Jerome famous. This disturbing story of sexual corruption shows marital fidelity as a perpetual struggle, with Dick Selwyn falling for the attractions of his wife's young cousin, Jessie. The link between mental and physical corruption is sustained through a central metaphor of a weed-infested garden, which perishes through neglect.

With its radical ending , this story of the dark side of passion casts an important light on late-nineteenth-century sexual politics and gender ideology. Jerome engages with contemporary debates on degeneration and the emergence of the New Woman, offering a powerful evocation of *fin-de-siècle* society.

Jerome's publisher Arrowsmith was nervous about the book's frank portrayal of adultery and it was never available for general sale during his lifetime. This new edition, with a critical introduction, bibliography and explanatory footnotes by Carolyn W. de la L. Oulton, reconsiders Jerome K. Jerome's important and neglected work.

ISBN: 978-1-906469-40-5 (also available in an ebook edition)

www.victoriansecrets.co.uk

Victorian Secrets

The Perfect Man: The Muscular Life and Times of Eugen Sandow, Victorian Strongman by David Waller

Eugen Sandow (1867-1925) was the Victorian Arnold Schwarzenegger – a world-famous celebrity, and possessor of what was then considered to be the most perfect male body. He rose from obscurity in Prussia to become a music-hall sensation in late-Victorian London, going on to great success as a performer in North America and throughout the British Empire.

Written with humour and insight into the popular culture of late-Victorian England, Waller's book argues that Sandow deserves to be resurrected as a significant cultural figure whose life, like that of Oscar Wilde, tells us a great deal about sexuality and celebrity at the fin de siècle.

"Hugely entertaining ... Waller skillfully places Sandow within the context of the age." Juliet Nicolson, *The Evening Standard*

"Waller...furnishes a narrative rich in stories reflecting Victorian life." Valerie Grove, *The Times*

"Waller's lively, colourful and fascinating book should help restore interest in an unjustly forgotten icon." Miranda Seymour - *The Daily Telegraph*

ISBN: 978-1-906469-25-2 (also available in an ebook edition)

www.victoriansecrets.co.uk

Victorian Secrets

Hope and Glory: A Life of Dame Clara Butt
by Maurice Leonard

Dame Clara Butt (1872-1936) was one of the most celebrated singers of the Victorian and Edwardian eras, a symbol of the glory of a Britain on whose Empire the sun never set. Standing an Amazonian 6'2" tall, Clara had a glorious contralto voice of such power that when she sang in Dover, Sir Thomas Beecham swore she could be heard in Calais. A friend of the royal family, Clara was made a Dame in recognition of her sterling work during the First World War. Her rousing performances of *Land of Hope and Glory* brought the nation together and raised thousands of pounds for charity.

Filling concert halls throughout the world, Clara was one of the first singers to undertake international tours, visiting Canada, Australia, New Zealand, South Africa, and Japan. She travelled with an entourage of over twenty people who fulfilled her every need. Her demands were many, but Clara never failed to delight her adoring audiences. At the height of her career, Clara was locked in rivalry with the celebrated soprano Nellie Melba, almost ending in a libel case when Clara wrote her memoirs.

In the first biography since her death, Maurice Leonard tells Dame Clara Butt's remarkable story, from humble beginnings in Sussex, to her dazzling apotheosis by an adoring nation. With humour and insight, Leonard reveals the woman behind the cultural icon.

ISBN: 978-1-906469-25-2 (also available in an ebook edition)

www.victoriansecrets.co.uk